Adobe® Edge Animate CC

FOR DUMMIES®

A Wiley Brand

by Michael Rohde

W9-ART-434

FOR DUMMIES®
A Wiley Brand

Adobe® Edge Animate CC For Dummies®

Published by
John Wiley & Sons, Inc.
111 River Street
Hoboken, NJ 07030-5774

www.wiley.com

Adobe® Edge Animate CC

FOR DUMMIES®

A Wiley Brand

About the Author

Michael Rohde (San Francisco, California) has worked as a web development professional and writer for 19 years. His experience ranges from marketing collateral to technical writing to website content. Mr. Rohde wrote a series of freelance articles for HTMLgoodies.com on the topics of CSS3, HTML5, and other trends in website development. This includes a series of articles on working with Joomla! as well as Adobe Edge Animate CC. His skills include Joomla!, SEO, content development, HTML, JavaScript, CSS, CMS, writing, page design, and web development. Michael is the Founder, Publisher, Editor, and Writer for his own site, GoozerNation.com, which won first prize in Amazon's Domino Project Associates Contest. Mr. Rohde currently lives in the Bay Area of Northern California with his wife and two children and works as the Senior Editor for Freeman, Sullivan & Co.

Dedication

This book is dedicated to my family. Much gratitude goes out to my parents; without them, I probably would have never earned my technical writing stripes. And to my wife and kids who sacrificed evenings and more than one weekend to allow me the time to write, rewrite, take screenshots, retake screenshots, and drone on and on over writing this book, which took a year to complete. To their credit, they encourage me to keep on writing. I love you all.

Author's Acknowledgments

This book would not have been possible without the encouragement, recommendations, and guidance that I received from many people across several different organizations. It all began with Brad Jones, currently of QuinStreet, who referred me to Wiley when I asked him how to get started writing books. Brad introduced me to Mary Bednarek, who then introduced me to Katie Feltman, who became my Acquisitions Editor. Later, I connected with Pat O'Brien, whose editing skills turned the book into what you see today. I want to thank them all for taking a chance on me as a first-time book author.

I also want to thank the good folks at Adobe, in particular Josh Hatwich, who invited me to join the Customer Advisory Board for Adobe Edge Animate. My participation on the board provided much of the content that I wrote for this book. In addition, I want to acknowledge Corrinna Rainwater of Adobe for providing her technical edits. Her contributions provided the extra details that helped me look like I knew what I was doing.

Publisher's Acknowledgments

We're proud of this book; please send us your comments at http://dummies.custhelp.com. For other comments, please contact our Customer Care Department within the U.S. at 877-762-2974, outside the U.S. at 317-572-3993, or fax 317-572-4002.

Some of the people who helped bring this book to market include the following:

Acquisitions, Editorial, and Vertical Websites

Project Editor: Pat O'Brien

Senior Copy Editor: Barry Childs-Helton

Technical Editor: Corrinna Rainwater

Editorial Manager: Kevin Kirschner

Editorial Assistant: Annie Sullivan

Sr. Editorial Assistant: Cherie Case

Cover Photo: © iStockphoto.com/Cary Westfall

Composition Services

Project Coordinator: Katie Crocker

Layout and Graphics: Jennifer Creasey, Joyce Haughey

Proofreader: Toni Settle

Indexer: Potomac Indexing, LLC

Publishing and Editorial for Technology Dummies

Richard Swadley, Vice President and Executive Group Publisher

Andy Cummings, Vice President and Publisher

Mary Bednarek, Executive Acquisitions Director

Mary C. Corder, Editorial Director

Publishing for Consumer Dummies

Kathleen Nebenhaus, Vice President and Executive Publisher

Composition Services

Debbie Stailey, Director of Composition Services

Contents at a Glance

Table of Contents

Introduction

*M*y interest in Edge Animate started when my editor at HTMLgoodies.com sent me an e-mail asking if I was interested in covering a couple of new software titles that Adobe was working on. The first title was Adobe Muse, a website creation tool aimed primarily at designers. The other title was Adobe Edge, which was later renamed as Adobe Edge Animate CC. As a person who prides himself on always wanting to learn new things, I took up my editor's offer, and I downloaded a free preview of Edge. From there, I wrote several articles for HTMLgoodies on how to use Edge and what it could do. My interest became so deep that I wanted to pursue writing a book on the topic. Now, more than a year later, you're holding that book in your hands.

I was lucky enough to be involved with the Adobe developers who created Edge Animate. I attended the Customer Advisory Board meetings online and took careful notes for each new preview release. I had to keep my mouth shut under terms of an NDA, and it was tough to not start writing articles right away on new features that were about to be announced. It was very exciting watching the software develop over the months. I saw new features added, then removed, then implemented back in. I provided some of my own input on what features I would like to see added and how the tool could be used.

Hopefully, through this book, I can convey everything I learned over the past year to you in a simple, easy-to-understand format that even the most inexperienced designer, animator, developer, or hobbyist can learn from and appreciate. It is my sincere wish that you learn how to use Adobe Edge Animate CC so that you can use it effectively in your day-to-day work. You can find me on both Facebook (www.facebook.com/AdobeEdgeAnimateForDummies) and Twitter (https://twitter.com/AnimateDummies).

Foolish Assumptions

I assumed absolutely nothing when I wrote this book. Except for maybe that you are a die-hard web content creator who yearns to learn the most advanced web techniques on the planet, which of course, this book provides for you. On the other hand, you really don't even have to be all that die-hard about wanting to find out how to make animations using HTML5, JavaScript, and CSS without even knowing how to code. All I ask for is at least a mild curiosity on what Adobe has built with Edge Animate and what it can do for you.

If you picked up this book looking for a replacement for Adobe Flash, then you may want to keep searching. Although it may be true that Edge Animate may eventually replace Flash, that isn't going to happen now or in the next year or two. I wrote this book assuming that you've never worked in Flash or even know the first thing about Flash. In fact, just forget about Flash altogether. You will never read a sentence that begins with, "Just like in Flash, you can. . . ." *Adobe Edge Animate CC For Dummies* is focused on the future, and there is very little discussion on the past.

How This Book Is Organized

This book was painstakingly organized, then torn apart, then put together again. The end result is a highly polished, extremely well put together book that will have you jumping from one chapter to the next. The editors did an excellent job of trying to make me, as the author, look good. Here's what we wound up with.

Part 1: Getting Started with Edge Animate

In the first part of this book, I walk you through the background of the Edge suite of tools that Adobe has put together as a means for web developers to help create the web. I also discuss browser concerns and compatibility, which, I hope, becomes an obsolete chapter in the coming years.

I also go into detail on how you can design interactive and adaptive presentations using Edge Animate. This includes the ability to reuse symbols for multiple projects, incorporating a responsive web design, figuring out the multi-featured publishing options, and more.

Also included in the first part is a process for creating an animation project with ideas on how to present your project online. After all, what good is an animation that lives only on your desktop — put it online and let the world see your creation!

The first part concludes with you actually using Edge Animate by drawing and editing elements. Hopefully, you find the entire book is filled with functional and effective instruction that you can use in your everyday work (or fun).

Part II: Adopting Tools and Techniques

The second part of this book dives in to a discussion on the tools and features of Adobe Edge Animate CC. I go into detail on using the Timeline, working with keyframes, and understanding how the Stage works.

I also start discussions on working with triggers, actions, labels, and adding attributes to cursors. All these features enable you to make animations that your audience can interact with.

Part II finishes with details on using the workspace and customizing it as you prefer. You can manipulate all of the frames and panels to appear to your liking. What's more, you can save your own custom layout for use with future projects.

Part III: Formatting and Animating

The third part of this book is all about the formatting and animating. At this point, you really get to the meat of the Edge Animate software. I go into detail on the Transform tool, setting visibility, positioning, and sizing. In addition, there are whole chapters on animating color, borders, corners, shadows, and more. This includes animating and formatting text boxes.

This part concludes with chapters on using the Elements panel, the Library panel, and even more on fonts. There's a ton you can do with Edge Animate, and these chapters are geared to make it all the more user-friendly.

Part IV: Putting Your Animation to Use

All the formatting and animating in the world would be pointless if you couldn't put your animation to use. That's where Part IV comes into play. I devote pages of text to explaining about the Edge Animate project structure and the files that Edge Animate generates, including files for use with Apple iBooks and Adobe's InDesign.

Getting your animation ready for publication goes beyond just clicking Save. You can set up several different types of publishing options depending on how and where you want to use your project. If you want to put your animation online, this part has you covered with discussions on putting your project into an existing web page, into a Joomla! or WordPress site, or on putting it online as a stand-alone page.

Part V: Creating Sample Projects

Part V was my favorite to write. This is where I could put to practical use everything taught in all of the proceeding chapters. While writing these sections, I tried to go as step-by-step as possible, but I also assumed that you took the time to become familiar with the basics. After all, you have to crawl before you can walk, and you have to walk before you can run.

After you start running through this part, you will be creating slideshows, interactive tutorials, and even animated children's books. You also find out how to synchronize elements and how to use easing and rotating effectively. In addition, I present examples on how to create navigation for one-page sites such as infographics or even a restaurant site. I even include how to incorporate your slideshow as a symbol into another site. I found it very cool to tie so many different aspects together for a cohesive project.

The last chapter in this part may prove the most beneficial in terms of discovering some very cutting-edge web techniques in terms of developing a responsive web design. Creating animations that can respond to screen size is a growing trend in web development, and the very first version of Adobe Edge Animate CC has you covered.

Part VI: The Part of Tens

The "Part of Tens" rounds this book out with a couple of top-ten lists. What *For Dummies* book would be complete without this section? Here, I present one list of the top ten users of Adobe Edge Animate CC and follow that up with a list of resources that are sprinkled throughout this book.

Icons Used in This Book

I use several icons throughout this book as a way to draw your attention to special information. Depending on the icon, this information is the type of stuff you can skip right over or give a quick glance, or in some really special cases, it's the type of information that you may want to study closely.

The Technical Stuff icon mainly refers to code that developers may like. These are the icons that many of you may want to glance over briefly, whereas others of you, perhaps the Cliff Clavens out there, might relish.

This entire book is full of Tip icons, ranging from special shortcut keys to performing tasks a different way than presented in the main text. Some tips contain useful information that doesn't quite fit with the other text but that I still want to get across to you.

 Ahhh, the dreaded Warning icon. This icon lets you know when pirates are about to attack. Whoops. Nope, that was for my other *For Dummies* book about sailing the high seas (that book doesn't exist, at least, not yet). The Warning icon mostly denotes when things may not work or when you could be in danger of losing your project. I recommend reading the warnings.

 The Remember icon presents information that's useful keep in mind for other times. You own the book, so you don't actually need to *remember* most of the stuff that's in it. Just open the book and follow the instructions when you need to.

Where to Go From Here

This book works a couple of ways. If you want to comprehend the capabilities of Edge Animate and make projects with it, simply start at the beginning and follow through, page by page, until you reach the Index at the back. It's worth the trip.

If you have a question about a feature, find it in the Index and jump straight to that page.

Occasionally, we have updates to our technology books. If this book does have technical updates, they'll be posted at www.dummies.com/go/ edgenaimatefdupdates.

I can't promise that every word will have you riveted to your seat with hands trembling in anticipation as you turn the page, but I can sincerely tell you that I wrote this book to show you, in the best possible way that I could, how to use Adobe Edge Animate CC.

If you're ready to see all about Adobe Edge Animate CC, turn the page. It's time to start!

Part I

Getting Started with Adobe Edge Animate

getting started with **Adobe Edge Animate**

In this part . . .

- ✔ Cruising the Adobe Creative Cloud
- ✔ Applying Edge Animate as a solution
- ✔ Exploring options
- ✔ Creating a composition
- ✔ Visit www.dummies.com for great Dummies content online.

Chapter 1

Introducing Adobe Edge Animate CC

*I*n this chapter, I show you the Adobe Creative Cloud and all the tools, services, apps, and software titles available; this includes Adobe Edge Animate CC. Adobe has fully embraced the cloud; now you can get the latest updates and features without having to wait for the next full version. A subscription to the Creative Cloud means access to all the latest developments.

What's even better is that Edge Animate is fully compatible with many of the titles in the Creative Cloud — with more features added regularly.

Edge Animate uses HTML5, which (even now) not all browsers support. Fortunately, Adobe provides features that help you when your audience isn't using modern browsers. Most likely you'll find there's more support for HTML5 these days than for Flash; the jury is still out on what this means for the future of Flash.

But onward: This chapter also provides an overview of creating a project in Edge Animate. You may recognize this process as being the same you use for many other different types of projects. It's all about the organization and planning.

Adobe Wants You to Create the Web

As part of introducing Edge Animate, Adobe also announced

✔ **Edge Suite:** An entire set of tools to help you create your part of the web.

✔ **Creative Cloud:** Everything you need to use Edge Animate is in the cloud.

✔ **Design and development features:** Edge Animate is great for both designers and developers.

✔ **Compatibility:** Edge Animate works with many different software tools.

✔ **Web-friendly animation features:** Adobe Edge Animate CC comes with a long list of features for creating modern web animations.

Introducing the Edge suite

In late September 2012, at the Create the Web event in downtown San Francisco, Adobe announced its entire suite of Edge tools and software. Through this event, Adobe reaffirmed its commitment to providing the best services for creative artists, web designers, and animators. It also cranked up support for HTML5 as the future of the World Wide Web. Flash animation is fading into the history books.

The Adobe Edge Suite is one part of the Creative Cloud that Adobe announced (as shown in Figure 1-1 and featured in its own sidebar later in the chapter) consists of these tools:

✔ **Edge Animate:** The main tool for turning static graphics and text into modern web animations.

✔ **Reflow** (planned for release after the publication of this book)**:** Geared toward helping designers to create a responsive web design.

✔ **Code:** You can use Code to preview CSS, edit code, and integrate other code for design work.

✔ **Inspect:** An excellent app that allows you to synch your desktop to your mobile device so you can install updates as they happen.

✔ **Web Fonts:** Free fonts that you can use with Edge Animate.

✔ **Typekit:** Another source of fonts that you can use with Edge Animate.

✔ **PhoneGap Build:** A tool for creating mobile apps with HTML, CSS, and JavaScript.

Figure 1-1:
The Adobe Edge Suite is available in the Creative Cloud.

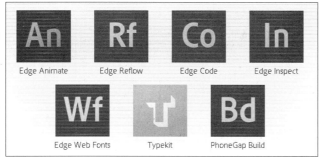

Your tools are in the cloud

All these tools and services are available through Adobe's Creative Cloud — a one-stop shop for the majority of Adobe's creative software (including Photoshop, After Effects, InDesign, Illustrator, Fireworks, Muse, and Dreamweaver). Most tools for most of these software products are compatible with Edge Animate.

You can get started with the Creative Cloud with a free membership for 30 days that includes 2GB of cloud storage and limited access to services. You can find more about the Creative Cloud online at http://html.adobe.com.

Creating animated web content

Adobe Edge Animate CC is a brand new software tool that allows everyone from beginners to expert web designers to create animated web content. What separates Edge Animate from other animation tools is that it uses the most advanced standards and methodology in its code. This rampant modernity includes the use of HTML5 and JavaScript — in particular, jQuery.

Adobe is providing the best of both worlds to accommodate all types of animators:

- ✔ If working with jQuery sounds scary, even if that's a good kind of scary, it shouldn't. Edge Animate does all the coding for you. All you have to do is conjure up the creative aspects of your design.

- ✔ On the other hand, if you do know how to code with jQuery and you like to dive in to the brackets, then Edge Animate provides a very functional code panel from which you can work.

Collaborating with other publishing tools

While Edge Animate is a terrific tool for creating online content, it doesn't actually publish your animation online. Fortunately, Edge Animate is compatible with several publishing tools, applications, and platforms. Here's a quick look at each tool and application.

iBook Files

If you weren't already aware, iBooks is one of the most popular and most downloaded apps for Apple devices, including iPhones and iPads.

By using Edge Animate to create your compositions, you can feel confident that your audience will see your animation play flawlessly on some of the most popular phones and tablets around. Even better, you can export your Edge Animate composition in formats that are compatible for use with Apple's iBook Author.

Adobe InDesign

InDesign is desktop publishing software that is also made by Adobe. It allows you to create pages for print, tablets, and other platforms and devices. InDesign is also part of Adobe's Creative Cloud and works well with Edge Animate. Exporting files from Edge Animate is a matter of clicking a few menu items and then it's only a matter of placing the files into InDesign.

InDesign outputs ePUB documents that work on the Apple iPad. The iBook app for the iPad uses the ePUB format. Through these tools, you are provided another way to incorporate your animation compositions into iBooks.

Adobe Dreamweaver

Adobe Dreamweaver has been helping budding web developers create websites since 2005, which is when Adobe acquired Dreamweaver from Macromedia. Using Dreamweaver, a web designer can whip up HTML websites and mobile apps with cross-platform compatibility, loads of features, and multiscreen previews. Now, with the release of Edge Animate 1.0, Adobe has updated Dreamweaver to include support for your animation projects: You can continue building websites in Dreamweaver *and* import your projects from Edge Animate.

Adobe Fireworks

Adobe Fireworks is another former Macromedia software product that you can use to create bitmap and vector graphics. Web designers use it in combination with Dreamweaver, and now Edge Animate, to create interfaces, onscreen designs, and interactive content for tablets and phones.

Adobe Muse

Adobe Muse is another tool for the website builder, aimed directly at design artists with little or no coding skill. Muse is brand new; a preview was released in 2012.

If you're a designer who's comfortable with creating print layouts, then working with Muse should come naturally. Plus, if you want your design site to feature a composition made in Edge Animate, such projects are easy to add to your Muse site.

Adobe Inspect

Adobe Shadow was renamed Inspect in late 2012.

Presently, Flash won't work on several types of devices — but Edge Animate will — and you'll want to preview your work on as many different screen sizes as you can. That's where Inspect comes into play. This tool allows you to view updates that you make to your animation on a variety of devices instantly.

Highlighting the Critical Features

Adobe Edge Animate CC is about more than just web animation. Some advanced web designers have already created entire sites using Edge Animate; don't be surprised if Edge Animate replaces Flash in the near future. The reason's a no-brainer: Because Edge Animate uses HTML5 and JavaScript, this expands your potential audience by making your content available to view on modern browsers and a wider range of devices — even those that block Flash.

The Edge Animate features that are most vital to web development include links, loops, interactivity, and a responsive web design. The limits on what you can do with Edge Animate rest mainly within the confines of your imagination. With Edge Animate, you'll create slide shows, logos, and sites; animated or not, with or without links, all text, all images, or a combination of text and images.

If you have a passion, or just have a passing interest in creating web animation, then you at the very least owe it to yourself to check out Adobe Edge Animate CC — and to continue reading this book.

Maintaining Browser Compatibility

Adobe Edge Animate CC works in all modern browsers — including the most recent versions of Chrome, Firefox, Opera, Safari, and Internet Explorer 9.

It also works on all tablets and smart phones that have modern browsers installed. For audiences that don't use modern browsers, Edge Animate does provide a fallback option that you can use so that your animation does not appear broken. This fallback option is discussed later in this section.

Compatibility is important for web content; if a browser doesn't support your code, then your animation won't work. No wonder Adobe Edge Animate CC creates code that works in all modern browsers.

A brief history of HTML

HTML5 is the slowly evolving next iteration of HTML (HyperText Markup Language), the coding language that developers use to create web pages. The very first version of HTML was introduced in the early 1990s. HTML2 was released in 1995. In 1997, HTML3 came out and was closely followed by HTML4 — the version that most web developers are familiar with — which is presently the predominant markup language.

Over the past few years, enterprising developers have turned their attention to creating web content with HTML5, even though it isn't the new standard for everyone — at least not yet. Modern web browsers, however, are already utilizing HTML5 functionality, and HTML5 will most likely become the norm for web development in the near future. Using and learning HTML5 now will put you ahead of the pack as the future of web development unfolds.

Concerns with HTML5 and older browsers

Many web developers are concerned that not all parts of HTML5 are compatible with all browsers. This is especially true with Internet Explorer. Where many features of HTML5 will work in browsers such as Chrome and Firefox, they will not always work in Internet Explorer. This leaves many web developers questioning how widely they should start using HTML5. It isn't in a web developer's best interest to create web pages that don't work in all browsers — but the future is still a bit murky, and lots of folks are content to use old browsers.

Adobe has addressed these issues with Edge Animate. You can feel safe and secure knowing that your Edge Animate web compositions will work in all modern browsers, including the current versions of Firefox, Chrome, Safari, and Internet Explorer 9.

You don't need to know HTML5, or even HTML, to use Edge Animate. But the more you know, the better off you'll be if you need to use the code to help implement it for viewing. The Edge Animate software creates the code for you while you build your web animation.

When you save your Edge Animate file, the software creates several different files. One of those files has the .html filename extension. The HTML5 code is within the .html file. You can view this file with any plain text editor such as Notepad. After you're done creating your composition, you can view the animation in a web browser — either from within the software, or by double-clicking the .html file, which opens and plays your animation in your default browser.

Desktop browser compatibility

Compatibility with the Microsoft Internet Explorer web browser is an issue that web developers have to contend with when developing sites. Microsoft has been slow to update Internet Explorer to be compatible with HTML5 — and code that works perfectly fine in Chrome, Safari, and Firefox doesn't behave well in earlier versions of Internet Explorer.

For example, if you code a border to have rounded edges, then your corners will appear rounded off in Chrome and Firefox; but view that same site in IE and suddenly your rounded edges appear square. Issues like this can ruin a website's design.

Browsers such as Firefox, Chrome, Safari, and Opera already support many aspects of HTML5. There are no concerns with Adobe Edge Animate CC compositions working perfectly in these browsers. These browsers also have built-in automatic updates for their users. Because of that, web designers and developers can feel certain that their users are most likely using the most current version of that browser.

What to do for Internet Explorer 8 and older versions

In an ideal world, everyone would upgrade their browsers regularly. Unfortunately, not everyone can do that, for whatever reason. Even though Internet Explorer 9 has opened the door to HTML5 compatibility, which means Edge Animate works in that version of the browser, not all IE users have upgraded their browsers. It's still not uncommon for many IE users to use versions 7 and 8 — and (to many designers' horror and dismay) IE 6 is still in use by many people.

Adobe Edge Animate CC compositions will not work in Internet Explorer 8 and older versions, just as HTML5 doesn't work in IE6.

However, the good news is that more and more web users are upgrading their browsers, and usage of IE6 is slowly dwindling. With that said, though, Edge Animate works in all modern portable browsers. If your main goal is to create animated applications for use on smart phones and tablets, then you're very much in luck.

If you're creating web animations for an audience who still uses IE8 and older browsers, that lurking obsolescence can be a concern when you're using Adobe Edge Animate CC. Say that you spend countless hours developing the perfect web animation and then put it online. You tested it in Firefox and IE 9, and it works perfectly. Then you walk across the hall to show it to your boss — and to your horror, it doesn't work because your boss is using IE 6. Well, in the real world, there's a good chance many of your clients and customers are also using an earlier version of IE that isn't compatible with Edge Animate. Fortunately, Edge Animate has you covered with at least two options: You can (a) use Google Chrome Frame support or (b) use *down-level browser support* — a feature that enables you to create a *poster* (a static image), or to use static HTML, to replace the animation — which keeps your website from appearing "broken." Your audience sees an image that looks the way it's supposed to look, even though it's not animated. (Chapter 14 details down-level support.)

Google Chrome Frame support

Edge Animate has a feature that enables you to use Google Chrome Frame support for browsers that don't support animation. As a next step to down-level browser support, you can publish Edge Animate content so that your audience can view it on IE 6, 7, or 8 using Google Chrome Frame. For the user who doesn't already have Google Chrome Frame, you can also control the experience of installing it.

Edge Animate has down-level Stages

The *down-level Stages* in Edge Animate are versions of the Stage that you can use to create and publish a down-level version of your composition that will be compatible with browsers that don't support HTML5 animation. (I go into detail on down-level Stage usage in Chapter 14.) The down-level Stages offer only minimal creation tools, but you can

- ✔ Import graphics and create text elements.
- ✔ Import a poster from the main composition.

Basically, the animations that you create and place online can detect the browsers your audience is using. If the code detects that someone is using a non-compatible browser for your animation, then it reverts to showing a poster image instead of the animation. This saves your website from appearing broken. Instead of seeing an animation that doesn't work, the audience sees a poster — a still frame — that you create from the animation.

Again, you don't have to know code for the down-level Stage support to work. Although coding for browser detection can be tricky, Edge Animate has that capability built in — and it's an option you can choose when you're ready to publish.

Compatibility with tablet and mobile browsers

Where Adobe Flash fails, Adobe Edge Animate CC works. It's well known that Apple doesn't allow Adobe Flash animation to work in its portable devices — and that includes the iPhone, iPod touch, and iPad. Steve Jobs, before his passing, stated that Flash had too many security vulnerabilities and other negative aspects for Apple to allow Flash to work with iOS.

Edge Animate, on the other hand, doesn't suffer from those issues. Your Edge Animate compositions will work just fine on Apple products — and on Android devices — whether tablets of all types, smart phones, and other devices that use modern mobile browsers.

Creating an Edge Animate Composition

The process for creating an Edge Animate CC composition isn't too different from creating any other type of content. When starting, you should consider what, where, and how you want your animation to appear. Will your animation be part of an existing website? Are you adding an animation to complement a book? Is your client requesting a brand new animated logo? Perhaps you want to create an advertisement to appear on the web? You can create all these projects using Edge Animate.

Here's the basic outline for creating an Edge Animate composition:

1. Determine how you and your audience will use this animation.

2. Collect your images and other assets.

3. Write an outline.

4. Create and save commonly used elements such as buttons for re-use later.

5. Start animating.

6. Save and export your finished animation.

Before you start animating, consider whether your animation will be viewed in an e-reader, in the browser, in iBooks, or be an app for use on both iOS and Android devices.

No matter the device, if it supports HTML5 and JavaScript, your Edge Animate project will run smoothly.

Gathering your assets

After you know what you want to create and where you want it to appear, it's time to start gathering your *assets* — electronically drawn images, photographs, paragraphs of text, or a combination of all three — that will make up the final animation. Edge Animate makes it easy to import or create these assets.

Creating an outlined approach to your animation

At this point you have defined the purpose of your animation and the art to make it beautiful. Now you need to create a *wireframe,* essentially an outline of how you want your animation to play. Sure, you can wing it and make it up as you go along, but an excellent idea is to picture your animation in your head, and then put down on paper how you imagine your animation will play from start to finish. This outline provides a base from which you can work.

Making symbols for frequently used elements

If you know your animation is going to contain many similar *elements,* or the same elements repeated over and over, you want to create those elements first. Elements are the different pieces that make up your animation. An element can be a box that you draw, a text box that you specify, an image that you import, and so on.

An element that you may want to reuse can be a button, or an asset that you re-use throughout the animation, or any type of navigation the audience can use.

After you create this element and have it behaving the way you want, you can then save it as a *symbol*. You can then export this symbol for use in other projects. That way, if this animation becomes a part of a series of animations and you want to re-use the same symbols, you'll be ahead of the game by having some assets already saved and ready to go when you create the actual animation.

 You can even save an entire animation project as a symbol. For example, if you create a slideshow animation, you can save that entire slide show as a symbol, which you can then export from Edge Animate — and then import into a different Edge Animate project. (Chapter 12 has the details on creating and working with symbols.)

Animators, start your animating

When you have a purpose for your animation, all of your assets are lined up and ready to go, and you've saved your multi-use elements as symbols, it's time to start animating.

To start animating, you import your assets onto the Stage. Then you use the Timeline to create keyframes. A *keyframe* represents an animation sequence. For example, if you animate a box moving from one side of the Stage to the other, that animation is represented in the Timeline as a keyframe. (I go into the details of working with keyframes and the Timeline in Chapter 4.) From there, you add actions to your elements for interactivity. As you create your animation, you can preview it to make sure the animation is behaving as you expect it to behave.

Saving and exporting your animation

When you finish creating your animation project, you want to save or export your composition for use by your audience or for use in another project or design tool. Edge Animate provides many options to export and save your work. Likewise, there are multitudes of options on how you can present your work both online, or in iBooks, or for use with other design tools. Chapter 15 has the details for putting your project online.

Adobe Edge Animate CC and the Creative Cloud

Adobe has embraced the cloud in a big way. Over the past few years, the term "cloud" has become a popular buzzword among the digerati (the tech gurus and their disciples) to mean all the documents, software, apps, pictures, and such that are stored online — which you can access through the Internet. When someone says, "it's in the cloud," the translation is, "it's available online."

Adobe's answer to the cloud comes in the form of a feature called the Creative Cloud — an online location where you can find the latest versions of the vast majority of Adobe creative software titles. No longer do you need to wait for new features to sprout and full-version cycles to run their course before you can receive software updates. By placing everything in the cloud, Adobe can update your software as needed — that's one of the main benefits of paying a subscription.

The software in the Creative Cloud includes Photoshop, InDesign, Flash, and much more. Brand new titles, as of 2013, include the Edge suite of tools.

The Edge suite of tools includes Edge Animate, Code, Inspect, Web Fonts, Typekit, PhoneGap Build, and an upcoming title currently called Reflow. Each of these tools serves a unique purpose, and they all tie in nicely together:

- Edge Code is all about coding the web. Currently in preview, you can use Code to preview CSS, edit code and integrate other code for design work. Code is based on an understanding of how HTML5, CSS3, and JavaScript work together and continually evolve. Adobe states that, "if you have the skills to use Edge Code, you also have the skills to customize the editor and contribute new features." You can find more information here: http://html.adobe.com/edge/code

- Edge Inspect is all about previewing the creative content that you create. Adobe knows that just because you might create your content on a desktop, that doesn't mean your audience will view it on a desktop monitor. Rather, your audience may view your content on a tablet, or a phone, or any other number of devices. Inspect allows you to wirelessly pair several different types of devices to the machine where you create the content. When you do this, you can then view the changes you make update instantly as you work. More information here: http://html.adobe.com/edge/inspect

- Edge Web Fonts is all about free web fonts. This large collection of fonts was gathered from sources such as Adobe, Google, and independent designers. Web Fonts is already available for use with Edge Code — and will eventually become a part of Edge Reflow as well. The fonts are served by Typekit, which leads us to . . . (More information here: http://html.adobe.com/edge/webfonts)

- Typekit is all about commercial fonts. Launched in September 2009 by Small Batch, Inc. (the folks behind Google Analytics), it was acquired by Adobe in October 2011. You can find over 700 fonts in Typekit and can search for them by classification, properties, or recommended use. Adobe makes it very easy to add these fonts into your websites by copying and pasting a couple of lines of code into the head tag of your HTML. More information here: http://html.adobe.com/edge/typekit

- PhoneGap Build is all about mobile. You can use PhoneGap Build to create mobile apps with HTML, CSS, and JavaScript.

With this tool, you build your app in the cloud, and Adobe keeps you current with the latest SDK (software development kit). Probably the most impressive feature to PhoneGap Build is that you can create iOS, Android, Windows Phone, Blackberry, webOS, and Symbian technologies, all from this one tool. More information here: `http://html.adobe.com/edge/phonegap-build`

✔ Reflow is all about responsive web design, an upcoming trend in web design that content developers are paying attention to. A responsive web design allows you to design once and have your creation look great no matter the screen size your audience is using. To get notified when a preview of Reflow becomes available, you can sign up here: `http://html.adobe.com/edge/reflow`

You can access all these tools and more through a subscription to the Creative Cloud. If you're unsure about spending money on cloud services, Adobe offers a free 30-day trial. This trial period gives you access to limited services and 2GB of storage. You can use the storage to save your projects. If your trial expires and you have projects saved in the cloud, you don't have to worry about losing your work. When you decide to start a paid subscription using the same account as the free trial, then your work is ready and waiting for you to return. Following this same line of thought, if you allow your paid subscription to run out, Adobe saves your projects in the cloud for a determined length of time. This allows you to renew your subscription later, and your work is still there; provided that you don't wait too long.

Finishing the process

Eventually, through this process, you've created an animation using HTML5 and jQuery — without typing a single line of code. Your audience may never know the technologies that made the animation they watch and interact with possible (for that matter, you may not fully understand the advanced coding techniques that make it possible — or ever have to). But that's the beauty of Adobe Edge Animate CC: It does all the heavy lifting behind the scenes, which allows you to sit back and do what you do best — create beautiful animated and interactive content that can respond to fit and form with any number of screen sizes and devices.

Presenting Your Project Online

After pouring your blood, sweat, and tears going through the process of creating your animation, you most likely want to put it online so that the world can enjoy your magnificent creation. There are many ways you can put your Edge Animate composition online or embed it in another tool for presentation, such as an iBook. Your animation can be a standalone web page, occupy part of a website as its own page, or be embedded in an existing page. You can add Edge Animate projects to content management systems (CMS) such as

WordPress, Joomla!, or Blogger. See Chapters 13 through 16 for more information on posting your animation online.

When you save your Edge Animate project, the software creates many different files for you. One of those files is written in HTML5. You can upload this HTML file, along with the other files that Edge Animate creates, to the web via FTP to your site or your client's site. Doing it that way allows you to create a single web page for your animation or make it part of a larger site.

It is also possible to embed your animation into an existing web page. If you want to do that, then you must still upload the files that Edge Animate creates for you to the folder structure of the site where the page lives. Then, you grab a snippet of code from the HTML file that Edge Animate created for you and place that snippet of code into the HTML file of the page where you want the animation to appear.

The snippet of code that you want to copy and paste from the Edge Animate HTML file to the HTML file of the page you want to embed your animation looks like this:

```
<!--Adobe Edge Runtime-->
    <script type="text/javascript" charset="utf-8" src="Untitled-1_edgePreload.
        js"></script>
    <style>
        .edgeLoad-EDGE-15449885 { visibility:hidden; }
    </style>
<!--Adobe Edge Runtime End-->
```

You also have to place a line of code such as this into the body tag of the page:

```
<div id="Stage" class="EDGE-13887483">
```

For more about this requirement, see Chapter 15.

The preceding code may look a little intimidating for those who don't know code, but there's really nothing to fret over. Basically, this code snippet is what calls your animation into action. The HTML file acts as a shell that triggers the JavaScript. Make sure that you upload all the files that Edge Animate creates for you, so that your composition doesn't appear broken. (See Chapter 15 for more information on putting your project on the web.)

The `.edgeLoad` line of code in this code snippet contains a unique number, in this case, 15449885. This number was created by Edge Animate to connect the HTML file to the JavaScript files. If you alter this number, you will break the connection between the files and your animation will not play correctly.

Chapter 2

Discovering Awesome Features and Tools

In This Chapter

▶ Getting to know the essential animation tools

▶ Creating interactive, responsive animations

▶ Exploring font, language, and publishing options

▶ Seeing how Edge Animate supports your coding habit

*A*dobe Edge Animate CC is a powerful, flexible program for creating and publishing animations for the web. In this chapter, I introduce you to many features of Adobe Edge Animate CC, including essentials such as the Stage, the Timeline, and familiar drawing tools. And I tell you about the options that Edge Animate provides for publishing and saving files, as well as choices it offers for your interface language and for web-friendly fonts. For those who like to dive below the surface, I describe the framework of the JavaScript API and working with native HTML in the code panels that Edge Animate places at your disposal. And — probably most important in this day and age of multiple screen sizes — you find out about creating a responsive web design that resizes itself to fit various devices.

Meeting Your Most-Used Animation Tools

Building even a basic animation in Adobe Edge Animate CC involves using three primary tools:

✔ **Stage:** The Stage is a live HTML window built directly into Edge Animate. It's where you draw elements such as rectangles, squares, and circles. Later on, you can add style and animations to those elements and even add actions such as links. You can also import images to the Stage — which you can also animate and make interactive for your audience. Finally, you can use the Stage to preview your animation.

✔ **Timeline:** This part of the screen is where you add keyframes and animation sequences that make your composition come alive. From the Timeline you can edit where, when, and for how long an animation sequence takes place.

✔ **Drawing toolbar:** You can draw rectangles, rounded rectangles, and even ellipses, including perfect circles, using the drawing tools. Also included is a Text tool so you can write text within your animation. Adding elements to your animation is one of the first steps in creating a composition in Edge Animate.

These three tools — the Stage, Timeline, and Drawing toolbar — are essential to creating an animation. The Stage is where your composition comes alive; the Timeline is where you plot your animation sequences; and the drawing tools help you create the elements that become the assets of your animation.

Putting a spotlight on the Stage

The majority of the Adobe Edge Animate CC interface consists of the Stage. The Stage is where you build your animations. When you first open Edge Animate, and you choose to create a new file, you're presented with a crisp, white, blank Stage from which you can start to build your project (see Figure 2-1).

Figure 2-1:
A blank
Stage to get
you started.

The Stage is located at the top center of the interface and has the following handy characteristics for creating your animations:

✔ **It is a live HTML window:** At first, the Stage may not look like much — but as you create your animation, you notice an abundance of functionality.

One of the Stage's best features is that you can watch your animation play on it. You don't necessarily have to switch to a browser to preview your work. Instead, you can preview your animation by watching it on the Stage — because the Stage is actually an HTML window. It's virtually the same as a standard web browser, but it's built right into Edge Animate.

✔ **It has rules and guides:** Two additional features to the Stage are the rules and guides shown in Figure 2-2:

- One ruler runs along both the top of the Stage; another runs down the length of the Stage on the left side. You can use these rulers to help place your *assets* (such as images and text) on the Stage.

- The *guides* are thin purple lines that stretch from the ruler across the Stage and to the opposite side of the screen. You can use these guides to help position your elements on the Stage. (*Elements* can be anything from drawn circles and rectangles to images to text boxes and other parts that make up the animation.)

Figure 2-2:
The Stage, with horizontal and vertical guides shown.

To place a guide on the Stage, place the cursor over the ruler, and then click and drag. The purple guide then appears. To move the guide around the Stage, click it and drag it.

After you place guides on the Stage, any elements (images, text boxes, and such) then snap to the guides. This helps you place elements exactly where you want them.

Engaging the intuitive, accurate, and flexible Timeline

Besides the Stage, the Timeline is probably the feature you use most often with Edge Animate. You find the Timeline at the bottom of the screen, and it contains many features, as follows:

✔ **Keyframes:** You use keyframes to direct when, and for how long, an animation unfolds on the Stage. The colored bars in the Timeline, shown in Figure 2-3, represent keyframes and indicate when an animation starts, stops, and for how long it will play. You can edit these keyframes with a click and a drag.

✔ **Mode toggles:** The Timeline also allows you to toggle different modes, such as Auto-Keyframes, Auto-Transitions, and the Pin, and you can choose different Easing attributes.

✔ **Animation enhancements:** From the Timeline, you can tweak your animation in multiple ways — for example, by adding actions (see Chapter 5), specifying filter elements (see Chapter 4), and enabling Timeline snapping (also Chapter 4).

Keyframes

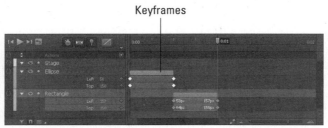

Figure 2-3:
The
Timeline.

Drawing with familiar tools

If you've ever used other drawing or image editing software, then you most likely recognize the drawing tools available in Edge Animate. If Edge Animate is the first artistic software you've used, then just relax as you discover that drawing elements such as rectangles and circles is as easy as clicking and dragging.

You can locate the drawing tools at the top of the screen, directly underneath the menu, as shown in Figure 2-4.

Drawing tools

Figure 2-4:
The drawing
tools.

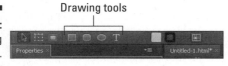

The drawing tools include a rectangle, a rounded rectangle, an ellipse for drawing circles, and a text tool for drawing text boxes.

Exploiting Features That Interact and Adapt

Adobe Edge Animate CC is about much more than moving elements around the screen. You can use many of its features to create interactivity for your audience — and fine-tune many more to configure the software to suit your preferences:

- ✔ **Interactivity:** You can build fully interactive animations with such controls and actions as buttons, links, and loops.

- ✔ **Symbols:** You can save elements you create (such as buttons) and use them again in a different animation.

- ✔ **Responsive web design:** Edge Animate enables you to build a composition that responds to browser and device window sizes.

- ✔ **Multiple publishing options:** Edge Animate offers numerous ways to publish your animation for use in different applications — such as different web browsers and iBooks — or you can import your Adobe Edge Animation into different Adobe products such as InDesign or Muse.

- ✔ **Font choices:** Edge Animate provides a multitude of font choices. If you're fussy about particular fonts, the good news is that if you can find a font on the web, you can most likely use it in your animation.

- ✔ **Choose your language:** If English is not your native language and you prefer to work in (say) German, Spanish, French, or Japanese, then Edge Animate has you covered.

Implementing interactivity intelligently

Adobe Edge Animate CC enables you to do much more than just draw and animate elements. You can also make those elements interactive, which allows your audience to click on items to make different actions happen. For example, you can make Stop, Play, and Pause buttons for an interactive slideshow. You can also create a menu by adding links that allow your audience to navigate to different parts of your animations — or to entirely different web pages.

When your audience moves the cursor around your animation, you can make different actions happen when the cursor moves over specific areas. This kind of cursor movement is called a *mouseover*. Or, if your audience is using tablets or smart phones to view your animation, you can allow them to simply tap an element to cause an action.

Using Symbols to make reusable objects

At first, using Symbols may prove a bit daunting, but after you gain experience working with them, they become indispensable.

So, what exactly is a *Symbol*? It's essentially a nested animation you create that has its own independent Timeline and interactive capabilities. For example, say that you find yourself creating the same element with the same actions over and over for many different projects. By saving that recurring element as a Symbol, you can reuse it and its associated actions for any project. A prime example of a Symbol is a button. If you find yourself recreating the same button — say, a Play button for a slide show — you may want to save that Play button as a Symbol for reuse later.

You can find your Symbols in the Library panel, as shown in Figure 2-5.

Figure 2-5:
How
Symbols
appear in
the Library
panel.

Edge Animate allows you to export and import Symbols. You can also copy and paste Symbols from one project to another for ease of use. You can even copy and paste Symbols that contain other Symbols. In addition, you can export a Symbol as a separate `.ansym` project and import it into another project. See Chapter 12 for information on creating and using Symbols.

If you do find yourself using Symbols regularly, then rejoice when you find that you can export and import more than one Symbol at a time. Edge Animate combines multiple Symbols into one `.ansym` file when you export them; you can have a number of them in a single directory without worrying about conflicts. Plus, you can import those multiple Symbols by using that one file instead of several — especially useful if, besides that Play button, you also want to reuse a Stop and Pause button as well.

Incorporating responsive web design

Right along with HTML5, *responsive web design* is the latest buzzword termi-nology when it comes to web development. A responsive web design allows your animation to resize appropriately depending on the size of the browser window. This can mean many things. Say, for example, someone is viewing your animation on a desktop computer. If the user resizes the browser window to make it bigger or smaller, the elements within your animation resize themselves appropriately, with the new sizes based on percentages. For example, if the browser window is maximized at 100%, the images and so forth in your animation appear at 100%. If the browser window is shrunk to 50% of its size, then your images also shrink to 50% of their normal size.

This is a very powerful feature because there is such a wide variety of screen sizes these days. You never know whether your audience is viewing your animation on a 60-inch display, a 4-inch iPhone, or anything in between. Tablets add to the diversity of screen sizes.

Adobe Edge Animate CC handles responsive design by using percentages instead of hard coded pixels. This enables you to concentrate on your anima-tion and not have to worry about how it appears on a myriad of screen sizes.

Counting your multiple publishing options

You have more than one way to publish animations these days — and Adobe Edge Animate CC has you covered, offering a multitude of options (as shown in Figure 2-6). You can publish your animation as a standalone web page or you can embed it in an existing web page. You also find options that allow you to export your animation for use in an iBook. You can even publish your animation as a static HTML page for use on older web browsers that don't support HTML5 or animations.

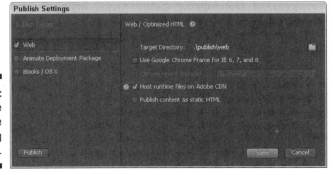

Figure 2-6:
The Edge
Animate
publishing
settings.

The static HTML files are still written with HTML5, and the animations still play. The difference is that the elements are not created via JavaScript when Edge Animate generates the static file. Instead, they exist in the HTML file. This arrangement is good for search engine optimization (SEO): Some search engines, when they find elements created dynamically with JavaScript, don't interpret those elements correctly.

Putting your best font forward

You can use a multitude of fonts on the web, and Adobe Edge Animate CC has you covered. In addition to a standard default list of fonts that are available to you (see Figure 2-7), Edge Animate also enables you to import fonts from around the web.

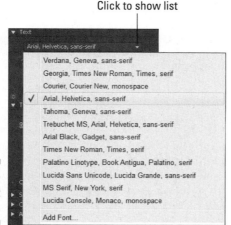

Figure 2-7:
Default font
list.

If none of these fonts satisfy your needs, you can import fonts from many different sources — including Google Web Fonts. You can also use Adobe Edge Web Fonts, which is built into Animate. And if you're familiar with Typekit (another free font tool), you can celebrate knowing that tool also works with Edge Animate.

Keep in mind that Typekit is a tool for the very experienced user: You can also use your own font, or one that you purchased, but you have to host the font on your web server. To do so, you have to create a style sheet with an `@font-face` rule and place it in the project file folder. Here's how:

1. **In Edge Animate, in the Web Font dialog box, type this line:**

   ```
   <link href="mystyle.css" rel="stylesheet" type="text/css">
   ```

   Another dialog box appears.

2. **In this second dialog box, input the name of the font as specified in the style sheet.**

If you need more information on how to write the Cascading Style Sheet (CSS) code for a custom font in the style sheet, you can find it here:

http://blog.freelancer-id.com/2010/06/02/custom-font-for-all-browsers/

I discuss fonts in more detail in Chapter 12.

Working in your language of choice

Adobe Edge Animate CC is global in many regards — including the language you see on menus and panels. If you feel more comfortable working in a language other than English, Edge Animate makes it easy for you to change the language used in the software to one of many popular languages.

From the Help menu, as shown in Figure 2-8, you can choose from several different languages. When you choose a language from the Help menu, that language appears in the software. The languages that you can choose from include German, English, Spanish, French, and Japanese.

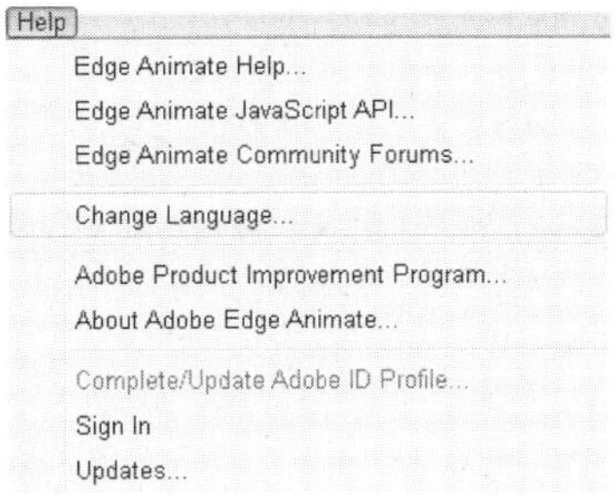

Figure 2-8:
The Change Language option from the Help menu.

| Help |
| Edge Animate Help... |
| Edge Animate JavaScript API... |
| Edge Animate Community Forums... |
| Change Language... |
| Adobe Product Improvement Program... |
| About Adobe Edge Animate... |
| Complete/Update Adobe ID Profile... |
| Sign In |
| Updates... |

If you do pick another language, you have to close and restart Edge Animate to see the change take effect. After you select the language that you want, the interface does not automatically update, simply close the program and then reopen it to see your newly selected language.

Digging into the Code

Adobe Edge Animate CC makes the creation of animations possible for a range of users — from those who consider working with code a challenge to experienced developers and engineers who eat code for breakfast. On the one hand, you really don't need any coding skills to create professional animations with Edge Animate; on the other hand, Edge Animate provides

- ✔ **Native HTML5 code,** which is very clean — no proprietary or unnecessary code. This helps make the code easier to read and understand for everyone.
- ✔ **A persistent code panel,** which gives you access to editing the code by hand.
- ✔ **JavaScript API** (application programming interface), which provides an opportunity to learn the details behind the code.

Designers without coding skills can relax knowing they can still create compositions without knowing any code at all. Meanwhile, experienced developers can salute Adobe for providing access to all of the background code.

Working in native HTML

While you work in Edge Animate, the software is constantly creating code behind the scenes. While you don't necessarily have to know any HTML or JavaScript to create animations, if you do happen to have some coding skills, then you can celebrate — Edge Animate creates very clean HTML code without any proprietary baggage.

If you want to get into the code, then consider the HTML file that Edge Animate creates as the only file that you may need to open. Edge Animate does create several other types of files, including JavaScript files, but those files are dense with code. If you are not a developer, then good advice is to steer clear of those files.

If you've already built several websites and don't want to create your animation from scratch, you're in luck: You don't have to start over from the beginning. A great feature of Edge Animate is that you can import existing HTML files — which gives experienced web developers a head start with Edge Animate.

HTML5 is the big thing with web development these days, right along with CSS3. If you're wondering what HTML5 is, the best way to describe it is that it's the future of the web. So, by using Edge Animate, you are placing yourself at the forefront of web technologies. And the best part is, you don't have to know how to code to use it; Edge Animate creates the code for you.

The HTML5 code generated by Edge Animate is clean and contains no extra code, as shown here:

```
<!DOCTYPE html>
<html>
<head>
    <meta http-equiv="Content-Type" content="text/html; charset=utf-8">
    <meta http-equiv="X-UA-Compatible" content="IE=Edge"/>
    <title>Untitled</title>
<!--Adobe Edge Runtime-->
    <script type="text/javascript" charset="utf-8" src="Untitled-1_edgePreload.
            js"></script>
    <style>
        .edgeLoad-EDGE-15449885 { visibility:hidden; }
    </style>
<!--Adobe Edge Runtime End-->

</head>
<body style="margin:0;padding:0;">
    <div id="Stage" class="EDGE-15449885">
    </div>

</body>
</html>
```

This HTML5 file simplifies animation playback. Here's why:

- ✔ After you upload the HTML file and the associated files (usually through FTP to your web host server), you and your audience can view the animation in a web browser.

- ✔ You can copy and paste a snippet of the code (shown next) into an existing web page, like this:

```
<!--Adobe Edge Runtime-->
    <script type="text/javascript" charset="utf-8" src="Untitled-1_
            edgePreload.js"></script>
    <style>
        .edgeLoad-EDGE-15449885 { visibility:hidden; }
    </style>
<!--Adobe Edge Runtime End-->
```

REMEMBER

If you copy and paste the code snippet just shown into an existing web page, you must also upload the associated JavaScript files, images, and so on that are part of the file and folder structure that Edge Animate creates when you save a composition. You also have to add a div with the composition ID into the body tag, as in this example:

```
<div id="Stage" class="EDGE-15449885"></div>.
```

Coding easily with the persistent code panel

You can use Adobe Edge Animate CC without knowing a single bit of code. However, if you are a developer who likes to hand-code, you can do so with the code window. You have two options when using the code window:

✔ **You can view the full code.** Figure 2-9 shows what you see: all the code in the actions file for the particular animation you're working on. This view is extremely helpful; you don't have to keep clicking back and forth between code snippets.

   Use the Full Code mode to view and edit your actions file. You can activate this mode by clicking the Full Code button in the top-right corner of the code editor.

✔ **You can view a specific action's code.** When you have the code window open, you see a list of actions on the left side. By clicking one of those actions, you can edit the code for only that action (see Figure 2-10).

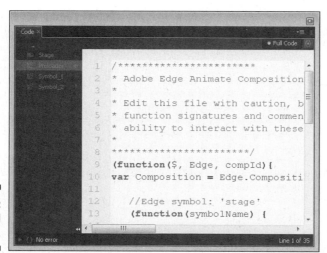

Figure 2-9: The Full Code panel.

Figure 2-10: Selecting a Specific Action to edit the code.

To open the code window, from the menu, choose Window and then Code as shown in Figure 2-11.

You can use a keyboard shortcut to open the code window by pressing Ctrl+E.

Figure 2-11: Opening the code window.

Pulling in the JavaScript API

An Adobe Edge Animate CC JavaScript API is available for the hardcore coders out there. For those who know nothing of JavaScript or writing code, don't fret; massive code-slinging isn't necessary in order to create animations. However, if you do like to lift the hood and poke around in the engine, then the JavaScript API provides an excellent resource.

You can find the JavaScript API here:

```
http://www.adobe.com/devnet-docs/edgeanimate/api/current/
index.html
```

API stands for *application programming interface* and is a common tool that programmers use for writing and debugging code. Of course, if you want to educate yourself on *how* to code, looking into the workings of APIs can get you started. Keep in mind, however, that APIs generally don't provide beginner-level information; they assume that you already know how to code.

The Adobe Edge Animate CC JavaScript API gives you plenty to explore:

✔ **Adobe Edge Animate CC overview:** This section of the API gives you a general introduction to the program.

✔ **Triggers, events, and actions:** These features of Edge Animate execute your code for you (such as looping) or when your audience interacts with different parts of the animation (such as clicking a button).

✔ **Tools and pointers for creating Symbols (reusable embedded animations):** Especially useful are the Edge Animate Symbols, which are self-contained behaviors, Timelines, and graphics.

  ✔ **JavaScript API:** This is the standard JavaScript interface, a handy tool in its own right, especially when you like to hand code specific aspects of your animation projects.

  ✔ **Advanced topics:** After you've got some coding practice under your belt, these topics offer some adventurous directions to explore (for example, creating multiple compositions in a page).

Figure 2-12 provides an example of what you can find in the API.

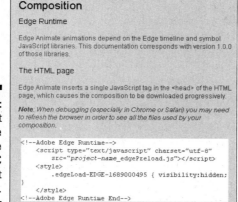

Figure 2-12:
An excerpt
from the
Adobe Edge
Animate CC
JavaScript
API.

Content of the figure:

Anatomy of an Edge Animate Composition

Edge Runtime

Edge Animate animations depend on the Edge timeline and symbol JavaScript libraries. This documentation corresponds with version 1.0.0 of those libraries.

The HTML page

Edge Animate inserts a single JavaScript tag in the <head> of the HTML page, which causes the composition to be downloaded progressively.

Note: When debugging (especially in Chrome or Safari) you may need to refresh the browser in order to see all the files used by your composition.

```
<!--Adobe Edge Runtime-->
    <script type="text/javascript" charset="utf-8"
        src="project-name_edgePreload.js"></script>
    <style>
        .edgeLoad-EDGE-1689000495 { visibility:hidden;
}
    </style>
<!--Adobe Edge Runtime End-->
```

Chapter 3

Working with a New Composition

*T*his chapter gets you working in Adobe Edge Animate CC. I discuss the Welcome screen and all of the informative links to tutorials and the help community — and I also show you how to make it all quiet.

I show you how to size the Stage so that it can have a static size or a responsive design that sizes the Stage to the size of the browser window.

Chapter 3 also discusses how to import existing web pages. Edge Animate can open simple web pages and turn any images into elements — which you can then animate or enhance with actions. (For more about elements and actions, see Chapter 5.)

Part of working with a new composition is knowing how to add images as assets that become part of the composition. This chapter discusses that vital bit of knowledge, and shows you how to build up what's on the Stage by drawing elements and adding text boxes.

Starting a New Composition

When you first open Adobe Edge Animate CC, you're greeted with a very informative Welcome screen, as shown in Figure 3-1. The Welcome screen has many components to it, which are grouped into three different sections.

On the left side of the screen you can open an existing file, create a new file, create a file from a template, or view a list of recent files.

The remainder of this section summarizes the Welcome screen and then branches off to cover two vital techniques:

- ✔ **Resizing the Stage:** You can size the Stage either by pixel count or by percentage.

- ✔ **Importing an existing web page:** You can open existing HTML files.

Also on the Welcome screen, down in the bottom-left corner, there are two little icons. You will most likely immediately recognize both of them. The Facebook icon takes you directly to the Edge Animate Facebook page; the Twitter icon connects you to the Edge Animate Twitter feed.

In the top-middle of the Welcome screen, you can find a menu that consists of

- ✔ **What's New:** This section provides a list of all the latest features, additions, and updates since the last release.

- ✔ **Getting Started:** The Getting Started section of the Welcome screen shows several boxes in the main part of the screen. From here, you can walk through several tutorials and examples that are built directly into Edge Animate (see Figure 3-1).

- ✔ **Resources:** The Resources section of the Welcome screen provides a list of links that you can click for additional help, tutorials, video, and FAQs from the community as shown in Figure 3-2. From the Resources section, you can also view and download sample projects as well as access the JavaScript API.

- ✔ **Quiet:** If you prefer a nice, quiet space from which to work when you open Edge Animate, all you have to do is click Quiet from the Welcome screen. Doing so removes the tutorials and lists that you may normally see.

Edge Animate remembers whichever Welcome screen option you choose. If you close the software with Quiet selected, then the next time you open Edge Animate, you see the Quiet Welcome screen. The same holds true if you close the program with any of the other options selected.

An Internet connection is required to gain access to many of the features listed on the Welcome screen.

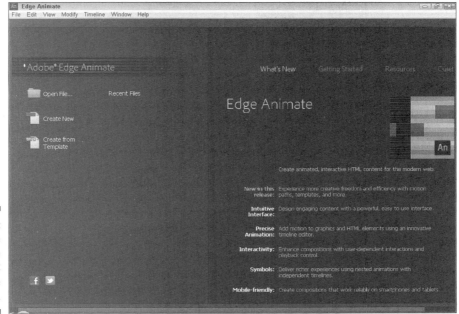

Figure 3-1:
The Adobe Edge Animate CC Welcome screen.

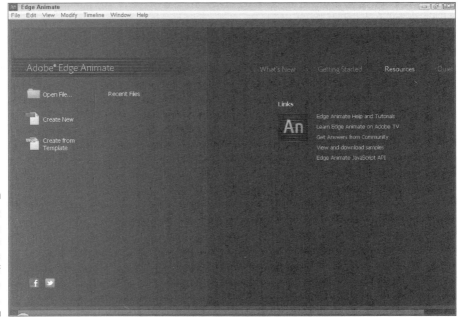

Figure 3-2:
The Welcome screen has a list of available resources.

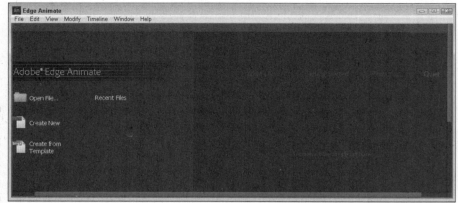

Figure 3-3:
The Quiet
option dims
out all the
clutter.

The first time that you open Edge Animate, you may want to start a brand-new composition. To do that, simply click the Create New icon from the left side of the screen (refer to Figure 3-1). Later, after you have some saved projects, you can click either Open File or Recent Files to open your existing compositions.

When you click Create New, Edge Animate presents a brand-new blank Stage from which you can start your work.

Resizing the Stage

The Stage is where you will place your elements, such as images, text, and drawn objects. The Stage is a live HTML window, which means that what you see on the screen, is what your audience sees when they view and interact with your composition. You can size the Stage a couple different ways:

- **Pixels:** Adobe Edge Animate CC enables you to set the Stage to remain a specific size no matter the size of the browser window.

- **Percentage:** For those who prefer a more responsive web design.

- **Testing responsive web design:** You may want to change the background color of the Stage to test the responsiveness of your design. (I go into detail on how to do this test in the next couple of sections.)

Sizing your Stage by pixel values

Most likely one of the first steps you'll want to take is to size your Stage properly. If you plan to insert your animation into an existing web page, first determine how much space you want your animation to take up on that page, and then size the Stage accordingly.

To resize the Stage, click the orange numbers in the Stage section of the Properties panel — in the far-left column near the top of the screen — as shown in Figure 3-4. Clicking the width or height numbers allows you to type in the exact dimensions (in pixels) that you want your Stage to have.

If you don't want to type in the numbers, Edge Animate gives you an alternative method for resizing the Stage: Simply place your cursor over one of the orange numbers. When the cursor turns into a double arrow (as shown in Figure 3-4), you can click and drag to increase or decrease the size of the Stage.

Sizing your Stage by percentage of screen size

If you want to create an animation that doesn't have to fit any specific dimension, then you should switch from pixels (px) to percentage (%), by clicking the toggle (see Figure 3-5). This is one step to creating a responsive web design. When you size the Stage by screen percentage instead of by pixel values, the Stage sizes itself according to the size of the parent element.

One example of a parent element can be the browser window itself — if the animation is a standalone web page. However, if the animation is one part of a web page, then the parent element can be a `div` element within which the animation is nested.

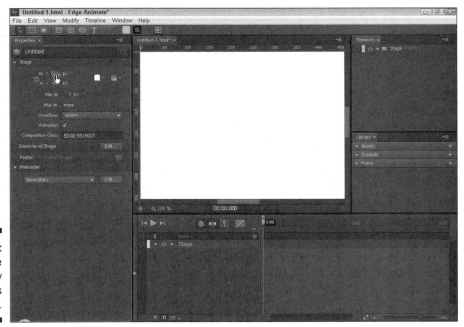

Figure 3-4:
Resizing the Stage by dimensions (in pixels).

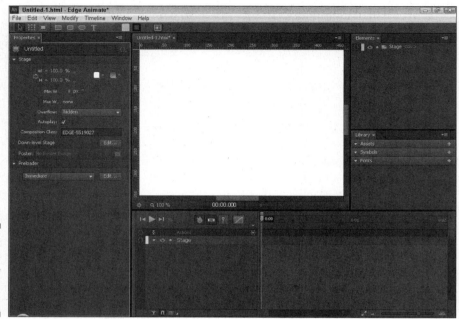

Figure 3-5:
Sizing the
Stage by
percentage
of screen.

To have your Stage fill the entire browser window, set the Stage width and height to 100%, as shown in Figure 3-6. To have your Stage fill half the browser window, set the Stage to 50%; and so on, depending on how much of the browser window you want your animation to occupy.

By default, the background of the Stage is white. Therefore you won't see any difference in the Stage when you switch between px and %.

To test the difference between using px and % for Stage size, change the background color of the Stage to something other than white, such as red. Then experiment with different percentages and px dimensions to see the different effects.

To change the background color of the Stage (as shown in Figure 3-6), click the white square to bring up a color picker.

You can tell Edge Animate to keep the width and height proportions the same by clicking the Link Width and Height icon (highlighted in Figure 3-7). By default, the Link Width and Height icon is turned off; with that default in effect, Edge Animate will not keep the width (or height) in the same proportion when you resize.

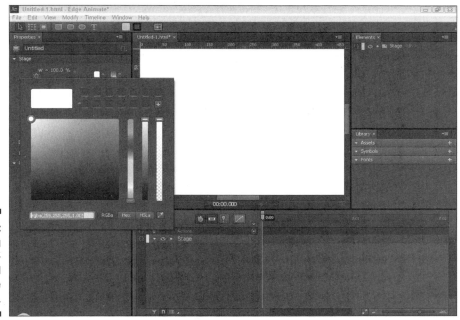

Figure 3-6:
Changing
the back-
ground
color of the
Stage.

Figure 3-7:
Using link
width and
height to
keep pro-
portions.

Importing HTML

Adobe Edge Animate CC is very HTML-friendly. If you have an existing —
albeit a very basic — HTML web page that you want to animate, then just
click Open File from the Welcome screen to start working with it.

Make sure all images and associated files are in the same folder as the `htm` file when you open it — or in a nested folder in the `htm` file. Otherwise they won't appear on the Stage.

When you're importing existing HTML, keep in mind the following:

- ✓ Edge Animate may not like your CSS files
- ✓ Images in your `htm` file appear in the Library panel.
- ✓ Text is imported as an element.

Possible issues with CSS files

Keep in mind that the simpler the HTML page is that you import, the easier it is for Edge Animate to open it.

If you do have trouble opening your `htm` file, try removing all associated CSS files. You may fret at the loss of that earlier work, but keep in mind that you can quickly replace all of that design work with Edge Animate.

If you open an existing HTML file with menus and such, you can animate the menus and elements but you can't reformat the color and some other aspects. The reason for this is that Edge Animate only allows animation sequences for imported HTML objects so as not to fight with any CSS styling you may have already applied. It can get a bit messy when you apply two styles to an element, which can lead to unexpected results.

Images appear in the Library panel

If the HTML page that you're importing contains images, then Edge Animate imports those images into the Library panel as an asset (see Figure 3-8).

Image   File name

Figure 3-8:
Here the
original
Edge
Animate
icon was
imported
as an asset
into the
Library
panel.

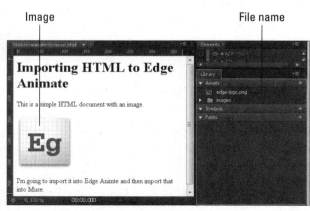

You can now treat the imported images as elements that you can animate or add interactive attributes; you can make the image move about the screen and/or make the image a link. For more information on the Library panel, see Chapter 12.

Text is imported as an element

When you import an HTML file with text, Animate imports that text as an element. You can select the text elements and animate them or add actions to them; however, you can't edit the text.

If the original HTML file used H1 or paragraph tags for text, then Animate recognizes those attributes and displays them in the Elements panel, as shown in Figure 3-9.

Paragraph tags

Figure 3-9:
Text is imported as an element.

Working with Templates

Templates were introduced in Edge Animate 2.0. This feature removes the necessity of reinventing the wheel every time you want to start a new composition. Sure, you could always start a new composition from a saved file, but Templates enable you to start a new project that already contains attributes and elements that you want to use without having to rewrite an existing saved file. Templates are very useful when you want to create several similar compositions and you want to start animating right away — without setting up your preferences from a brand-new composition or having to remove or swap out elements from a saved file. You can find the Templates from the main menu under File (as shown in Figure 3-10).

From the File menu, you can

- ✔ **Create from Template:** Here's where you start a new composition from a saved Template, to do this, you must first save a Template and then import that Template into Animate. When you click Create from Template, the Template Viewer opens and you see thumbnails of your imported Templates (as shown in Figure 3-11). Then you choose the Template you want to work with.

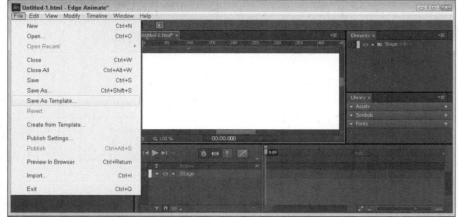

Figure 3-10:
Access the
Templates
from the File
menu.

Figure 3-11:
Choose a
Template
from the
Template
Viewer.

✔ **Save As Template:** this saves your current composition as a Template. Saved Templates include anything and everything in your composition. This includes Symbols, images, text, fonts and custom amendments you made including the size of the Stage. When you click Save As Template, and then choose a spot to save the file, Animate creates an `antmple` file. When you save a Template, you are then prompted to import that Template. I suggest you do that, so you can select it later when you choose Create from Template.

If you try to open an `antmple` file from your file directory and that file has already been imported, you'll get this message:

```
The Animate Template file contains a template that is already imported.
                Overwrite the existing template?
```

You can then choose Yes or No. If you try to open an `antmple` file from your file directory that has *not* already been imported, then Edge Animate imports that Template for you. You can then open that template by clicking Create from Template.

If you decide you no longer want a particular Template to appear in the Template Viewer, click the garbage can from the Template Viewer when you hover over a particular Template thumbnail, as shown in Figure 3-12.

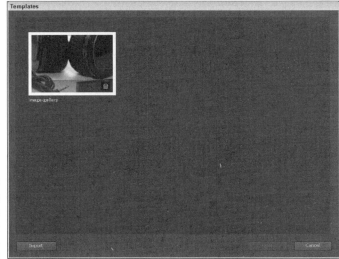

Figure 3-12: Delete unwanted Templates.

When you delete a Template, the saved Template file remains on your hard drive (or in the specific file directory to which you originally saved it). Deleting a Template simply removes it from Edge Animate; you can no longer choose it from the Template Viewer.

Drawing and Editing Elements, Importing Images, and Writing Text

Adobe Edge Animate CC provides drawing tools so that you can create rectangles, rounded rectangles, and ellipses on the Stage — which then become elements that you can animate and add actions to. The same is true for importing images and writing text. Figure 3-13 shows where you can find the drawing tools directly under the main menu.

Drawing tools

Adobe Edge Animate CC provides a range of tools you can use to create elements:

- ✓ **Drawing tools:** You can draw rectangles, rounded rectangles, and ellipses (including circles).

- ✓ **Editing the corners:** If you want to edit the roundness of your corners, Edge Animate provides ways to make it happen.

- ✓ **Importing images:** As a designer, you most likely have some choice images that you want to animate. Now you can.

- ✓ **Writing text:** There is a very good chance that you want to add some text to your composition. Animate makes that task easy for you.

Drawing rectangles

Drawing a rectangle is as easy as clicking the Rectangle tool and then clicking and dragging inside the Stage.

When you animate the rectangles you draw, they become elements on the Stage. Then you can turn them into Symbols, assign them actions and triggers, and so on.

When you draw an element on the Stage (such as a rectangle) and other elements are already on the Stage, Edge Animate automatically shows pink guidelines (see Figure 3-14). These guidelines can help you create equal-size elements and align your elements evenly with each other.

Figure 3-14:
Use the
guidelines
to help
create
equal-size
elements.

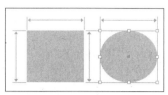

Creating rounded rectangles

The Rounded Rectangle tool is similar to the Rectangle tool, except the corners are round instead of square.

You can affect how round the corners are by experimenting with the way you click and drag when you draw a rounded rectangle. For example, you can draw a circle, a pill shape, or a square with slightly round corners — and just about anything in between. Figure 3-15 shows some of the different shapes you can draw with the Rounded Rectangle tool.

Figure 3-15:
Drawing
different
shapes with
the Rounded
Rectangle
tool.

Drawing ellipses

The Ellipses tool makes it easy to draw circles. Just select the Ellipses tool (as highlighted in Figure 3-13), and then click and drag to draw a shape with rounded corners. Figure 3-16 shows a perfect circle element.

To draw a perfect circle, hold down Shift while you click and drag. This key-press forces the proportions of the elements to retain the circle shape no matter how you click and drag.

Figure 3-16:
Draw a perfect circle with the Ellipses tool by holding Shift.

Editing the Corners of Elements

No matter what type of element you draw — rectangle, rounded rectangle, or ellipse, or circle — you can then select it and edit each corner (if it has corners) independently. To do so from the Properties panel, find Corners, and then (if necessary) click the white arrow to display its attribute settings.

Figure 3-17 shows the Corners attributes in the Properties panel. In this example, you can edit eight different points on the element, and the top-right corner is set to 0 so the corners are straight. The other corners are set to 50 so that the corners are round.

Square corner

Figure 3-17:
Use the Corners attributes in the Properties panel to edit corners.

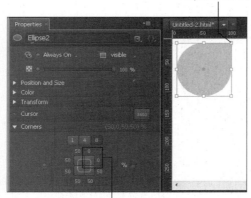

Square corner settings

To edit all the corners at once, select 1, edit the orange number on the right, and then press Enter. All the corners become uniform, as shown in Figure 3-18.

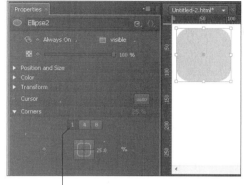

Figure 3-18: Editing all corners at once from the Corners attributes in the Properties panel.

Select 1 to make corners uniform

Importing images

You can import images from the menu bar; click File➪Import. A navigation window opens, prompting you to select an image. Navigate to where you saved your image, then select the image, and finally choose Open from the navigation window.

Adobe Edge Animate CC supports drag and drop. Instead of clicking through the File menu, you can drag an image from your desktop directly onto the Stage.

When you have an image in your composition, several new options appear in the Properties panel, as shown in Figure 3-19.

Figure 3-19: New options in the Properties panel.

Writing text

Adding text to your Edge Animate project is a matter of a few clicks and typing. And the best part is that the text you type is considered *selectable* type while it's viewed in a browser. Edge Animate will not convert your text into an image for the final output — which means search engines can parse your text and index it for search results. Ultimately, using text in Edge Animate helps — or at least doesn't hurt — your website's SEO (search engine optimization).

Adobe Edge Animate CC is considered SEO-friendly; it places text in the JavaScript file *as* text, not as an image *of* text. Therefore, search engines can find any text that you type into Edge Animate and use in the final animation placed on your site.

To insert text into your Edge Animate composition, click the Text tool, which is located directly under the main menu bar in the top-left corner (see Figure 3-20).

Figure 3-20:
Selecting
the Text
tool.

Text Tool

With the Text tool selected, click and drag over the Stage. You see a thin, blue rectangle appear as you click and drag. When you release the left mouse button, you also see a gray text box with a blinking cursor (as shown in Figure 3-21).

Figure 3-21:
A blank text
box.

Part II

Adopting Tools and Techniques

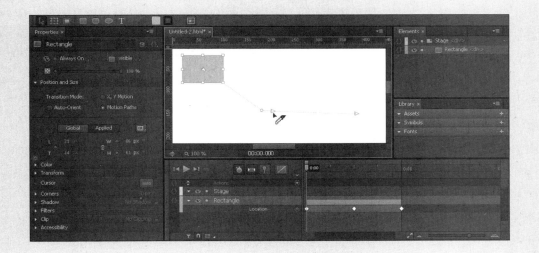

Visit www.dummies.com/extras/adobeedgeanimatecc for great Dummies content online.

In this part . . .

✔ Operating the Timeline

✔ Managing actions

✔ Customizing your workspace

✔ Visit `www.dummies.com/extras/adobeedge animatecc` for great Dummies content online.

Chapter 4

Using the Timeline for the First Time

In This Chapter

▶ Playing, rewinding, and fast-forwarding from the Timeline

▶ Toggling the different Timeline modes

▶ Animating with Motion Paths

▶ Keeping the Timeline at peak efficiency with keyframes and animation sequences

▶ Fine-tuning the Timeline view to match your preferences

The Adobe Edge Animate CC Timeline is a crucial part of the software. The Timeline is where you determine when different actions take place and which elements are affected. You can find the Timeline at the bottom of the screen. This chapter covers many elements of the Timeline, including the finer details — including the creation of animation sequences, also known as transitions.

Controlling the Timeline

The Timeline is located at the bottom of the interface. It has Play controls such as Play, Rewind, Fast Forward, and Return to Last Play Position (see Figure 4-1).

The Play controls include the basics and one that proves extremely convenient:

✔ **Play, Rewind, and Fast Forward:** These are the basic controls you'll find on any kind of media player, and Adobe Edge Animate CC has them for your use.

✔ **Return to Last Play Position:** Sometimes you don't want to return to the beginning of an animation when you finish watching it. That's especially true when your animation starts to get long and (say) you have a particular section that you want to tweak. This control gets you back to the point at which you last stopped playing the animation, as often as you like, with no fuss.

Play, Rewind, and Fast Forward

When you have your animation ready to test or view, you can click Play to watch the animation play out on the Stage. Likewise, you can click Fast Forward or Rewind to (respectively) advance the animation quickly or back it up just as fast.

The Return to Last Play Position will return to the point in the Timeline to where you left the Pin.

Play controls

Figure 4-1:
The Play controls on the Timeline.

You can also press the spacebar on your keyboard to play the animation. The animation will play in its entirety if the Playhead (explained in detail later in this chapter) is at the end of the Timeline. You can also watch your animation unfold simply by clicking and dragging the Playhead back and forth over the Timeline.

Return to Last Play Position

By default, the Return to Last Play Position icon is grayed out, because the last play position was at the beginning of the Timeline. When you start to create your composition, you can move the Playhead further out along the Timeline. Doing that activates the Return to Last Play Position button as shown in Figure 4-2.

Return to Last Play Position   Playhead

Figure 4-2:
The Return to Last Play Position and the Playhead.

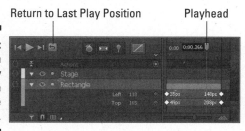

When you click the Return to Last Play Position after you play the composition, Edge Animate brings you back to where the Playhead was on the Timeline, as opposed to bringing you all the way back to the beginning.

Toggling the Timeline Modes

Directly after the Play controls are another set of tools where you can set the Keyframes mode, set the Auto-Transition mode, and you can also toggle the Pin and set the Easing attribute. These tools are shown in Figure 4-3.

Figure 4-3:
Keyframe tools are to the right of the Play controls.

Keyframe tools

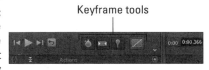

Adobe Edge Animate CC uses keyframes for animations. Keyframes appear as white diamonds in the Timeline. The green horizontal bars in Figure 4-2 represent the transitions (animation sequences) between keyframes for a rectangle element that moves from the left corner to the bottom-right corner over a period of 5 seconds. That's a lot of information, and you can find it all within the Timeline and keyframe.

Adobe Edge Animate CC contains several toggle modes within the Timeline area:

- ✔ **Keyframes:** You can toggle them on or off if you want or don't want Edge Animate to create keyframes automatically for you while you're creating your composition.

- ✔ **Auto-Transition:** You can toggle this feature on or off if you want or don't want Edge Animate to create animation sequences automatically when you move elements around the Stage.

- ✔ **Playhead and Pin:** When it comes time to start animating, make sure the Pin is toggled on, otherwise Edge Animate won't create animation sequences.

- ✔ **Easing:** You may not necessarily call this a toggle, but you can choose your preferred Easing attributes; your choices affect the way Edge Animate brings your elements to life.

Keyframes modes

To create keyframes automatically, you must first activate keyframes by clicking the red Stopwatch icon. By default, when you first start a new animation, the Stopwatch is red but has gray lines running through it (as shown in Figure 4-4).

Click to activate keyframes

Figure 4-4:
Here the default state of the Auto-Keyframe mode is disengaged.

You'll want the Stopwatch to appear red as you create your composition so that Edge Animate automatically creates keyframes for you. Simply click the Stopwatch to activate Auto-Keyframes and turn the Stopwatch red (as shown in Figure 4-5).

When the Stopwatch is disengaged, you don't have to click the Stopwatch to enable it. Simply toggle the Pin and Auto-Keyframes will become enabled. You can learn more about toggling the Pin and moving the Playhead in the following sections.

Figure 4-5:
Here Auto-Keyframes are enabled.

If you click the Stopwatch and it dims to gray instead of red, then you'll need to manually insert your keyframes.

If you want to arrange elements on the Stage without triggering keyframes, then make sure the Stopwatch is dimmed by clicking it, as shown in Figure 4-6. When the Stopwatch is gray, that means Auto-Keyframes are disabled.

Figure 4-6:
Auto-
Keyframes
are disabled
when the
Stopwatch
is gray.

Click again to disable keyframes

Auto-Transition mode

By turning Auto-Transition mode on or off, you toggle the capability to create smooth transitions between keyframes. *Transitions* are the animations that you create to show (for example) an element moving from left to right on the Stage (transitions are also referred to as *animation sequences*). When you create a new file, the Auto-Transition mode is enabled for you (as shown in Figure 4-7). You'll also see a colored arrow between the Pin and the Playhead. This orange-colored bar-with-arrows is discussed in detail later in this chapter, in the "Animating forward" and "Animating backward" sections.

Figure 4-7:
Here the
default state
for Auto-
Transition
mode is
enabled.

Auto-transition mode

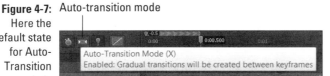

When Auto-Transition mode is turned on, Edge Animate creates an animation effect when you move elements around the Stage, provided you've toggled the Pin and Playhead as outlined in the next few sections.

You'll know when you've created an animation: The color-coded bars appear between the keyframes, as shown in Figure 4-2.

If you click the Auto-Transition icon, it dims, and Edge Animate will not create an animated sequence. Instead, Edge Animate only inserts the keyframe diamonds; you won't see the colored bars (see Figure 4-8).

Figure 4-8:
When Auto-Transition is turned off, Edge Animate won't create animations.

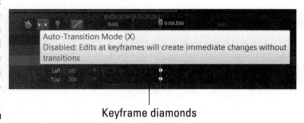

Keyframe diamonds

If you want animation sequences to appear when you move elements around the Stage, make sure that the Stopwatch icon is red and the Auto-Transition mode is enabled. If you want to move elements around on the Stage without creating keyframes or animation sequences, then disable both the Stopwatch and the Auto-Transition icon. You also have to toggle the Pin, as discussed next.

Toggling the Pin

When you start creating animation sequences, you need to toggle the Pin. When you first start a new composition, the Pin is turned off, as shown in Figure 4-9. In this state, you can't create animation sequences.

Pin is turned off

Figure 4-9:
Here the default state of the Pin is turned off.

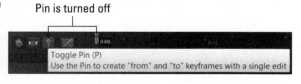

To create animation sequences, you turn on the Stopwatch, make sure the Auto-Transition mode is on, and then click the Pin icon. The Pin icon activates (as shown in Figure 4-10) and turns light blue.

Click the Pin

Figure 4-10:
Click the Pin to activate it.

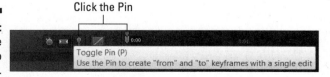

With the Pin turned on, you can now move it up and down the Timeline to determine where and for how long you want an animation sequence to last. You can find more details in the following sections.

Easing tool

The Easing tool is the last icon right before the Timeline. You can use the Easing tool to affect how animations play. To add Easing to an element, select an element's transition from the Timeline, and then select an attribute from the Easing menu (as shown in Figure 4-11).

For example, if you want your element to bounce like a ball, choose Ease Out from the left column, and then choose Bounce in the right column.

The default setting for Easing is Linear, which has no effect on your elements. If you change Easing from Linear to something else, then all new elements that you create will default to this new Easing attribute. You can have different Easing attributes for each element on the Stage. To edit a particular element's Easing attribute, you must select that element's transition from the Timeline.

If you're mathematically inclined, you'll appreciate the graph on the far right, which shows the effects of the Easing attributes.

Figure 4-11:
The Easing
attributes.

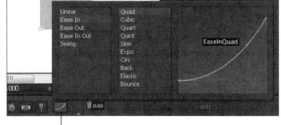

The Easing tool

The Playhead and the Pin

The Playhead and the Pin are located along the time markers in the Timeline. You'll use them for a couple of different tasks. The first task is to determine the points in time where you want an animation to start and end. The second task is to tell Edge Animate where you want to start viewing your animation when you click Play.

The Pin is the blue icon on top; the Playhead is the yellow chevron below it.

When you're ready to start animating, you'll want to drag either the Pin or the Playhead down the length of the Timeline. Dragging either the Pin or the Playhead down the Timeline, as shown in Figure 4-12, determines whether your animation plays forward or backward. This is discussed in more detail in the following sections.

Playhead

Figure 4-12:
The
Playhead
and the Pin.

Working with Keyframes and Animation Sequences

It's important to get a handle on working with keyframes and animation sequences so you can create them and edit them to do what you want. The following sections introduce you to all the parts of Edge Animate that you need for creating keyframes and animation sequences. Here's where you actually create those keyframes and animation sequences — which boils down to getting familiar with these processes:

- **Creating keyframes:** When you start animating, depending on how you set the Pin and the Playhead, you can create transitions that play either forward or backward, depending on how you create them.

- **Selecting keyframes:** After you create keyframes, you can select them so that you can edit them.

- **Editing keyframes:** After creating a keyframe, and then selecting it, you can edit it.

- **Copying and pasting keyframes:** You can copy and paste the keyframes you want to reuse. This should save you plenty of time; you don't have to recreate the same keyframe over and over for similar animation sequences.

Creating sequences

To create a keyframe and an animation sequence (transitions), follow these steps.

1. **Place an element on the Stage with the drawing tools or by importing an image.**

2. **Toggle the Pin so that it turns light blue.**

3. **Click and drag either the Pin or the Playhead down the Timeline.**

   The differences between moving the Pin and moving the Playhead are described later in this section.

   The amount of space that separates the Pin from the Playhead determines the length of time the animation takes to play out.

4. **Click and drag the element around the Stage, for example, move the element from the top-left corner down to the bottom-right corner.**

   Edge Animate adds color-coded bars to the Timeline.

To preview your animation, click Play or press the spacebar.

Animating forward

Where you place the Pin and the Playhead on the Timeline affects your animation sequence. For example, you may be scratching your head and wondering why, when you play your animation, the element goes from the bottom-right corner up to the top-left corner instead of the other way around.

To animate forward — that is, to have the animation sequence play in the same direction in which you moved the elements on the Stage — you must move the Playhead farther down the Timeline than the Pin so that you see a yellow bar-with-arrows (as shown in Figure 4-13).

Figure 4-13:
Animating forward by moving the Playhead down the timeline.

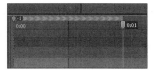

Animating backward

If you want your animation to appear in a backward sequence relative to the direction in which you move the element on the Stage, then move the Pin farther down the Timeline than the Playhead: You see a blue bar-with-arrows, as shown in Figure 4-14.

Figure 4-14:
Animating
backward
by mov-
ing the Pin
down the
Timeline.

 Adobe Edge Animate CC is full of keyboard shortcuts. One of them is Shift+P, which reverses the direction of your timespan from blue to orange (or vice versa). This comes in useful when you realize you want to play an animation sequence in the opposite direction.

Animating with Motion Paths

Motion Paths enable you to create animation sequences that follow a curved path, or a loop, such as a bird in flight or an image that dances across the stage. Animate provides plenty of options to working with Motion Paths, as described in the following sections. You can toggle Motion Paths off or on from the Properties panel as shown in Figure 4-15 (be sure to select an element on the Stage so you can see the Motion Path property).

 Toggle the Auto-Orient option so that the element's rotation follows the Motion Path. If you leave Auto-Orient off, then the element's rotation is not affected by the Motion Path.

 Use the Layout Defaults from the toolbar to set Motion Paths as a default for all new elements that you add to the Stage (see Figure 4-16). When you change the Layout Defaults, the settings for all previously existing elements are not affected.

With Motion Paths toggled on, when you create an animation sequence for an element, you will see a thin blue line with arrows at each end; these arrows represent the direction of the element's movement (see Figure 4-17). This blue line indicates the path the element travels during the animation. Remember to toggle the Pin and set the Playhead to create an animation sequence.

Figure 4-15:
Toggle
Motion
Paths off or
on from the
Position and
Size panel.

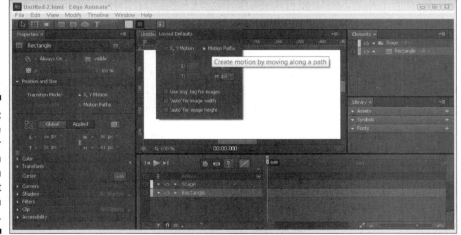

Figure 4-16:
Set the
default for
Motion
Paths from
the Layout
Defaults in
the toolbar.

To move a Motion Path around the Stage without adding a new anchor point, hover the mouse over the thin blue line (at a place in the line with no anchor points), hold down Cmd or Ctrl, and then drag with the mouse.

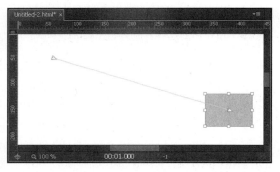

Figure 4-17:
The thin blue line indicates the Motion Path for the element.

Adding an anchor point

When you first draw a Motion Path (dragging an element across the Stage with the Pin toggled), Animate creates a straight path. To add curves to your path, you must insert anchor points. To add an anchor point, hover the mouse over the thin blue line until you see the pen tool as shown in Figure 4-18.

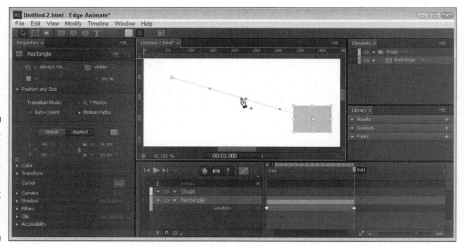

Figure 4-18:
The pen tool indicates that you can edit the Motion Path.

With the pen tool showing, click and drag with your mouse to insert an anchor point and to add a curve to the Motion Path. This action also creates a *Bézier handle*. You can use the Bézier handle to further manipulate the curve of the Motion Path by clicking and dragging those points, as shown in Figure 4-19.

Figure 4-19: Motion paths can have Bézier handles to help you create the perfect curve.

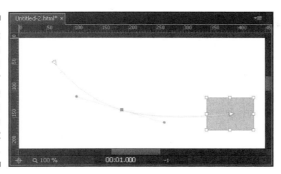

Figure 4-19: Motion paths can have Bézier handles to help you create the perfect curve.

To delete, or remove an anchor point, hover on the existing anchor and use the keyboard shortcut Ctrl+Click for the PC or Cmd+Click for a Mac.

Creating a sharp point instead of a curved path

While curved paths are pretty awesome, 90 degree angles can look pretty sharp as well (pun intended). To create a sharp angle in your Motion Path, you have to remove the Bezier handle from the anchor point. To remove the Bezier handle, position the mouse over the Bezier handle and use the keyboard shortcut Alt+Click (Option+Click for Mac). When you do that, the Bezier handle is removed from the Motion Path and the anchor point becomes a sharp angle as shown in Figure 4-20.

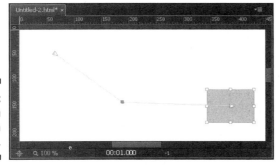

Figure 4-20: A Motion Path with a sharp angle.

Keyframes and Easing with Motion Paths

You can split up a Motion Path to have more than one keyframe. The keyframe diamonds in the Timeline represent different Motion Paths (also known as animation sequences or transitions). To add a keyframe to a Motion Path, place the Playhead and Pin in the portion of the Timeline where you want to add the keyframe, then simply click the diamond from the Timeline next to the transition you want to add a keyframe to as shown in Figure 4-21.

Figure 4-21:
Add key-
frames to a
Motion Path
to create
separate
animation
sequences.

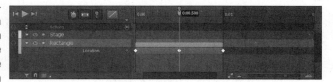

Breaking a single Motion Path into more than one transition can be useful. For example, you can add one Easing attribute to the first keyframe of the path and have a different Easing attribute assigned to the second part. To do that, select the first keyframe transition from the Timeline (see Figure 4-22) and then add an Easing attribute to it (see Chapter 17 for more details on Easing). Then select the second Motion Path sequence and add a different Easing attribute. You can then preview the entire animation sequence on the Stage (press the Space Bar to preview on the Stage or press Ctrl+Return to preview in a browser).

Figure 4-22:
Select the
animation
sequence
from the
Timeline
to edit the
Easing
attribute.

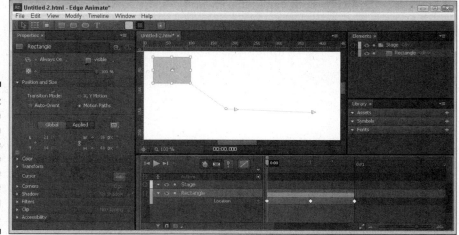

Splitting and joining Motion Paths

Motion paths are fully editable. Meaning you can bend and twist them to your will as well as splitting them apart and putting them back together.

To split a Motion Path, you have to first add a keyframe diamond to the animation sequence as discussed in the last section. Adding the keyframe to the path creates two separate Motion Paths that happen to be connected. To split these two Motion Paths, hover the mouse pointer over the middle arrow that was created when you added the keyframe diamond (as indicated in Figure 4-22), and then Ctrl+Click (Cmd+Click) and drag to separate the two Motion Paths. Figure 4-23 shows the saw cursor that appears when you Ctrl+Click over an arrow.

To join two Motion Paths together, simply click an end arrow and drag it over to the other Motion Path's end arrow until they snap together.

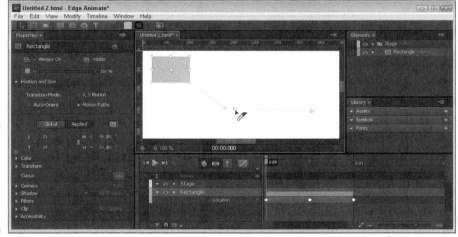

Figure 4-23: Separate the Motion Paths when you see the saw icon.

Don't be alarmed if you see the element attached to only one of the separated paths. If you move the Playhead up and down the Timeline, you'll see that the element is still attached to both Motion Paths. Previewing the animation also shows that the element is still associated to both of the Motion Paths. It's just that one of the Motion Paths will appear as if it doesn't have the element simply based on where the Playhead is on the Timeline.

If you split a Motion Path and place one segment on the far side of the Stage and the other path on the opposite side of the Stage, then you'll see your element follow the first path and then jump to the second path. To exaggerate this effect, try adding time in the Timeline between when the first Motion Path ends and the second starts. To separate the keyframe diamonds (and the animation sequence), place the cursor over the second animation sequence and then click and drag down the Timeline (see the next two sections on selecting sequences and editing sequences for more information). See Figure 4-24 as an example.

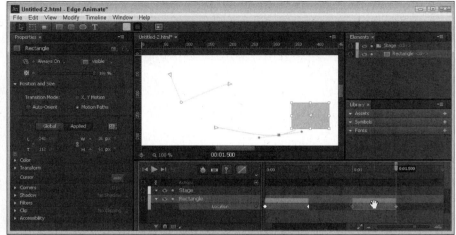

Figure 4-24:
Add time
between
the Motion
Paths
to delay
the jump
between
paths.

You cannot set Motion Paths to use percentage-based layouts to create a responsive layout (see Chapter 21 on how to build a responsive web design). As a work-around, you can nest your Motion Path element inside a group, parent, or Symbol and then set the parent to use percentage based positioning (see Chapter 11 for nesting elements, Chapter 21 for layout preferences and layout defaults, and Chapter 12 for information on Symbols). You can also use this nesting method to set the Motion Path relative to top, right, bottom, and left.

Experiment with the Transform Origin point when animating with Motion Paths. The element's travel along the Motion Path is based on the origin point, which doesn't necessarily have to be the center of the element itself. For more information on origin points and the Transform tool, see Chapter 7.

Selecting sequences

After you create keyframes and animation sequences, you may want to select them so you can edit them. You have several ways you can select keyframes.

- ✔ Place the cursor over the top bar (also called the *rollup bar*). When the cursor turns to the shape of a hand, as shown in Figure 4-25, you can click to select all associated animation sequences.

- ✔ Select keyframes by clicking and dragging with the mouse.

  You can select several keyframes at once.

- ✔ Hold the Shift key down while clicking different keyframes to select more than one at a time.

Figure 4-25:
Select
keyframes
and
animation
sequences
by clicking
the
rollup bar.

Edge Animate also allows you to select just one animation sequence by clicking a specific colored bar.

You can edit animation sequences and keyframes after you've selected them.

Editing sequences

Adobe Edge Animate CC provides an easy means to not only move keyframes and animation sequences, but you can shorten or lengthen them as well.

Moving sequences

To move keyframe and animation sequences either up or down the Timeline, simply select the color-coded bar and then drag it while keeping the left mouse button depressed.

You can move multiple keyframes in the same manner. To select more than one keyframe at a time, hold the Shift key down while clicking different keyframes.

Lengthening or shortening sequences

Not only can you move where the keyframe appears in the Timeline, you can also lengthen or shorten the keyframe so that the animation takes a longer or shorter time to play.

To lengthen the keyframe, move the mouse cursor to either end of the keyframe until the cursor turns into a double-arrowed line (see Figure 4-26). Then simply click and drag.

Figure 4-26:
Lengthening
or short-
ening
animation
sequences.

Copying and pasting keyframes and sequences

Adobe Edge Animate CC allows you to copy and paste keyframes and animation sequences. This makes it easy to create multiple instances of the same animation.

To copy a keyframe, simply select it and then use Ctrl+C. Then place your Playhead at the point in the Timeline at which you want to paste the keyframe. Finally, use Ctrl+V to paste in the keyframe.

Before you paste in the keyframe you copied, make sure the Playhead is located at the point in the Timeline where you want it to appear. Otherwise you might paste the keyframe into a section of the Timeline that isn't where you want it. The keyframe that you're pasting into the Timeline will appear wherever the Playhead is located.

Finer Details of the Timeline and Stage Controls

Edge Animate offers many ways to configure the Timeline and Stage; you can adjust them to your own liking. This includes an easy way to center the Stage, magnify the Stage, filter elements, and turn Timeline snapping on or off.

The finer controls for the Stage and Timeline include these:

- **Centering the Stage:** If you start moving, adjusting, resizing, and so forth, you may need to re-center the Stage for better viewing.

- **Magnifying the Stage:** For those times you want to see every last pixel of your elements.

✔ **The Playhead and Pin timestamp:** Edge Animate provides more than one way to move the Playhead and Pin up and down the Timeline.

✔ **Filtering elements:** Sometimes you only want to see certain elements.

✔ **Timeline snapping:** Do you like your elements to snap into a precise place on the Timeline or do you prefer more freedom?

✔ **Configuring the grid view:** You can set the grid view to your preference so that you either see a grid or you don't.

✔ **Viewing more or less of the Timeline:** Sometimes you may want to see the entire Timeline for your composition; sometimes you may want to zoom in.

✔ **Adding more time:** If you run out of time, you can always add more!

You might be wondering how Edge Animate determines the vertical order in which elements appear in the Timeline. It all depends on how the elements are arranged. The element that is most in front (appears on top of all other elements) is the first element listed in the Timeline. The element that is most in back (appears behind all other elements) is the last element listed in the Timeline.

Stage controls

There are a couple of controls for the Stage that enable you to center it and magnify it.

✔ **Centering the Stage:** If, for some reason, the Stage has gone off-kilter on you and you want a one-click solution to re-center the Stage on your screen, then simply click the Center the Stage icon. This icon is located in the bottom-left corner of the Stage (as shown in Figure 4-27).

✔ **Magnifying the Stage:** If you want to zoom in on the Stage, you can use the magnification tool (as shown in Figure 4-28). You can either click the orange number and type in a specific zoom level or place your mouse pointer over the number and then click and drag to adjust.

Figure 4-27:
Center the Stage on your screen with the Centering the Screen icon.

Centering the Screen

Magnification tool

Figure 4-28:
Magnifying
the Stage.

Timeline controls

Adobe Edge Animate CC provides several tools to help you configure the
Timeline so that it appears just the way you want.

- ✔ **Playhead and Pin stamp:** Provides a means to show you where the
  Playhead is in the Timeline and the length of time for the animation
  sequence. The Playhead is represented by the yellow numbers on the
  left, and the Pin is represented by the blue numbers on the right (see
  Figure 4-29). You can place your cursor over these numbers and then
  click and drag to change the location of the Playhead and Pin on the
  Timeline.

Playhead Pin   Playhead Pin

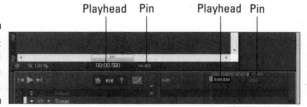

Figure 4-29:
Playhead
and Pin
stamp.

- ✔ **Filtering elements:** Edge Animate provides a way for you to see only the
  elements with animation sequences or to see all of the elements at once.
  This doesn't affect what you see on the Stage, but it does affect what you
  see in the Timeline. In Figure 4-30, on the left, the filtering is turned off,
  and you see all of the elements; on the right, filtering is turned on, and
  you see only the animated elements. The Filter control is identified.

Figure 4-30:
Filtering
elements.

Filter control

✓ **Configuring the grid view:** If you want to see precise measurements in the Timeline — anywhere from a full second to a 30th of a second — you can set that view (as shown in Figure 4-31); you can pull up your choices and toggle the grid view on or off.

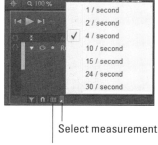

Figure 4-31: Configuring the grid view.

Select measurement

Toggle grid view

✓ **Timeline snapping:** If you choose to turn on the grid view, then you can have the Pin and Playhead snap to the grid by turning on Timeline snapping (as shown in Figure 4-32).

Timeline snapping

Figure 4-32: Toggling Timeline snapping.

✓ **Magnification scrollbar:** You can view more or less of the Timeline by scrolling the magnification bar (as shown in Figure 4-33). You can click to view the entire Timeline, click to either zoom the magnification in or out, or click and drag the icon on the scrollbar.

Magnification

Figure 4-33: The magnification scrollbar.

Click to view the Timeline   Zoom in/out

✔ **Inserting more time into the Timeline:** You can add more time into your Timeline at any point while you're designing your composition. From the main menu, click Timeline and then choose Insert Time, which is about halfway down the menu. When you do that, a dialog box opens (as shown in Figure 4-34).

Figure 4-34:
Inserting
more time
into the
Timeline.

Inserts blank time in the timeline at the playhead position.

Amount of time to insert:

00:00.000

Insert Time   Cancel

Place the Playhead in the Timeline at the point at which you want to insert more time.

Chapter 5

Working with Triggers, Actions, Labels, and Cursors

*O*ne especially powerful feature of Adobe Edge Animate CC is the capability to add actions, triggers, labels, and cursor attributes to your composition. These tools are what you use to make your animation interactive so your audience can participate in what your animation is doing instead of having to sit there and watch passively.

By placing *labels* in the Timeline, and associating them with actions and triggers, you can identify specific points in the Timeline, and you create a simpler means of controlling actions and triggers (as opposed to using time-stamps). Through the use of labels, you don't have to open the code box to change, for example, the point in time at which you want the animation to play when a trigger or action is called. Rather, you just have to slide the label up or down the Timeline to edit the action or trigger. Using labels helps you skip a step — opening the code box — if you need to edit your actions to reflect a different point in the Timeline.

When you place interactive elements into the Timeline, it's a good idea to change the *cursor attribute* to provide a visual clue to your audience. Knowing that an element is (say) clickable, sizable, or what have you makes the audience more inclined to interact with the composition. If the cursor never changes, then your viewers may never know they could have clicked instead of just sitting there.

Inserting Stage Triggers

Adobe Edge Animate CC enables you to add *Stage triggers* — essentially commands that control how the animation plays. A Stage trigger occurs when the animation reaches a certain point in the Timeline where you've placed a command to make something happen onscreen. A typical command launched with a Stage trigger is *looping* — having an animation repeat when it reaches the end (or at some other point you designate). Figure 5-1 shows a list of available Stage actions.

Figure 5-1:
List of triggers you can use for the Stage.

You can also add actions to the Stage along with triggers. For more information on adding Stage actions from the Elements panel, see Chapter 11.

Adding triggers to the Stage

To add Stage triggers, you have to perform a number of steps in a certain order. The following procedure shows how to add a loop to your animation through a Stage trigger:

1. **Create an animation sequence to which you can add the Stage trigger.**

   For example, draw an element on the Stage using the drawing tools (see Chapter 3) and then create an animation sequence (see Chapter 4).

2. **Position the Playhead on the Timeline where you want the Stage trigger to fire.**

You could, for example, set a trigger at the end of the animation.

3. Click the Insert Trigger icon as identified in Figure 5-2.

Insert Trigger

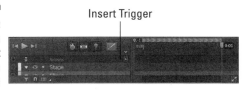

When you click the Insert Trigger icon, the Trigger menu opens (refer to Figure 5-1).

4. With the menu open, click a trigger item on the right, for a loop, choose Play from.

Doing so inserts code into the window on the left (see Figure 5-3).

Code   Selected item

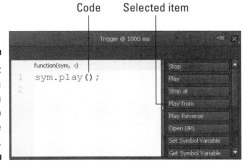

5. Click the X in the top-right corner of the Trigger box to close and save your trigger.

You see a Trigger icon in the Timeline, as identified in Figure 5-4.

Trigger icon

To see your loop in action, you need to preview it in a browser. To preview your animation in a browser, from the main menu, click File and then Preview in a Browser (see Figure 5-5).

File	Edit	View	Modify	Timeline	Window
New					Ctrl+N
Open...					Ctrl+O
Open Recent					▶
Close					Ctrl+W
Close All					Ctrl+Alt+W
Save					Ctrl+S
Save As...					Ctrl+Shift+S
Save As Template...					
Revert					
Create from Template...					
Publish Settings...					
Publish					Ctrl+Alt+S
Preview In Browser					Ctrl+Return
Import...					Ctrl+I
Exit					Ctrl+Q

Figure 5-5: Click Preview in Browser to see your triggers in action.

Congratulations! You now have a loop within your animation.

You can add a label or designate a time in the Trigger box if you want your animation to loop back to a certain point in the Timeline instead of returning to the beginning. (I describe how to create and insert labels in the next section.)

If you want to designate time instead of a label, you can do that as well. Simply type in the ms (milliseconds) value in the parentheses in the Trigger box as shown in Figure 5-6. For example, if you want your animation to loop back to 0:01 in the Timeline, then type in **1000**; if you want to loop back to 0:02 in the Timeline, then type in **2000**.

Time value

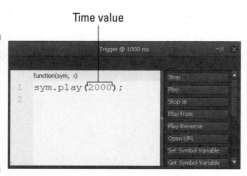

Figure 5-6: Designate a time in the Trigger Box to tell Edge Animate what point to play from.

You can edit Stage triggers a couple of different ways:

✔ You can move where the triggers are in the Timeline by clicking and dragging the Trigger icon (refer to Figure 5-4) up and down the Timeline.

✔ Double-click the Trigger icon to open the coding box. You can then edit the trigger from within the coding box.

Labeling Key Points

You can add labels into the Timeline for use with Stage triggers and element actions. Say you want your animation to jump back to a certain point in time when it reaches the Stage trigger. You can use a label to determine where the animation jumps back to in the Timeline.

Using labels with Stage triggers has a unique advantage over using time-stamps. You can drag a label up and down the Timeline to change the point, for example, where a loop is to begin. This is nice, because you don't have to open the coding box to make the edit, which is what you would have to do if you used a timestamp.

Creating labels

To insert a label into the Timeline use the main menu; click Timeline and then Insert Label (Figure 5-7).

A label appears in the Timeline where the Playhead is located. You can name this label (as shown in Figure 5-8).

You can name this label as you see fit, but name it appropriately so you can remember later why you put it there. For example, if you want a slideshow presentation to loop back to the 1-second mark instead of looping all the way back to the beginning, then you insert the label at the 1-second mark and name it something like **Restart Slide Show**.

When you have a label inserted into the Timeline, you can go back and edit your trigger or action.

You can move the label up and down the Timeline by clicking and dragging. This comes in handy when you start making more advanced animations and you're constantly finding good reasons to adjust exactly where you want the loop (or whatever) to start. Without a label, you'd have to keep opening up the Trigger box, adjusting the ms value, and fuming about having to do that.

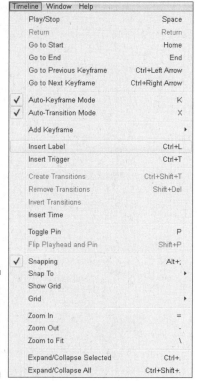

Figure 5-7:
Insert a
label Into
the Timeline
from the
main menu.

Label name

Figure 5-8:
Name the
label.

You can change the name of the label by double-clicking it from the Timeline. Note that if you change the name of the label on the Timeline, then you have to go back to the trigger or action and update the name of the label in the code box as well.

Associating labels with actions and triggers

If you decide to add a label to your Timeline after you create a trigger or action, you can go back and edit the trigger or action to use the label.

✔ To edit a trigger, double-click the Trigger icon (as shown in Figure 5-4).

✔ To edit an action, select the element, right-click, and then choose Open Actions For.

With the Trigger/Action dialog box open, edit the code to show a label instead of a number of ms (milliseconds), as shown in Figure 5-9.

You have to use the single quotation marks for the label to work:

✔ When you type the label correctly, the text appears orange.

✔ If you forget the single quotation marks, the text appears purple.

Labels are case-sensitive. Therefore, if your label says `Restart Slide Show` but you type *Restart slide show* or *Restart Slideshow* in the Trigger box, your trigger won't work. Be sure to type the label exactly as it appears on the Timeline in the Trigger box.

Figure 5-9:
Trigger with
a label.

Label

When you're using a specific ms value to identify a trigger, you need not use single quotation marks around the number; simply typing the number is sufficient. If you want to use a label, however, then you must use single quotation marks — one at the beginning and one at the end of the label. If you type in the label without the single quotation marks, the text appears in black to signal that the label is incorrect. If you use the single quotation marks correctly when you type the label, the text turns orange.

To use labels with Symbols and playback actions, see Chapter 12.

Inserting Element Actions

Adding actions to an element is similar to adding a trigger to the Stage. Two main differences exist between a Stage trigger and an *element action:*

✔ An element action requires that your audience do something to make the action happen.

For example, your audience must click or mouse over an element to trigger the element's action. For a Stage trigger, the audience doesn't have to do anything at all because the Stage trigger fires when the animation reaches the point where the trigger is located. Figure 5-10 shows a list of available actions that you can designate so that your audience can fire an element action.

✔ The *Actions box* for an element allows you to designate the type of interaction your audience must use to execute the action.

Stage triggers don't work the same way as actions; they execute when the animation reaches a certain point in the Timeline, whatever the audience is (or is not) doing. They don't require interaction.

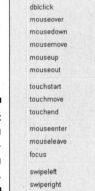

Figure 5-10:
Actions you
can desig-
nate to an
element.

```
click
dblclick
mouseover
mousedown
mousemove
mouseup
mouseout

touchstart
touchmove
touchend

mouseenter
mouseleave
focus

swipeleft
swiperight
```

Element actions require interaction from the audience. These interactions include:

✔ **Click or dblclick:** Choose these options if you want your audience to click or double-click an element for the action to occur. You can use the swipe actions in the same way as Click, for mobile-focused experiences.

✔ **Mouse:** Use mouseover, mousedown, and other such actions if you want your audience to move the mouse over, into, or off of an element.

✔ **Touch:** The touch actions refer to mobile devices and touch screens and act the same as a click. If you plan for your animation to work for both desktop and mobile, then using just Click is sufficient.

✔ **Focus:** This action is tied to using the Tab key on the keyboard to enable your audience to select (or tab through) different elements; it has its own section of the chapter to detail the additional steps needed to implement it.

Adding actions to elements

One of the actions you may want to add to an element is to have it open a new URL. This capability is handy for creating menus or building links to other relevant content.

You can follow this same basic procedure for most of the other actions as well. (The additional steps for working with focus are coming up in the section directly after the steps for adding actions to elements.)

To start adding actions to an element, you must first create an element, as described in Chapter 3. With an element on the Stage, follow these steps:

1. **Select an element, right click and choose Open Actions For (as shown in Figure 5-11).**

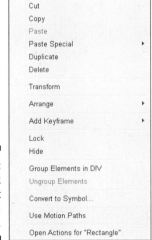

Figure 5-11:
Right-click
an element
to open a
large menu.

After you click Open Actions from the menu, a blank *coding box* (the place where you type in your commands) opens.

2. **From the menu on the right, choose Open URL.**

Edge Animate populates the box with code, as shown in Figure 5-12.

By default, Adobe Edge Animate CC uses the URL to adobe.com when you click Open URL. If another destination for the link suits your purpose better, simply replace the adobe.com URL with a URL that goes to where you want to send your audience.

Add action   Remove action

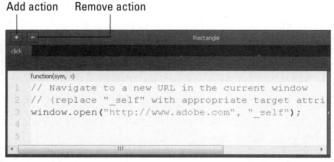

Figure 5-12:
The Actions coding box looks like this with code in it.

You can use multiple actions on an element:

✔ To add an action to an element, with the Actions coding box open, click the + in the upper-left corner, as indicated in Figure 5-12.

✔ To remove an action from an element, click the –.

✔ When you have more than one action associated with a single element, then Edge Animate displays all of the actions in a tab view (as shown in Figure 5-13). Simply click the tabs to display the relevant code for each action.

Click tab to display code

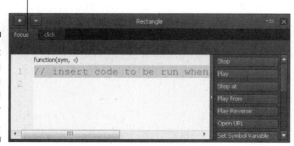

Figure 5-13:
You can have more than one action per element.

3. **From the menu on the right, choose Open URL.**

4. **Update the URL within the code box, which is highlighted in orange text.**

5. **Close the coding box to save your work.**

6. **Preview your animation in a browser to test your work.**

To test to make sure that your link works, click the link with the mouse.

On most websites, when you place your mouse over a link, the cursor changes from an arrow to a hand. Using the procedures described in this chapter, you can set cursor attributes to provide visual clues to your audience to indicate, for example, where links are or to show if you can select an element.

Congratulations! You now have a loop within your animation.

If an element already has an action associated with it, then when you click Open Actions, Edge Animate immediately opens the coding box instead of the menu shown in Figure 5-11. When that happens, and you want to add a second action to that element, then click the + (as shown in Figure 5-12).

Using focus as an action

Focus is an action that requires a couple more steps. You need to set the Tab Index from the Properties panel to get it to work. This section discusses specifically how to use the Tab Index with the Focus action.

Focus in Edge Animate is a jQuery event. From the jQuery API, "Elements with focus are usually highlighted in some way by the browser, for example with a dotted line surrounding the element." In Edge Animate, you can highlight an element by setting the tab index. For more information on focus, see http://api.jquery.com/focus.

To get started with the Focus action, follow these steps:

1. **Create an element on the Stage, as described in Chapter 3.**

2. **Select the element.**

3. **At the bottom of the Properties panel in the Accessibility section, assign a number to the element in the Tab Index (as shown in Figure 5-14).**

4. **To test that your element now has a tab assigned to it, preview your animation in the browser.**

    Press the Tab key and the browser highlights your element:

    • In Google Chrome, the highlight appears as a golden border.

    • In Firefox and Internet Explorer, the highlight appears as a dotted line.

Figure 5-14: Setting the Tab Index to get Focus to work.

Assign a number

5. **Close the browser window and return to Edge Animate.**

6. **Right-click the element, choose Open actions, and then choose Focus.**

   The coding box opens, and the following code appears:

   ```
   // insert code to be run when an element gains focus
   ```

7. **Choose an action from the menu on the right (such as Open URL).**

8. **Update the URL and then close the box to save your changes.**

When you preview the animation in a browser and press the Tab key, when that element is highlighted — in effect, when it gains focus — the action is triggered. In this case, the new URL loads.

Adding Cursor Attributes

When you create, say, a button that your audience can interact with, your users expect some kind of signal to show them that part of the animation is clickable. A clear way to provide such a signal so your audience can interact with an element is to change the shape of the cursor. You do that by specifying attributes for the cursor. Read on.

Cursor attribute types

Edge Animate provides a large choice to choose from when it comes to *cursor attributes,* such as a pointing finger that indicates a link. As shown in Figure 5-15, you can change the cursor to represent different types of interactivity, including these:

- **Pointing finger:** Indicates a link to click.

- **Watch:** Indicates that something is loading and/or that the audience should wait for something to happen.

- **Sizing:** Indicates that the audience can resize something such as a window or a column or a row.

Figure 5-15:
Edge
Animate
provides a
wide range
of cursor
attributes.

Good animators always provide as many visual clues to their audience as possible. That's how your audience realizes when and where an element of your composition is available for interaction.

Adding cursor attributes

Adobe Edge Animate CC allows you to change how the cursor looks by changing its attributes. This section shows you how to change the cursor into a pointer when you hover over a button in your composition.

To change the attributes of the cursor, follow these steps:

1. **Select an element, such as a button.**

2. **From the Properties panel, click the Cursor Style icon as indicated in Figure 5-16.**

3. **Choose a cursor attribute from the menu (see Figure 5-15).**

Figure 5-16:
Click the
Cursor
Style but-
ton to open
the Cursor
Attributes.

Cursor Style

To test that your cursor attribute is working, simply preview it in a browser. When you hover the mouse pointer over the element, it should change to a pointing finger, as shown in Figure 5-17.

Figure 5-17:
Here the
cursor
changes to
a pointing
finger when
you hover
over a
button.

Pointing finger

Chapter 6

Embracing the Workspace

*A*dobe Edge Animate CC is a dynamic software tool. The flexibility of the tool provides you the means to configure the interface to your choosing. You can close all the panels if you prefer to view only the Stage and the Timeline. Or you may want to maximize the Assets panel so that it takes up the entire screen. You can tab panels, stack them side by side, or place one on top of the other. And if the screen becomes entirely too cluttered, all you have to do is revert to the default view. However, if you finally get all the panels arranged in the manner best suited for you, you can save that view as a custom workspace.

The settings in the Properties panel constantly update as you click from one type of element to the next. Each different type of element — drawn rectangle, imported image, or text box — has its own unique set of properties. Not all properties are completely unique; some remain consistent no matter their type.

Clicking and Dragging the Panels

The Adobe Edge Animate interface consists of a main menu along the top and a series of *panels* and *frames* border the Stage. The panels contain the buttons, toggles, and switches that enable you to design. The frames contain the panels — and you can configure those as well, moving and resizing them as you see fit. You can even revert to the default view or create several different types of views:

  ✔ Stacked

  ✔ Tabbed

  ✔ Default

  ✔ Side by side

You can customize the location and size for the Properties panel, the Elements panel, and the Library. Each of these panels has two small icons in the top-right corner:

✓ **Drop-down arrow (shown in Figure 6-9):** Use this icon to undock or close panels and frames. You can also use it to maximize frames.

✓ **Click and Drag:** Use this icon to move panels around the workspace.

You can click and drag the panel by placing the cursor over the Click and Drag icon at the far right, as indicated in Figure 6-1.

Click and Drag icon

Figure 6-1: The Click and Drag icon for panels.

You can move each panel into any onscreen position and location, whether by clicking and dragging the name of each panel or clicking and dragging its icon.

Creating a stacked view

You can stack panels on top of each other. For example, you can click and drag the Properties panel to the top portion of the Timeline. While you click and drag, Edge Animate highlights — using a purple shade — where you are dragging the panel. Figure 6-2 shows the purple shade.

Figure 6-2: The purple area shows where the dragged panel will appear.

If you drag the Properties panel to the top portion of the Timeline (refer to Figure 6-2), the Properties panel appears stacked on top of the Timeline (as shown in Figure 6-3).

Figure 6-3:
Properties
panel now
stacked on
top of the
Timeline.

Creating a tabbed view

If the stacked view appears too cluttered for your taste, then you may prefer a tabbed view for the panels. You can drag a panel so that it's tabbed with another panel: The dragged panel becomes a tab; the panel it's dragged to becomes another tab. To make this happen, you can drag (for example) the Properties panel so that the purple shade is inside the Timeline, as shown in Figure 6-4.

Figure 6-4:
Creating
tabbed
panels.

By dragging one panel into the center of another panel, you create a tabbed view (as shown in Figure 6-5).

When the panels are tabbed, you can click the different tabs to see the different panels.

Tabbed panel

Figure 6-5:
Tabbed
panels for
the Timeline
and for
Properties.

Moving a panel back to its original position

After you move a panel around, you may decide you liked it better where it was before. In that case, you can simply click and drag that panel back to its original position.

If you move the Properties panel to a tabbed view with the Timeline, and want to revert the positioning, then click and drag the Properties panel (you can drag it from the name of the panel) over to the far-left side of the screen. A thin green shade appears, along with a hollow image of the panel, when you've dragged the Properties panel far enough over (Figure 6-6).

Figure 6-6:
A green line
and a hol-
low image
of a panel
show where
the panel
will appear.

Stacking panels side by side

The options are nearly endless as to where and how you can arrange the workspace. Another option besides stacked or tabbed is to place the panels side by side, as shown in Figure 6-7.

Figure 6-7:
Side-by-side placement of panels.

This side-by-side stacking was done by dragging the Properties panel onto the left side of the Library panel, as shown in Figure 6-8.

Figure 6-8:
Purple shading shows where the panels will appear when stacked side by side.

Manipulating the Panels and Frames

Adobe Edge Animate CC is a flexible and customizable tool that enables you to work the way you want. You configure the panels and frames in various ways that include these:

- ✔ Undock panels and frames so they can float about the interface.
- ✔ Maximize the frame so you can see much more information.
- ✔ Save customized views tailored to your preference.

Undocking panels

If stacking or creating tabs isn't your style, then you can undock the panels, which allows them to float around your workspace. In each case, you can undock either the panel or the frame, as shown in Figure 6-9.

Drop-down arrow

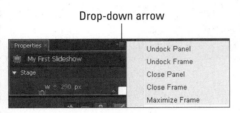

Figure 6-9: When you want to undock, click the drop-down arrow to open the menu.

Undocking a panel separates it from the workspace so you can freely move the panel around onscreen (as shown in Figure 6-10).

Figure 6-10: An undocked panel.

If you click the red X in the top corner, the panel closes.

To reopen an undocked panel, from the main menu click Window and then choose which panel you wish to open. Any panels currently open have a check mark next to them. Closed panels don't have a check mark (as shown in Figure 6-11).

Window	Help
	Workspace ▶
✓	Timeline
✓	Elements
✓	Library
✓	Tools
	Properties
	Code Ctrl+E
	Lessons
	Untitled-1.html
✓	slide-show-animation.html

Figure 6-11:
Opening
or closing
panels from
the Window
menu.

Undocking frames

Each frame can hold multiple panels when you've grouped the panels in a
tabbed view. If you have panels tabbed together and you choose Undock
Frame from the menu shown in Figure 6-9, then all the tabbed panels undock
from the workspace and you can float them around the interface at will (as
shown in Figure 6-12).

Figure 6-12:
Undocking
a frame
in tabbed
view.

You can close the frame (and all of the panels with it) by clicking the X.

Maximizing the frame

Another option for viewing frames and panels is to expand to maximum view. You can do this by choosing Maximize Frame from the menu shown in Figure 6-9. When you click Maximize Frame, your chosen panel fills the entire workspace.

The shortcut key to maximize a frame is one you may find especially useful. Simply place the cursor over the panel and press the ` key, which is located in the top-left corner of your keyboard, just to the left of the 1, showing the tilde (~) above the ` character. You can restore the frame size by choosing Restore Frame Size from the menu, as shown in Figure 6-13.

Drop-down arrow

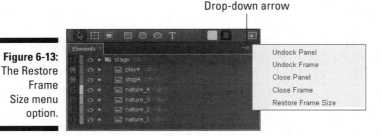

Figure 6-13:
The Restore
Frame
Size menu
option.

When you choose the Restore Frame Size option, the frame reverts to the way it appeared before you chose to Maximize Frame.

Saving a custom workspace view

When you get your workspace customized to exactly the way you want it, you can save that view and use it again on future compositions or the next time you open Adobe Edge Animate CC.

To save your custom workspace, from the main menu, choose Window⇨Workspace⇨New Workspace (as shown in Figure 6-14).

When you choose New Workspace, a dialog box appears. You can then name your customized workspace in that dialog box, as shown in Figure 6-15.

After you name your workspace and click OK, your newly named workspace appears in the Workspace menu (Figure 6-16). In this example, the custom workspace was named *My Workspace*.

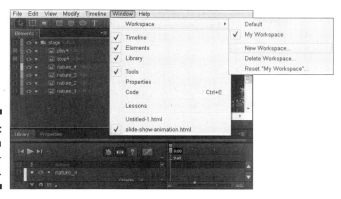

Figure 6-14:
Saving a new workspace.

Figure 6-15:
Naming your new workspace.

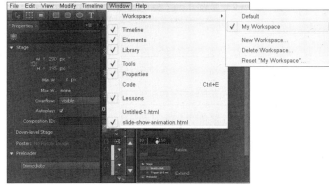

Figure 6-16:
Your custom workspace appears in the Workspace menu.

From the Workspace menu shown in Figure 6-16, you can choose your custom workspace or you can revert back to the default workspace by clicking Default. If, during the course of animating, your custom workspace gets moved around and you want to reset it, then you can click Reset "My Workspace."

You can also Delete Workspace and create even more New Workspaces.

When you close Edge Animate after customizing your workspace, the software shows the same customized workspace the next time you open Edge Animate, regardless of whether you saved that view. If you were hoping the interface would revert to the default view, you can reset (go back to) the default by clicking Window⇨Reset "Default" (as shown in Figure 6-17). See the next section for more details.

Reverting to the default view

It's fun to move and resize the different panels and frames around the interface. However, if you get carried away and you start to think you broke something or you can't figure out how to undo what you just did, don't worry: You can always revert your workspace to the way you want it to be.

Sorry, but pressing Ctrl+Z on your keyboard doesn't undo moving panels around the workspace.

To revert your workspace to the default view, from the main menu choose Window⇨Workspace⇨Reset "Default".

If you're working from a custom saved view, the Workspace menu appears a bit differently. In Figure 6-17, the top arrow shows how to revert to the default view; the bottom arrow shows how to revert to the saved custom view.

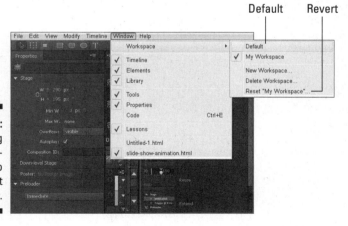

Figure 6-17: Resetting the workspace to the default view.

Choosing Window⇨Workspace⇨Reset "Default" restores your workspace to looking the way it did the first time you opened Edge Animate.

The Constantly Changing Properties Panel

The Properties panel (found along the left column) constantly updates itself depending on which type of element is selected. If you select a drawn element such as a rectangle, Edge Animate displays different configurations in the Properties panel than if you select a text box or an image. This keeps the clutter down in that you only see what you need, or can, work with for a certain type of element. Some properties are consistent, and appear no matter what type of element you select; other properties are specific to certain types of elements. Examples of consistent properties include: ID, Class, Actions, Display block, and Position and Size. All of these are discussed in detail in the following pages.

In addition to formatting and animating from the Properties panel, you can also:

✔ Edit the `Title` tag

✔ Set the class name

✔ Add actions

✔ Enable your audience to tab through elements

Specific properties for the Stage

Your first view of the Properties panel occurs when you start a new composition (Figure 6-18). This initial view shows properties for the Stage, including:

✔ **Title tag:** You can edit the title tag for the HTML page from the Properties panel.

✔ **Actions:** You can add actions to the Stage from the Properties panel.

✔ **Size dimensions:** You can edit the size of the Stage from the Properties panel.

✔ **Overflow:** These attributes include Visible, Hidden Scroll, and Auto. You can find more information on Overflow in Chapter 8.

✔ **Toggle Autoplay:** If you don't want your animation to automatically start playing when the page loads, make sure this check box isn't checked. If you do uncheck the box, then make sure to add an action to an element — such as a Play button — so your audience can start the animation.

✔ **Composition ID:** I recommend leaving the Composition ID alone. Edge Animate uses this ID in the HTML file for reference.

✔ **Down-level Stage:** This simpler version of the Stage accommodates browsers that don't support HTML5 or CSS3. Chapter 14 provides details of the down-level Stage.

✔ **Poster:** Used with the down-level Stage. Chapter 14 contains additional information.

✔ **Preloader:** Used for setting what your audience first sees while your animation is loading to the screen.

This is best used for large compositions that may not load immediately upon launch. Chapter 14 contains additional information.

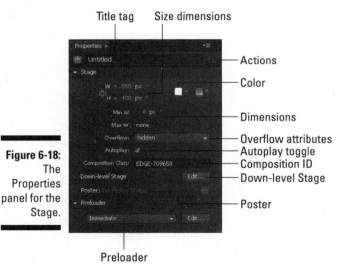

Figure 6-18:
The Properties panel for the Stage.

You can find more information on Stage properties in Chapter 3, where I discuss resizing the Stage by pixel or by percent. Chapter 13 also provides additional information on configuring the Stage for a responsive web design; Chapter 20 provides a sample project on creating a responsive web animation.

You can edit the Title tag not only from the HTML file, but also from the Properties panel. The Title tag is important because, if your animation is a standalone web page, the text used for the Title tag appears in the tab of your web browser. (Figure 6-19 shows the Title tag in the Firefox browser.) Therefore it's good practice to give the Title tag a name relevant to your content.

Title tag

If you open the HTML file, you can edit the Title tag (shown in bold in the lines of code presented here). Saved changes appear in Edge Animate when you reopen the file.

```
<!DOCTYPE html>
<html>
<head>
    <meta http-equiv="Content-Type" content="text/html;
    charset=utf-8">
    <meta http-equiv="X-UA-Compatible" content="IE=Edge"/>
    <title>Page Title</title>
<!--Adobe Edge Runtime-->
    <script type="text/javascript" charset="utf-8"
        src="properties-panel_edgePreload.js"></script>
    <style>
        .edgeLoad-EDGE-10260726 { visibility:hidden; }
    </style>
<!--Adobe Edge Runtime End-->

</head>
<body style="margin:0;padding:0;">
    <div id="Stage" class="EDGE-10260726">
    </div>
</body>
</html>
```

Consistent properties for all elements

The Properties panel appears in the left column of the default view of the interface. This is where you can configure, toggle, set, animate, etc. all of your different elements, including the Stage (see the previous section).

Depending on the type of element that you select, different properties appear in the Properties panel, but some of them remain consistent (as shown in Figure 6-20):

- **ID:** Name an element in this box, which then appears in the Timeline.

- **Class:** You can specify the user class for a specific element. If you aren't a developer and see yourself strictly as a designer, you may not use this box; if you do know JavaScript and CSS, you may use this feature. When you type a name into the Class box, and then open the `.js` file from the folder structure, you should see that your content elements now have a user class assigned.

- **Actions:** You can assign actions to elements from the Properties panel. See Chapter 5 for more information.

- **Display block:** This is where you can set when an element is Always On, On, or Off. If an element is On, you can see it; if it's Off, it's hidden from view. You can also set the Overflow properties to Visible, Hidden, Scroll, or Auto. Opacity is another property that you can set from this block. See Chapter 8 for more information.

- **Position and Size:** You can use these settings in association with building a responsive web design. Here you can set an element's *anchor point* (which determines the point of an element that Edge Animate considers the center, thus affecting how certain animations display the element). You can also position the element on the Stage and change its actual size. You can even use Layout Presets. For more information, see Chapter 8.

- **Transform:** In this block, you can skew and rotate elements. You can also change the scale of the element and move the origin point. Additional information is found in Chapter 7.

- **Cursor:** If you want a specific type of cursor to appear when your audience hovers the mouse pointer over an element, you can set that from here. See Chapter 5.

- **Shadow:** Whether your element is a rectangle, ellipses, a text box, or an image, you can add a shadow to make it stand out. You can even animate that shadow. Chapter 9 contains additional information.

- **Clip:** You can use clip to cover or uncover portions of an element. For example, you can animate an image so that parts of the element slowly appear or disappear. Chapter 9 has the details.

- **Accessibility:** Refers to setting a tab index for elements. This allows your audience to use the Tab key on the keyboard to select different elements (as discussed in Chapter 5).

You can assign a title to images, rectangles, and other drawn elements, including text boxes. These titles appear when your audience hovers their mouse over the element, or if they use Tab to select an element or elements. To assign a title to an element, simply type in the box as indicated by the red rectangle in Figure 6-20.

Figure 6-20:
Consistent
properties
for all types
of elements.

Specific properties for specific elements

You use properties in Edge Animate to format and add style to elements. Elements can be anything from a drawn box to images to text. When you select one of these types of elements from the Stage, different properties appear in the Properties panel.

Each different element type has different properties that you can configure from the Properties panel. The element types include:

✔ **Drawn:** Objects you create, such as rectangles, rounded rectangles, and ellipses.

✔ **Images:** Pictures you insert, which have their own sets of properties.

✔ **Text:** The text boxes that you create, which have their own unique properties as well.

Drawn elements

When you select a drawn element — rectangle, rounded rectangle, or an ellipse — new properties appear in the Properties panel. Although text boxes are considered drawn elements, they have their own special properties, detailed in the next couple of sections.

Color section

In the Color section, you can set the background color of the element (refer to Figure 3-7), the border color, the border type, and the thickness of the border (as shown in Figure 6-21).

Background

Figure 6-21: Setting the drawn element's background color, border color, border type, and thickness.

Corners section

The Corners section is where you can set the roundness of the corners — or even animate the corners so that a square box turns into a circle. (In Chapter 9, I discuss how to set up that animation sequence.)

In Figure 6-22, you can see that you can configure up to eight different corners of an element. If you click the 4, then you can configure four corners. If you want to set all of the corners at once, then choose 1.

You can set the Corner settings as either px or percentage.

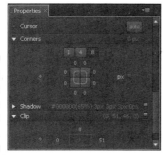

Figure 6-22:
Set the
roundness
of the
corners.

Image elements

You can set images as either *img* or *div*.

- ✔ **As an img:** Edge Animate treats the element as an image using the image tag in HTML.
- ✔ **As a div:** Edge Animate treats your image as a background image.

You can set the image to either img or div from the Properties panel, near the top, as shown in Figure 6-23. Use the image tag (img) when the image includes actual content (for example, a graph); use a div tag with a background image when the image is only decorative.

Figure 6-23:
Setting
specific
proper-
ties for div
background
images.

Swap images

Also shown in Figure 6-23 is the capability to swap out one image for another, as indicated by the red arrow. This is useful if you don't have the final art ready, but you do want to start animating. The next subsection details how to do this extremely handy trick.

Swapping images in your animation

In this case, you can use filler art to get started; when the final art is ready, all you have to do is follow these steps:

1. **Make sure that your replacement image is added to the Library panel. If it is not, add it as follows: From the Library panel, click the + icon (as shown in Figure 6-24).**

   Your chosen replacement image is added to the Assets section of the Library panel.

Figure 6-24:
Adding an
image to
the Asset
Library so
you can use
it to replace
another
image.

Click to add

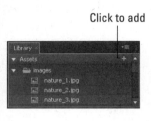

2. **Select the image element you want to replace from the Stage.**

   The image becomes highlighted.

3. **Click the arrows in the Image section of the Properties panel.**

   A box with a list of images from the Library panel appears.

4. **Choose a replacement image.**

   The replacement image becomes highlighted.

5. **Insert the replacement image into your animation by clicking anywhere on the interface, besides the box.**

   The new image replaces the old image.

6. **Test your animation with the new image by previewing in a browser.**

   The new image does its thing in your animation.

Background image

If you choose div to set the image as a background image, then the Properties panel appears (refer to Figure 6-23), and you have the opportunity to set the location and size of the image as indicated by the orange rectangle.

Image tag

If you choose img instead of div, then Edge Animate assigns an image tag to that element. When this happens, the Properties panel updates and appears as shown in Figure 6-25.

If you designated your image as an img, you can now name an ALT tag for your image. The ALT tag appears in place of the image if your audience has images turned off in their browsers. A typical ALT tag would show Cute Kitten in place of an image showing, say, a cute kitten.

Alt tags are also good for *search engine optimization (SEO)*. SEO is a marketing term for web developers, which basically translates into best practices for the best search results. Search engines can't read images, but they can read ALT tags, so by adding an ALT tag to your image you provide a way for search engines to index your content.

Alt tag

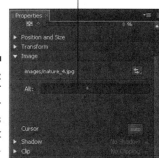

Figure 6-25:
Add an ALT tag to your images as best practice.

There is a difference between ALT tags for images and the *accessibility title* — text that appears as a pop-up when you hover your mouse pointer over an element (refer to Figure 6-20, #10) — for all different types of elements:

✔ ALT tags provide a way for search engines to index your images for search results. The text assigned to an ALT tag appears in place of the image if the image cannot be displayed.

✔ Accessibility titles provide a way to add pop-up text that appears when someone hovers the mouse pointer over an element.

Text box elements

Edge Animate is very font-friendly. When you select a text box, the Text properties appear in the Properties panel, as shown in Figure 6-26. You can set many text properties:

- ✔ Font style (refer to Figure 2-7)
- ✔ Font size
- ✔ Font weight
- ✔ Font decoration
- ✔ Left, center, or right alignment

You can animate the font size, as when you make text appear to shrink or grow. You can also animate the font color if (say) you want to have your text slowly (or quickly) change from one color to another. See Chapter 10 for more information on animating text.

Unfortunately, you can't animate a change from one font style to another.

To add new fonts, see Chapter 11.

Click to set font properties

Figure 6-26:
Set such
Font proper-
ties as size,
color, type,
and justifi-
cation.

Part III
Formatting and Animating

Visit www.dummies.com/extras/adobeedgeanimatecc for great Dummies content online.

In this part . . .

- ✔ Applying Transform
- ✔ Managing appearance
- ✔ Operating graphic effects
- ✔ Visit www.dummies.com/extras/adobeedge
  animatecc for great Dummies content online.

Chapter 7

Animating with the Transform Tool and Properties Panel

● ●

In This Chapter

▶ Animating powerfully with the Transform tool

▶ Applying Transform attributes by clicking and dragging or entering numbers

▶ Centering on the center point

▶ Animating border radius, spinning, skewing, scaling, and rotating with the Transform tool

● ●

*T*he Transform tool allows you to animate the Skew, Scale, Rotation, Border Radius, and Location of an element simply by clicking and dragging. The Transform tool is located directly to the right of the Select tool, as shown in Figure 7-1.

You can also use the Transform tool to spin elements, which is different from rotating elements (also described in this chapter).

Figure 7-1:
The Transform tool.

Transform

File Edit View Modify Timeline Window Help

Transforming with the Transform Tool and Properties Panel

Here's a handy feature of Edge Animate: Much of what you can do with the Transform tool, you can also do from the Properties panel. While you're making your animation, you may want to switch back and forth between the Transform tool and the Properties panel. The difference is that the Transform tool allows more fluidity while the Property panel provides more accuracy and precision by using numbers.

Turning a selected element into a transform selection

If you right-click an element on the Stage, a menu appears from which you can choose Transform (along with several other options), as shown in Figure 7-2. When you click Transform, elements you select appear as a transform selection.

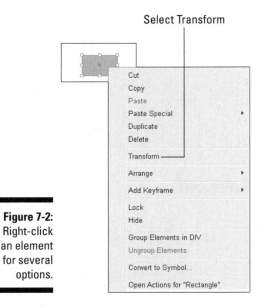

Select Transform

Cut
Copy
Paste
Paste Special ▸
Duplicate
Delete

Transform

Arrange ▸
Add Keyframe ▸

Lock
Hide

Group Elements in DIV
Ungroup Elements

Convert to Symbol...

Open Actions for "Rectangle"

Figure 7-2:
Right-click an element for several options.

You can also click the Transform tool icon, as shown in Figure 7-1. When you click the Transform tool, the element changes from a blue border to a black border with several selection points, as shown in Figure 7-3.

Transform box

Figure 7-3:
Regular
boxes and
transform
boxes.

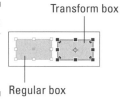

Regular box

Transform elements have their own properties

When you have the Transform tool selected on an element, new items appear in the Properties panel, as shown in Figure 7-4.

Figure 7-4:
The
Transform
Origin
feature.

When you have a Transform box onscreen, you can animate it several different ways, as described in the rest of this chapter. I highly encourage you to be creative with the Transform tool to create unique animations.

Understanding the Center Transform Origin

The *center point,* indicated in Figure 7-5, determines where the center of an element is located. Where you place the center point has an effect on the animation.

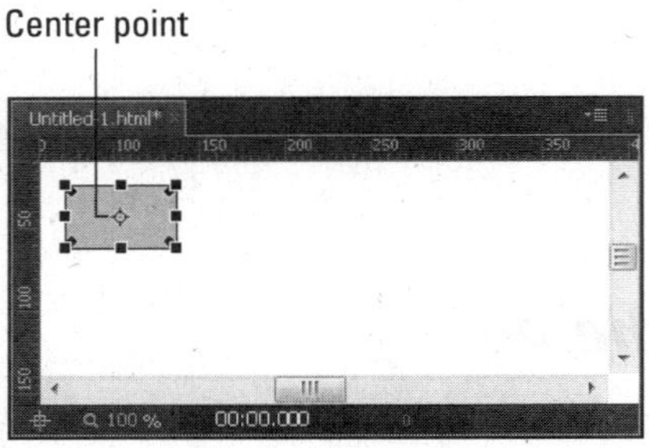

Center point

Figure 7-5: The little blue dot known as the center point.

Positioning the center point

You can move the center point around, and thus affect how an animation plays out, by using either of two features:

- **The Transform tool:** All elements have a center point when you click the Transform tool. You can move that center point by clicking and dragging it with your mouse. You can even drag the center point outside of the element for an exaggerated animation.

- **The Properties panel:** You can position the center point through the Properties panel from the Transform section, as shown in Figure 7-6. Note that this feature has X and Y coordinates; these determine where the center point appears in the box. X and Y coordinates of 50% represent the center of the element.

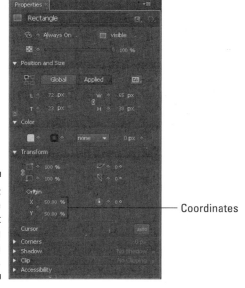

Figure 7-6:
Moving the center point by changing the Origin Properties.

— Coordinates

Animating with the center point

You can experiment by placing the center point in different parts of the element and seeing how that affects the animation. Here's a step-by-step explanation of how to create an animation sequence with the center point on a text box:

1. **Draw a text box on the Stage and type in something like** Text Box.

2. **Select the Transform tool (refer to Figure 7-1).**

3. **Click and drag the center point so it's over the top-left part of the first letter, as shown in Figure 7-7.**

Center point

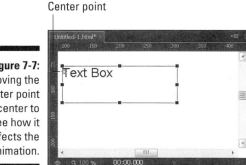

Figure 7-7:
Moving the center point off-center to see how it affects the animation.

Text Box

4. Set the Pin and the Playhead in the Timeline.

Toggle the Pin, and then drag the Playhead down the Timeline so that you see the chevron arrows (as shown in Figure 7-8).

Figure 7-8:
Setting up the Timeline to create an animation sequence.

5. On the Stage, place your cursor over the bottom-right corner of the text box so that the cursor turns into a semicircle-with-arrow, as shown in Figure 7-9.

6. Click, hold down the mouse button, and swing the mouse around in a circular motion.

You should see the text box rotate as you move the mouse. The box swings around as if a pin was stuck in the top-left corner.

7. When you're done swinging the box, release the mouse button.

Edge Animate creates an animation sequence, which you can then preview.

To experiment, move the center point back to the center and then try rotating the box again. You should see a very different animation in that the center of the box is now actually in the center instead in the top left of the box. The difference is that the box is now rotating from the center of the box instead of from the top left.

Figure 7-9:
Grab the corner of the box to rotate.

Rotate

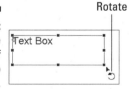

Here's something to try for fun:

1. **Create a long animation sequence so that you can slowly see how the point of origin affects the rotation of the text box.**

2. **At the beginning of the sequence, set the center point in the top-left corner.**

3. **At the end of the sequence, position the center point in the lower-right corner.**

4. **Preview the animation to see how the center point gives the appearance of the text not only rotating, but also moving across the Stage as well.**

   You can also scrub the Playhead up and down the Timeline to see the origin point move across the box.

Creating Animations with the Transform Tool

The Transform tool enables you to create many different types of animation sequences. In this section, I cover:

- Border radius
- Moving an element across the Stage
- Spinning elements

Animating the border radius

You can animate the border radius of an element with the Transform tool so that you can change square corners to rounded corners. Figure 7-10 shows where to click and drag to change the radius of the corner. This allows you to take an element with square edges and animate it so that it transitions to having rounded corners.

To animate the transition of square corners to rounded corners, with the Transform tool selected, place the mouse pointer near one of the squares in the corner of the element.

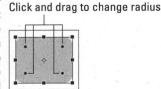

Figure 7-10:
Using the
Transform
tool to
animate
rounded
corners.

Click and drag to change radius

Click and drag one of the corner squares inward toward the center point. The farther you click and drag, the more the square corners round off (Figure 7-11).

If you want to animate the corners rounding off, remember to set the Timeline so that Edge Animate creates keyframes and an animation sequence: Toggle the Pin, make sure the Stopwatch is red, and separate the Pin and the Playhead on the Timeline as shown in Figure 7-8.

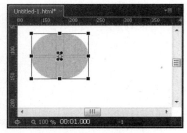

Figure 7-11:
Rounding
corners by
using the
Transform
tool.

If you click and drag one of the corners, then all four corners round off in synch, but they won't stay to scale if you start dragging to the left or right (as compared to evenly dragging inward). If you want to ensure that all the corners stay in scale relative to each other, then press Shift on the keyboard while you click and drag.

If you want to round off only one of the corners, then press Ctrl on the keyboard (or for the Mac use Cmd) while you click and drag. You can also use the Corners section of the Properties panel to set specific configurations.

Animating the location of an element

You have several different ways you can animate an element from one location to another (having it move across the Stage). One way is to use the Transform tool by following these steps:

1. **Set the Playhead and Pin in the Timeline to designate when the animation will start and how long you want the animation to last.**

2. **Click the Transform tool from the toolbar (as shown in Figure 7-1) and then select an element from the Stage.**

   The pointer changes to a four-way cursor (as shown in Figure 7-12).

Cursor

Figure 7-12:
Using the
Transform
Tool to
animate the
location of
an element.

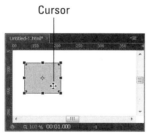

3. **Click, hold, and drag the element across the Stage to where you want it to appear, and then release the mouse button.**

   The element is now animated to move across the screen.

4. **To test your new animation, you can run the animation on the Stage or you can preview it in a browser.**

5. **To save your animation, you can press Ctrl+S or, from the main menu, choose File⇨Save.**

Spinning elements

In this section, I show how to make an object spin using the Transform tool, which is different from rotating.

Here's how to make an element spin.

1. **Create an element on the Stage.**

   In this example, I use a text box with the word *Spin* in it.

2. **Set up the Playhead and Pin in the Timeline to designate how long you want the animation to last.**

3. **With the element selected, click the Transform tool (refer to Figure 7-1).**

4. **Place the cursor over the left-middle selector on the box so that you see the double arrow (as shown in Figure 7-13).**

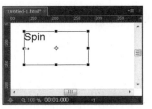

Figure 7-13: Click and drag the middle-left selector to start spinning.

5. **Click, hold, and drag the mouse to the right.**

The element transforms as you drag.

Use the pink guideline to help you determine when the element is completely flipped over. The guideline automatically appears as you click and drag.

6. **When the element appears reversed — that is, appears as its mirror image — stop dragging and release the mouse button (see Figure 7-14).**

Releasing the mouse button generates an animated keyframe automatically. This is the first half of your spin animation; the remaining steps complete it.

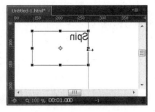

Figure 7-14: The mirror image.

7. **Adjust the Playhead and Pin in the Timeline as shown in Figure 7-15.**

To do so, move the Pin to the end of the first animation sequence, and the Playhead farther along from there.

Figure 7-15:
Adjust the
Playhead
and Pin in
the Timeline
to create
the second
half of the
spin.

Figure 7-15:
Adjust the
Playhead
and Pin in
the Timeline
to create
the second
half of the
spin.

You can move the Pin and Playhead together by placing the mouse over the onscreen chevron. When you see the pointer change to a hand, you can click and drag the Playhead and Pin together down the Timeline.

8. **With the Playhead and Pin in position, place the cursor on the right-most middle selector, and then click and drag to the left until the element appears the same as when the first half of the animation started.**

   You should now have two animation sequences. If you want the element to spin continuously, you can add a loop (as described in Chapter 5).

Adobe Edge Animate CC has several Paste Special options, shown in Figure 7-16. They include a Paste Inverted option, which comes in handy if you want to replicate the opposite of a keyframe. In this example on how to make an element spin, you can use the Paste Inverted option to create the second keyframe. After creating the first keyframe, copy it and then paste it using the Paste Inverted option.

Figure 7-16:
The Paste
Special
options from
the Edit
menu.

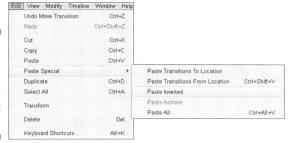

Animating with the Transform Tool or the Properties Panel

You can also use the Properties panel to create three of the same animation effects that you create with the Transform tool:

- ✔ Skewing
- ✔ Scaling
- ✔ Rotating

Using the Transform tool gives you more fluid control over the animation. When you use the Properties panel, you set specific numbers — which provides greater precision in creating the animation.

Skewing elements

Skewing your elements is a very cool effect. In Adobe Edge Animate CC, to *skew* your element means to animate your element through a transition of oblique angles or to change its direction or position suddenly. The best way to figure out what skew does is to experiment with it.

One example of skewing is to bring text onto the Stage. You can use skewing as an alternative approach to fading text in or scrolling it. Skewing gives the effect of the text shrinking in size as the different angles twist the words around.

Transform tool

With the Transform tool and element selected, place the cursor directly along an edge as shown in Figure 7-17 so that you see the double lines with half-arrows. You can now click and drag to skew the element.

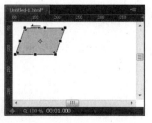

Figure 7-17:
Skewing with the Transform tool.

If you don't want to animate the skew effect, be sure you disable the Auto Keyframe mode when you use the Transform tool.

If you do want to animate the skew, then set the Pin and Playhead at different points in the Timeline when you use the Transform tool and make sure the Stopwatch is red.

Properties panel

To use Skew via the Properties panel, follow these steps:

1. **Import an image or create an element.**
2. **Adjust the Timeline Playhead and Pin to where you want the skewing to happen.**
3. **From the Properties panel, adjust the number of Skew degrees (see Figure 7-18).**

You can specify both horizontal and vertical Skew values for the object. These values affect the object on its X and Y axis (respectively). To find the best effect, try using both values at varying degrees; also adjust the length of the animation.

After you set the Skew values, you can test the effect as follows: Move the Pin in the Timeline forward or backward to allow at least a 5-second duration (to provide enough time that you can really see the effect in action), and then reset the Skew values back to 0 to display the object without any Skew at all.

Adjusting the length of the animation for Skew has a dramatic effect on how the animation plays out. With a longer animation, the Skew effect has more time to show the different angles the object is twisted through before settling back to 0 (or whatever final value you set for the object).

 — Skew degrees

Figure 7-18:
The Skew feature in the Properties panel.

The most you can skew an element is 89 degrees. If you use a value higher than 89, Edge Animate reverts the value to 89. You'll probably want to use a skew value much lower than 89 for your final composition. A value of 89 twists and transforms the element greatly and may be a bit much.

Scaling elements

Scaling means essentially that you can change the size of an element while keeping its proportions consistent if you want. You can:

- ✔ Scale elements with the Transform tool
- ✔ Scale elements from the Properties panel

Scaling with the Transform tool

If you prefer to use a click-and-drag method for scaling elements, you can use the Transform tool to do just that by following these steps:

1. **Click the Transform tool (refer to Figure 7-1) to select it.**

2. **Place the cursor over one of the corner selectors on an element.**

   As shown in Figure 7-19, you see a diagonal cursor with an arrow at each end.

3. **Click, hold, and drag the corner selector.**

   If you drag outward, you make the element larger; if you drag inward, you make the element smaller.

Figure 7-19:
Using the Transform tool for scaling.

To keep the element's proportions the same, hold down Shift while clicking and dragging.

Scaling with the Properties panel

You can shrink and grow objects through a Scale feature on the Properties panel. You can Scale objects both horizontally and vertically.

The Scale feature has a Link Scale attribute that enables you to synch the proportions (see Figure 7-20). When the Link Scale attribute is on, the horizontal and vertical sizes remain in synch — but only when you're modifying the values from the Properties panel. With the Link Scale attribute turned off, you can set two different values for horizontal and vertical.

Scaling your text is different from animating the font size. To animate the font size, see Chapter 9.

Horizontal and vertical sizes

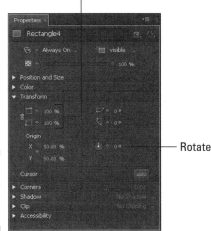

——————— Rotate

Figure 7-20:
Scaling has
a Link Scale
attribute.

Shrinking elements

To make an element shrink, go to the Properties panel and click the diamonds next to Scale with the percentages at 100% (see Figure 7-20). Clicking the diamonds creates keyframes.

Next, toggle the Pin and slide out the Playhead in the Timeline to the point where you want the shrinking to stop. Last, adjust the percentages in the Scale feature to a value lesser than 100%. This should create an animated keyframe for you in the Timeline.

Scaling an element can create a neat trick by making your object appear to flip over. To see this in action, create an animated keyframe where the object starts at 100% and ends at –100%. The animation shrinks the element down to nothing, and then makes it reappear flipped upside down. The negative percentage is what flips the object over.

Growing elements

To make your element grow larger, start the keyframe with the object at a value lesser than or equal to 100%. Then slide out the Playhead in the Timeline to the point where you want the growing to stop (making sure to keep the Pin at the point where you want the animation to start). Then go back to the Properties panel and increase the percentage to the size desired. Provided the Stopwatch is still red, Edge Animate creates a new animated keyframe for you.

Rotating elements

You can *rotate* elements in your composition, like the wheels of a car, which is different from making an element spin (as discussed earlier in this chapter).

In this section, I show you how to:

✔ Use the Rotate feature from the Properties panel to make your text appear to rotate.

✔ Make a rotation animation appear as if it's happening very quickly or very slowly.

For information on how to rotate an element with the Transform tool, look in the beginning of this chapter, in the section, "Animating with the center point."

This technique to make elements rotate also works on imported images.

Determining how fast to make the element rotate

After you have a text box or an image ready to rotate, you need to determine how long you want the animation to last.

✔ If you want the rotating to happen quickly, separate the Playhead from the Pin in the Timeline for about a half-second or so.

✔ If you want the text or image to rotate more slowly, then move the Playhead further down the Timeline away from the Pin.

The shorter the duration of the animation, the quicker it happens. The longer the animation lasts, the slower it plays out. For a quick animation, create a very short keyframe. For a slow animation, create a long keyframe.

Using the rotate feature

Go to the Properties panel and find the Rotate feature as shown in Figure 7-21. Click the diamond next to Rotate to set the position of your object at the start of the animation sequence. Then set up your Timeline to make an animation sequence.

There are two ways to change the rotation of an object from the Properties panel:

✔ Click and drag the thin white line on the Rotate circle in a circular fashion

✔ Input a degree value by clicking the orange 0 and typing in the number of degrees you want the object to rotate.

If you type in the degrees manually and press Enter, the thin white line on the circle rotates to the degree value you indicated. This provides a helpful visual clue to the angle created by the number of the degrees you entered.

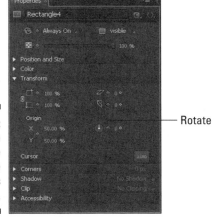

Figure 7-21:
The Rotate feature in the Properties panel.

Rotate

For the keyframe to appear, the Stopwatch icon in the Timeline must be red.

After you create the animation sequence, you can press the spacebar to play the rotating animation.

If you want to change the speed of the rotating effect, place the cursor at the end of the keyframe in the Timeline so that you see the double-arrow cursor. Then click and drag to create either of the following effects:

- ✔ Slow down the rotation by increasing the length of the keyframe.
- ✔ Speed up the rotation by decreasing the length of the keyframe.

Chapter 8

Formatting Element Visibility, Positioning, and Sizing

*I*n Chapter 8, I present how to animate and format several aspects of the elements you use in your animation. This includes formatting and animating visibility: You can choose when, where, and for how long an element appears on the Stage by using visibility.

In addition, scroll bars and the Overflow property enable you to work with content that is larger than the container. For example, scroll bars provide your audience with a way to access and read text that doesn't fit entirely on the screen.

When creating animations, you expect to size and position elements as needed — and Edge Animate responds with a ton of positioning and sizing features. This includes a variety of layout presets.

Setting the Visibility of Elements

You can format and animate the *visibility* of an element — that is, whether the viewer can see an element on the Stage. Even if you turn Visibility off and you no longer see the element on the Stage, you can still select it from the Elements panel or the Timeline and work with it. You have these options:

> ✔ You can turn Visibility Off, On, or Always On.
>
> ✔ You can animate the Visibility setting so that elements appear or disappear as the animation plays.

Element Visibility on the Stage

If your composition starts to get cluttered with too many elements, you can turn the visibility of specific elements off and on to help clean up the clutter. When you turn off an element's visibility, it disappears from the Stage but it's still present; you can still see it when you preview your animation in a browser.

Figure 8-1 shows where the Set Element Visibility icon is in the Timeline and how it appears when it's turned on or off. For more information on setting the visibility of elements on the Stage, see Chapter 11.

Figure 8-1: Setting an element's visibility on the Stage from the Timeline.

On

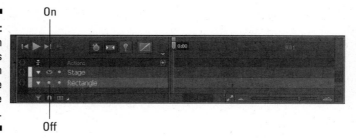

Off

Animating the visibility of elements

You can use the Element Display feature on just about anything in Edge Animate, including text boxes, images and rectangles. The Display feature is found in the Properties panel (as shown in Figure 8-2).

The default is Always On, which means your audience will always see the element on the Stage.

Always On, or Off, or On

Use the Display feature to toggle elements from one state to another, whether Always On, On, or Off. Click the tiny arrow next to Always On to open the menu shown in Figure 8-3.

Element Display

Figure 8-2:
The Element
Display
feature.

Figure 8-3:
The Display
feature
menu.

The Element Display feature is useful in that you can tell Edge Animate when you want a certain element shown in the animation. This comes in handy if, for example, you want a bit of text to appear late in the animation and then for it to disappear. Instead of adding in Opacity attributes to make text appear at a certain point in the Timeline — by animating the Opacity from 0% to 100% — you can simply use the element Display feature. More information on Opacity is found in this chapter.

The default setting for the Element Display feature is Always On. So, if you want your audience to always see the element, then you don't have to do anything to make sure your element is always on.

To toggle an element from Off to On, you need to first create an element such as a rectangle. Then, from the Properties panel, click the drop-down arrow for Display and choose Off. Doing so inserts a keyframe (diamond) into the Timeline as shown in Figure 8-4 — which also shows the Display setting, which appears in the Timeline along with the keyframe.

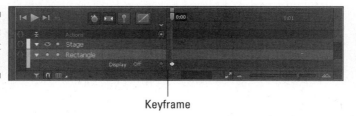

Figure 8-4:
Element
Display off.

Keyframe

From the Timeline, you can toggle the Display between off and on, but in order to revert to Always On, you have to do that from the Properties panel. When you revert the element to Always On, Edge Animate warns you that any keyframes will be removed (as shown in Figure 8-5).

Figure 8-5:
Reverting
to Always
On removes
any key-
frames
associ-
ated with
Display.

Don't be alarmed to see your text box suddenly disappear from the Stage when you turn it to Off. Likewise, don't worry when you realize you can't select the turned-Off element from the Stage. In essence, when an element is Off, it may as well not be part of the composition at all. However, you can still select it from the Elements panel in the top-right corner and you can also see it listed in the Timeline. That's how you know the element still exists.

Follow these steps to animate the visibility of an element from Off to On to Off again:

1. **Create an element on the Stage.**

2. **Move the Playhead to the point in the Timeline at which you want the element to become visible.**

3. **Select the element and then choose On from the Display menu.**

   Doing so automatically turns Visibility to Off for the time leading up to when it's On.

4. **Move the Playhead to the point in the Timeline at which you want the element to become invisible.**

5. **Choose Off from the Display menu.**

Congratulations! You have now created an animation in which an element starts off invisible, becomes visible, and then disappears again. To test that it works, you can preview the animation in the browser or you can view from the Stage.

Figure 8-6 shows how your Timeline should appear after you complete the quick steps for animating Visibility. The shaded areas represent when the element is off. The Timeline segment between the two hollow diamonds represents the time during which the element is visible.

Figure 8-6:
Timeline
for an ele-
ment's
Visibility
going from
Off to On to
Off again.

Adding scroll bars, hidden, visible, or auto

Overflow is a nice added touch in Adobe Edge Animate CC. You can find it in the Properties panel, as indicated in Figure 8-7.

Overflow

Figure 8-7:
Use the
Overflow
tool in the
Properties
panel for
scroll bars.

Overflow gives you some handy ways to control the visibility of your elements. You can

- ✔ Add scroll bars to an element.

- ✔ Allow for content that is larger than the size of the element or Stage to be in one of two states:

  - • **Visible:** Useful when you want all of the content to appear even if it overflows the container (see Figure 8-9) or the Stage.

  - • **Hidden:** Useful when you want to hide certain content.

- ✔ Use an Auto feature in which Edge Animate determines whether to have scroll bars present.

Overflow is a CSS property. Auto, Visible, and Hidden are all values of that property.

When you click the drop-down arrow for the Overflow attribute in the Properties panel, several choices appear as shown in Figure 8-8.

Figure 8-8:
Overflow
attributes
include
Visible,
Hidden,
Scroll, and
Auto.

You can set the Overflow properties to any type of element.

Visible Overflow property

Visible allows any overflow content (content that doesn't fit on the Stage or within a *container*) to still appear, both on the Stage and in the browser. In Figure 8-9, the container is the blue-outline box with selection points.

Figure 8-9:
Visible
allows
content that
extends
past the
container to
appear.

Hidden Overflow property

The *Hidden* Overflow property keeps any content that overflows the container hidden from immediate view onscreen until your audience scrolls to it (as shown in Figure 8-10).

Figure 8-10:
The Hidden
attribute
covers
content that
extends
past the
container.

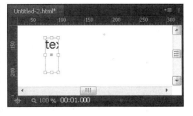

Scroll Overflow property

The *Scroll* Overflow property inserts scroll bars into the element's container or the Stage, as shown in Figure 8-11. With the scroll bars available, the user can scroll around within the box. Figure 8-11 shows an example.

Figure 8-11:
Scroll bars
enable your
audience
to scroll
through text
or other
content.

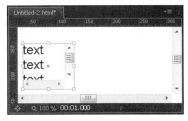

Auto Overflow property

Auto enables Edge Animate to do the thinking and determine if any content overflows the container. If content does overflow the container, then Edge Animate automatically adds scroll bars (as shown in Figure 8-12). With Scroll enabled, the scroll bars appear both on the bottom and on the right (refer to Figure 8-11). However, if you use Auto, Edge Animate knows to add only the right scroll bar, and the bottom scroll bar won't appear because it isn't necessary.

Figure 8-12:
Auto enables Edge Animate to do the thinking on adding scroll bars.

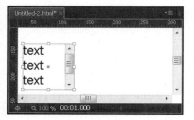

Animating with Opacity

Opacity is the condition of lacking transparency or translucence; when an object is opaque, you can't see through it (you knew that). And Adobe Edge Animate CC enables you, through the Opacity tool, to have elements slowly fade in or out or simply appear as mere see-through shadows. Figure 8-13 shows where you can find the Opacity tool on the Properties panel.

Opacity

Figure 8-13:
Set the Opacity to 50% to make an element see-through.

Figure 8-14 shows an image at 50% Opacity placed over a rectangle. At 50% Opacity, you can see through the image and make out the rectangle behind it.

Figure 8-14:
Using
Opacity to
allow your
audience to
see through
elements.

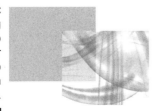

Here are some quick steps on animating with Opacity. In this example, I show you how to make an image slowly appear on the Stage:

1. **Select an element on the Stage, such as an image.**

2. **From the Properties panel, move the Opacity slider down to 0% (as shown in Figure 8-13).**

3. **In the Timeline, toggle the Pin and then move the Playhead down to specify as long a time as you want the Opacity animation to last.**

   The farther you separate the Playhead from the Pin, the longer the animation, and the more slowly the image appears.

4. **With the Playhead set, go back to the Opacity slide bar and drag it up to 100%.**

   Edge Animate creates a keyframe animation sequence after you set the Opacity the second time.

You can now preview the Opacity animation from the Stage or in a browser.

Configuring Positioning and Sizing

Adobe Edge Animate CC has no shortage of settings when it comes to positioning and sizing. Many of these features work best when nesting elements, so you may want to check Chapter 10 to understand how the Element panel works. Positioning refers to the coordinates of the element relative either to the Stage or to the parent element when one element is nested inside the other. You can also use a position attribute to affect how you want the element to react when you size it.

Setting the relative position

Specifying the *relative position* of an element affects which corner of your element is manipulated when you resize it. You can find the Position and Size attributes in the Properties panel (as shown in Figure 8-15). Be sure to select an element from the Stage to have these attributes appear.

When I refer to *relative position* in the context of Edge Animate, note that it doesn't mean the same as *relative positioning* in Cascading Style Sheets (that is, the distinction between Position: absolute and Position: relative). In strict CSS terms, Edge Animate 1.0 uses only absolute positioning.

Here's how to test the way relative position works in Edge Animate:

1. **Make sure the top-left corner of the element is highlighted (as indicated in Figure 8-15).**

2. **Adjust the width or height of the element by using the W and H attributes (as indicated in Figure 8-15).**

   Notice that when you adjust the width or height, the top-left corner of the element stays where it is, while the rest of the element shrinks or grows.

3. **Select the bottom-right corner, resize the element, and see what a difference it makes.**

   The bottom-right corner stays in the same location while the other three corners are affected.

Top left corner

Figure 8-15:
Setting the relative position to affect how elements are manipulated.

Height and width

Global or Applied settings

You may wonder about the difference is between *Global* and *Applied* settings. Here's the essence:

- ✔ **Global** settings coordinate elements relative to the Stage.
- ✔ **Applied** settings use underlying property values to affect elements.

I go into further detail in the next two sections to provide a better sense of what these properties do.

When you switch between Global and Applied, it affects all elements on the Stage. It isn't possible to have some elements configured as Global and some as Applied; it's an all-or-nothing deal. However, switching between Global and Applied doesn't affect relative positioning applied to a specific element. For example, if you set an element with Top Right positioning, it remains in that setting whether you choose Global or Applied.

Using Global settings for position

When you use Global settings, the position coordinates always appear as x and y axis points (as shown in Figure 8-16). You can use keyframes with the position points, which means you can animate the position of an element; for example, you can have the element move from the left of the Stage to the right.

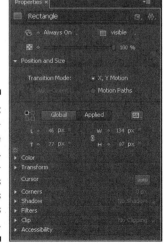

Figure 8-16: Global settings, the default, make coordinates appear as x and y axis points.

To get a better sense of how Global settings work, try the following:

1. **Draw four rectangles on the Stage and click Global.**
2. **Set the first element using the top-left square as shown in Figure 8-15.**
3. **Set the second element using the top-right square.**
4. **Set the third element with the bottom-left square.**
5. **Set the fourth element with the bottom right.**
6. **Switch to the Stage by clicking an empty part of the Stage.**
7. **Adjust the height and width of the Stage as shown in Figure 8-17.**

   Notice how the four different elements are affected.

When you adjust the width of the Stage, elements set with the top-right and bottom-right positioning are affected. When you adjust the height of the Stage, elements set with the bottom-left and bottom-right positioning are affected. The element set with the top-left positioning isn't affected at all when you change the dimensions of the Stage.

Height and width

Figure 8-17:
Adjust the height and width of the Stage to see how that affects elements.

Using Applied for position

The first difference you may notice between Global and Applied is in the Properties panel:

✔ When you choose Global and then select an element, you see x and y axis points.

✔ When you choose Applied, you see axis points based on the relative position if one element is nested inside another element.

For more information on nesting elements, see Chapter 10.

You can nest certain types of elements into another element by dragging them over that other element.

Figure 8-18 shows an element set with Applied Top Left positioning. Notice the axis points are shown with L (left) and T (top). If you choose Right Bottom positioning, then the axis points appear as R (right) and B (bottom). And so on for the other positions.

Axis points

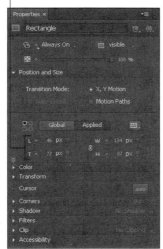

Figure 8-18:
Applied
settings
with top-left
positioning.

If your element is nested inside another, as shown in Figure 8-19, then the relative position is shown in relation to the parent item. For example, if you select an ellipse that is nested inside a rectangle, then you see the position of the ellipse from the rectangle. If you choose Global, then you see the relative position from the Stage.

Figure 8-19:
Nesting
items by
dragging
one over
another.

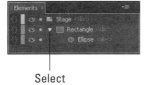

Select

The Global and Applied settings don't modify any settings, instead, they provide a means to display the relative positioning between nested elements.

Layout presets

Adobe Edge Animate CC conveniently provides *Layout* presets. You can select different Layout presets instead of configuring the settings yourself. There are different Layout presets depending on the type of element that you select from the Stage. There are different presets for the two major types of elements used in your animation:

- ✔ **Text boxes and other drawn elements** have their own presets.

- ✔ **Images:** Different settings appear depending on if the image is an img or a div. See Chapter 6 for more information.

Layout presets make more sense when the Stage's width and height are formatted by percent.

Text boxes and drawn elements

The different Layout presets for text boxes and drawn elements such as rectangles and ellipses include these:

- ✔ **Scale position:** Sets elements to use % instead of px for the position (as shown in Figure 8-20).

- ✔ **Scale size:** Sets elements to use % instead of px for the size (as shown in Figure 8-21).

Figure 8-20: Using the Scale Position layout preset.

Figure 8-21: Using the Scale Size layout preset.

Images

If you have your image set as an img, then different options appear under Layout presets than if you set the image as a div (see Chapter 6). Both img and div provide the same Layout presets — scale position and scale size — as drawn elements.

Img sets the image as a regular image on the Stage. Div sets the image as a background image.

For regular images, you can select a Scale Image Layout preset (as described in Figure 8-22).

Figure 8-22:
Layout presets for images set as img from the Properties panel.

Images set as div that act as background images have even more options, as shown in Figure 8-23.

Figure 8-23:
You can choose from four different background Image Layout presets.

Presets

To get an idea of what each different Preset Layout does, simply click the box for the description, then click Apply.

There's one more place to configure default layouts up near the main menu. If you click the Layout Defaults icon (as shown in Figure 8-24), a menu appears that enables you to select a default setting for relative positioning, px (pixels), or percent; you also get to choose how to use images.

Layout Defaults

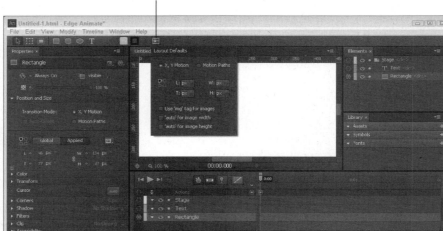

Figure 8-24:
Set the
Layout
Defaults for
elements
and images.

Minimum and maximum sizing

Hidden away at the bottom of the Position and Size section of the Properties panel, you can find a little icon that reveals two more sizing options for setting minimum width and/or maximum width (as shown in Figure 8-25).

The best way to use the minimum and maximum settings for an element is when you design a *responsive web animation* in which you create elements that change dynamically in proportion relative to the size of the Stage and browsers. (Chapter 12 goes into more detail on creating a responsive web animation.)

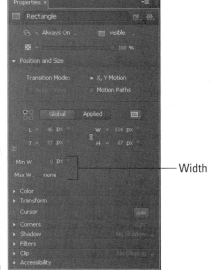

Figure 8-25:
Set the minimum and maximum widths for a responsive web design.

— Width

Chapter 9

Animating Background Color, Borders, Corners, Shadows, and Clipping

● ●

In This Chapter

▶ Applying colors

▶ Cutting corners

▶ Enlightening shadows

▶ Clipping elements

● ●

*I*n this chapter, I present many more formatting and animating options. I cover how to use background color for elements and how to add a border to elements. You can even animate the background color to transition from one color to another. In the same regard, you can animate the borders as well.

Adobe Edge Animate CC provides you the features necessary to animate the rounding-off of corners. If you want that square to turn into a circle, you can do that; you can also add shadows to your element. In this chapter, I show you a few different examples of using shadows.

Last but not least, clipping is a featured tool in Edge Animate. Use clipping to veil and unveil elements. This is a cool technique to use if you want text to gradually appear on the Stage.

Applying Color

Adobe Edge Animate CC has a few different options for using color, some of which are quite powerful. You can add background color to drawn elements such as rectangles and ellipses, but you can't add background color to text boxes or images. You can also add color to borders— as well as format and animate the border to appear solid, dashed, or dotted. You can add colors in two ways: by using the Eyedropper tool to sample colors from the Stage or by setting RGBa, Hex, or HSLa numeric values. In addition, Animate boasts a robust Color Gradient tool with many options. I discuss all these features in the following sections. You can find the Color properties in the Properties panel when you have a drawn element (other than a text box) selected, as shown in Figure 9-1.

Border color

Gradient color   Border formatting

Background color   Border width

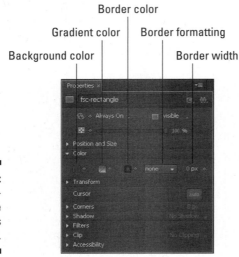

Figure 9-1:
Color prop-
erties in the
Properties
Panel.

To apply background color or a border to a text box, simply place a rectangle with a colored background or formatted border behind the text box, as shown in Figure 9-2. The following section describes how to set background colors, which you can also use for adding color to text. (You can find the steps that show how to format borders in the section that follows the discussion of using gradient colors.)

Figure 9-2:
Place a
colored
rectangle
behind a
text box
to provide
background
color.

Using the color graph

You can choose a background color and border color in a couple of different spots in Adobe Edge Animate CC, as shown in Figure 9-3. You can set the background and border color from either up near the main menu in the toolbar or from the Color section in the Properties panel.

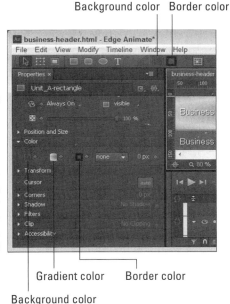

Background color   Border color

Figure 9-3:
Open the Color properties from either the Properties panel or the near the main menu.

Gradient color   Border color

Background color

You don't have to select the border to change its color. You set the color of the border just as you would set the background color. The border color icon is directly to the right of the background color.

You can select colors either by appearance or by numeric value.

When you click the Background Color icon or the Border Color icon, a color graph appears as shown in Figure 9-4. From this graph, you can choose the background or border color for your element.

The color graph gives you many options for picking a color. When you first open the color graph, the box in the top left appears gray. When you choose a new color, the box splits in two, showing you the current color on the left and the original color on the right. If you want to revert to the original color, simply click the right side of the box. When you find a color that you like, you can save it for later use by clicking the + icon near the saved colors (as shown in Figure 9-4).

Current Color   Revert to color   Saved colors

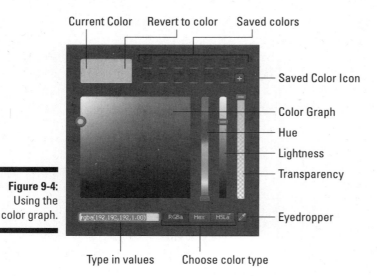

Saved Color Icon

Color Graph

Hue

Lightness

Transparency

Eyedropper

Figure 9-4:
Using the
color graph.

Type in values   Choose color type

To actually choose a color, you can click and drag the circle around the graph, or you can use the first slider to change the hue. The second slider affects how light or dark the color appears. The third slider affects transparency, which is useful if you want to see other elements that might be placed under the element you are adding color to. Another option is to change the color by typing in specific RGBa, Hex, or HSLa color values in the text box.

If you have an image or other element on the Stage that has a color you want to use, then you can use the Eyedropper tool to sample a color for use on a selected element. When you select the Eyedropper tool, you see a target with a large ring around it as shown in Figure 9-5. As the target passes over the Stage, the color it will sample is shown in the ring. When you pass over the color you like, simply right click and that color is automatically applied to the selected element. You can also save this color by pressing the + icon.

You can animate the background and border color as indicated by the presence of a keyframe diamond. It's possible, for example, to animate a rectangle so its background changes from red to black. Here's a quick procedure for animating colors:

1. **Draw an element, such as a rectangle, on the Stage. Make sure the Auto-Keyframe Mode is on (the Stopwatch is red).**

2. **Use the color graph from the Properties panel to choose a background color, such as red.**

3. **Move the Playhead down the Timeline for as long as you want the animation to last.**

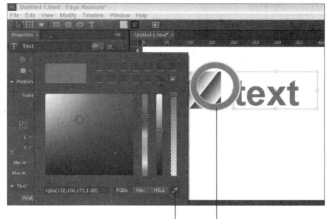

Figure 9-5:
Use the
Eyedropper
to sample
colors from
the Stage.

Eyedropper   Target

4. **Use the color graph to choose a new color, such as blue.**

- If the Stopwatch is red, then you just created an animation in which the background color of the rectangle slowly changes from red to blue.

- If you made the sequence last long enough, you'll see the element turn purple during the animation as the colors change from red to blue.

- For more precise control over which color you want to use, you can directly input numeric values for either RGBa, Hex, or HSLa values, as shown in Figure 9-4.

Using the color gradients

The Gradient Color icon is located directly to the right of the Background color icon in the Properties panel as shown in Figure 9-1. The Gradient color graph works a lot like the background color graph — but with one big, obvious difference: You can use *gradient colors,* meaning that you can fade a color from, say, a dark purple to a light purple, or from a light gold to a dark black. Figure 9-6 shows the Color Gradient color graph with the additional gradient feature on the right side.

No gradient

Linear gradient

Ellipse gradient

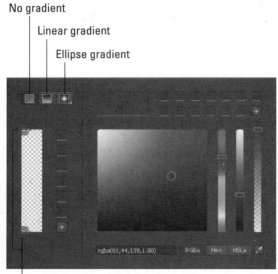

Figure 9-6:
Color
Gradient
color graph.

Gradient slider bars

To create a gradient color, first draw a rectangle or ellipse on the Stage and then choose the Color Gradient icon from the Properties panel. With the Gradient Color graph open, choose your starting color. Animate automatically picks white as your secondary color. To update the secondary color, click the bottom slider and then choose a second color. The element on the Stage updates as you change the colors so you can see the final outcome as you're working. You can slide both of the sliders up and down to indicate where you want colors to begin and end in relation to the element.

Linear gradients

When you start choosing gradient colors, Animate picks the Linear option for you, with the first color appearing at the top and the second color appearing at the bottom. You can change this arrangement to fit your needs. For example, if you want the gradient color to start in the top-left corner and end in the bottom-right corner, you can change the gradient angle as shown in Figure 9-7. Simply click and drag the Gradient Angle icon or click the orange number and type in your preferred angle.

To have your gradient color pattern repeat itself, you can click the Repeat option at the bottom of the color graph. To help exaggerate this effect, slide the top and bottom sliders close together (as shown in Figure 9-8).

Gradient angle appears for linear gradients

Figure 9-7:
Configuring the gradient angle.

Have gradients repeat

Sliders

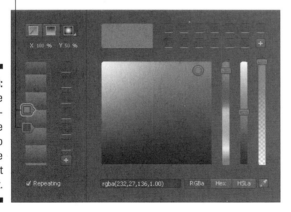

Figure 9-8:
Slide the two sliders close to each to exaggerate the Repeat effect.

You can add as many sliders — therefore as many color stops — as you like (as shown in Figure 9-9). That way, for example, you could have red fade into orange, which fades to yellow, which fades to green, which . . . well, you get the idea. To add a slider, simply click inside the bar and a new slider appears. To remove a slider, simply click and drag the slider off the bar.

Add multiple sliders by clicking within the bar.

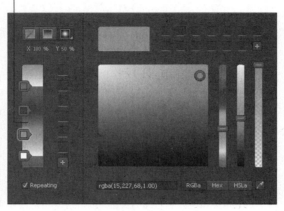

Figure 9-9:
A color gradient with several color stops.

Radial gradients

If linear gradients aren't what you are looking for then Animate also offers elliptical and circular gradients. Directly to the right of the linear gradient icon, you can find the radial gradient icon. If you long-click this icon, a menu appears with several radial options, as shown in Figure 9-10.

Long click for options

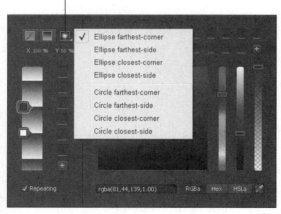

Figure 9-10:
Radial options for gradient colors.

You can change the center point of where your radial gradient originates. For example, if you don't want your radial gradient to start from the center of the element, you can adjust the X and Y axis points as shown in Figure 9-11.

When you change the X and Y properties, you can see the changes to the radial gradient appear on the Stage in real time.

Change the origin of the gradient

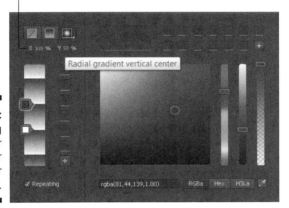

Figure 9-11:
Configuring
the center
point of your
radial color
gradient.

You can save your gradient settings just as you can save your background colors. On the gradient side of the color chart, click the + icon (as shown in Figure 9-12), and Animate saves your current gradient settings in that row of vertical boxes.

Save the color gradient

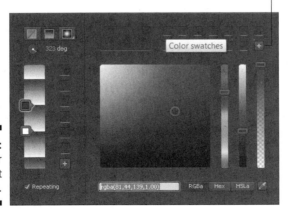

Figure 9-12:
Saving your
gradient
colors.

You can animate the colors in a gradient, but you can't animate from a linear gradient to a radial gradient; you can only animate the colors — say, from gold to black.

Choosing a border style

You can choose the style (None, Solid, Dashed, or Dotted) for the border of a rectangle, rounded rectangle, or ellipse, as shown in the drop-down menu of Figure 9-13. You can choose whatever color you want for the border, using the same type of color-picker tool as for the background.

To update the width of the border, simply click the orange 0 that is located next to the Border Style drop-down arrow.

You can animate the width of the border as you can any property that has a diamond keyframe icon next to it. Note however, that you can't animate the border type (for example, animating a solid border to become a dotted border).

Figure 9-13: Choosing the border type for rectangles and ellipses from the Properties panel.

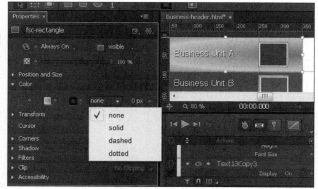

Rounding Corners

Corner properties in Edge Animate is a powerful tool (Figure 9-14 provides a glimpse). The Corner properties allow you to set how much of a curve the borders have on your rectangles. For example, if your rectangle has square corners, you can use the Corners properties to round them off.

Figure 9-14:
The Corners
properties
allow you
to round
off corners
or square
them.

Corner properties

Not only can you use the Corners properties to round off square corners, you can also change the radius for each corner. This means you can set one corner square, another corner with a small radius, and another corner with a large radius.

One, four, or eight different points

Figure 9-15 shows a composite of the three different views of the Corners tool:

- ✔ Option 1 affects all four corners by changing the orange number.
- ✔ Option 4 allows you to specify the roundness of each corner individually.
- ✔ Option 8 allows you to specify the roundness of each corner, and each corner has two different specifications that you can adjust for roundness.

Figure 9-16 provides an extreme example of how you can change the look of a rectangle by manipulating eight different points. Take note of how each corner is contorted differently according to the settings you make from the Properties panel.

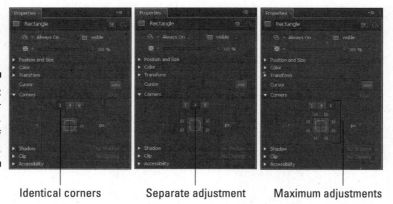

Figure 9-15:
One, four, or eight differ-ent points of a rectangle.

Identical corners   Separate adjustment   Maximum adjustments

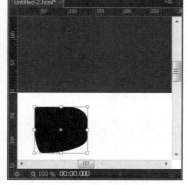

Figure 9-16:
Experiment with dif-ferent configura-tions for your rect-angles.

By toggling the px switch, you can choose between using px or percentage to specify how your corners look. Also, setting the border radius to 50% creates a circle.

Animating rounded corners

What's really great about the Corners tool is that you can animate how round, or square, the corners appear. For example, you can start with a circle that transforms into a square. Here's how you can do that:

1. **Start off by drawing a perfect circle.**

   Hold down Shift while drawing the circle with the Ellipse tool to maintain even proportions.

2. **Slide the Playhead down the Timeline to where you want the animation to end, leaving the Pin at the beginning of the animation.**

3. **Select the circle and adjust the corner radius to 0.**

   Doing so creates an animation that transforms your circle into a square.

4. **Preview the animation on the Stage or in the browser.**

This is great stuff to learn, but what if you want just the opposite — say, to transform a square into a circle? In that case, repeat the preceding procedure, and when you finish, select the keyframe animation sequence and copy it. Then paste the copied sequence into the Timeline using Edit, Paste Special, Paste Inverted (Figure 7-16).

Adding Shadows

You can create some pretty sweet animations and effects using shadows.

The Blur feature of the Shadow properties can create some interesting imagery, as shown in Figure 9-17.

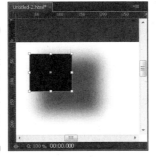

Figure 9-17: Experiment with the Blur property for interesting effects.

Shadow properties

As an extreme example of pushing the Shadow properties to the edge, you can create a shadow that appears as simply blurred or as a gradient. Note, in Figure 9-18, that the element need not be on the Stage (and here it isn't). In this section, I show you how to create an effect such as this by explaining each of the Clip properties.

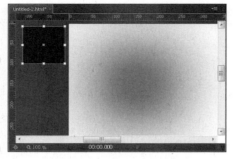

Figure 9-18:
All systems
are "Go" in
this Shadow
effect.

To enable the Shadow tool, you must toggle the switch as indicated in
Figure 9-19. You can choose, if you want, to configure a *Drop Shadow* or
an *Inset Shadow*. Drop shadows appear outside the borders of the element
(making it appear to float) and inset shadows appear along the inner edges of
the element.

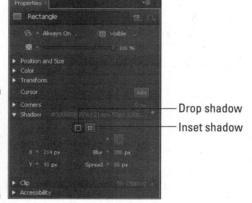

Figure 9-19:
Toggling
the Shadow
switch to
enable the
properties.

Besides setting a drop or inset shadow, you can also configure these options:

- ✔ **X and Y axis points:** These settings determine exactly where the
  shadow appears in relation to the element.

- ✔ **Blur:** Your shadow can have anything from straight corners (0 blur) to
  an appearance of foggy haze (1000 blur).

- ✔ **Spread:** This setting controls how big, or how little, the shadow appears
  in relation to the element.

- ✔ **Color:** You can open a color graph to choose a color for the shadow.

Animating shadows

You can animate shadows in Adobe Edge Animate CC, and the opportunities it presents are pretty powerful.

Shadow does provide keyframe diamonds for each of the properties — X, Y, Blur, Spread — allowing you to animate shadows. In this example, I provide an example of an element and a shadow appearing as if they come together, after which the shadow shrinks to become a blurry edge of the element. Follow these steps to create the example:

1. **Select an element from the Stage and set the Shadow properties as shown in Figure 9-20.**

   On the right of the figure, you see the element is mostly off the Stage; the shadow has square corners and doesn't even touch the element.

Clipping tool

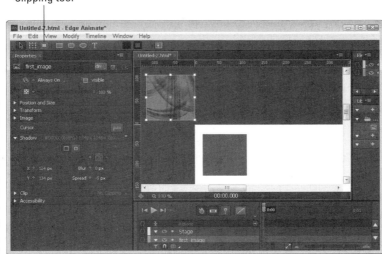

Figure 9-20: Setting the Shadow properties at one extreme and then animating to the other.

2. **Set the Playhead and the Pin in the Timeline so that you can create a keyframe animation sequence.**

3. **Change the settings in the Shadow properties (as shown in Figure 9-21).**

   By changing the settings, you create a keyframe animation sequence.

4. **Play the animation on the Stage or in the browser.**

   Note how the shadow and the element come together, and the shadow first softens and then frames the border.

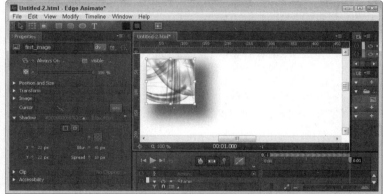

Figure 9-21:
The end effect of shadow and element coming together.

Using Filters

Adobe Edge Animate CC has a set of properties called Filters, which are similar to what you would find in software such as Adobe Photoshop. You can find these Filters in the Properties panel (as shown in Figure 9-22). You get the Filters properties to appear in the Properties panel by having an element selected. You can apply the individual Filters — Invert, Hue-Rotate, Contrast, Saturate, Sepia, Grayscale, Blur, and Shadow — to text boxes, drawn elements, divs, symbols, and images. You cannot apply the Filters properties to the Stage itself. Using the Filters properties is a versatile way to create special effects such as fuzzing out images in the background.

You can pick and choose which Filters you want to affect your element by clicking the X after each Filters property you want to use. A grayed-out X indicates that a particular Filters property will not affect the element; a bright X shows that it will affect the element.

The Filters properties are still highly experimental; they work best in Chrome, Safari, iOS 6, and Blackberry 10.

Click the Xs to toggle the Filters

Figure 9-22:
The Filters
Properties.

Unveiling the Clipping Tool

Adobe Edge Animate CC features a *Clipping* tool, which you can find just under the main menu as shown in Figure 9-23. Clipping is an animation effect used to unveil or veil an onscreen element; you can animate the effect of an element appearing left-to-right or top-to-bottom.

Selecting the area

The following procedure demonstrates how to use the Clipping tool:

1. **Select an element on the Stage and then click the Clipping tool.**

   The element takes on a green outline, as shown in Figure 9-24.

2. **Click and drag the selectors (the mini squares on the outline) from the green box.**

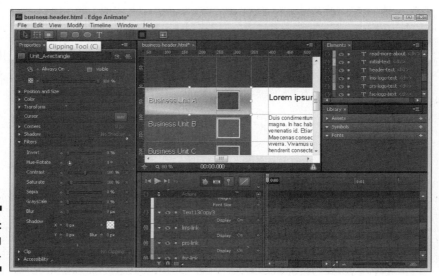

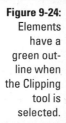

Figure 9-23:
The Clipping
tool.

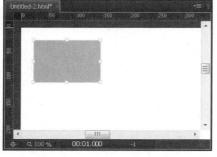

Figure 9-24:
Elements
have a
green out-
line when
the Clipping
tool is
selected.

Doing so selects the areas of the element that you want clipped.

- The solid gray area inside the green outline shows which parts of the element are visible.

- The diagonal lines that create a shaded effect show which parts of the element will appear clipped (see Figure 9-25).

At this point, your element appears half-visible.

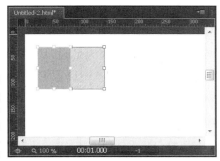

Figure 9-25:
A partially
clipped
element.

To undo the magic just done in the previous steps — creating an animation that unveils the clipped portion of the element to your audience — follow these steps:

1. **If the element isn't already clipped, select the Clip tool and drag the left-middle green selector on the element all the way to the right.**

   Doing so completely clips the element.

2. **Position the Playhead and the Pin in the Timeline to designate when the unveiling starts and how long you want the animation to last.**

3. **Grab the left-middle selector again and drag it to the left until the entire element is unclipped.**

   The result is an animated sequence keyframe that unveils the element.

You can watch this animation play on the Stage or preview it in a browser.

Adjusting the properties

You can use the Clip feature in animations to reveal or hide parts of an element; you have two ways to do it. In addition to the Clipping tool, Adobe Edge Animate CC features a Clip section in the Properties panel that you can use to clip or cut off portions of an element (text, images, or whatever). Figure 9-26 shows the Clip section in the Properties panel.

You must toggle the Clip switch to enable the properties.

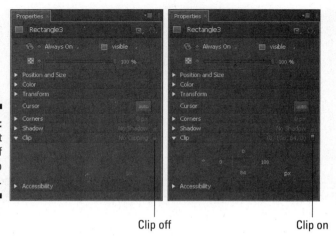

Figure 9-26:
The default
setting of
the Clip
attributes.

Clip off   Clip on

The px controls affect the element in a circular fashion: The top px (orange number) affects the top of the image, the right px affects the right side of the image, the bottom px affects the bottom of the image and the px on the left affects the left side of the image.

In order to see the green border and the clipped area, you must select the Clip tool (refer to Figure 9-23).

The following steps show how this use of the Clip feature works:

1. **Click the clipped element to select it.**

2. **Click the Clip tool.**

   The element acquires a green border, and the clipped area becomes visible.

3. **Clip exactly 50 px of the element from the top down by setting the orange number on top to 50 and the number on the right to the width of the element (as shown in Figure 9-27).**

   Adobe Edge Animate CC is smart enough to provide the width and height of the element for you.

4. **Click the keyframe diamond to set your chosen properties in the Timeline.**

   If you don't want to type in a number to specify how much Clip property to apply, you can click and drag on the orange number to increase or decrease the clip area.

Figure 9-27:
Click the
diamond
to create a
keyframe.

Diamond

5. **Set the Pin and the Playhead in the Timeline, and then set the Top and Left value for the Clip property to 0.**

    The resulting animation unveils the clipped area of the element.

    You can preview the complete animation, showing both the veiling and unveiling of the clipped part of the element, on the Stage or in a browser.

    If you set the bottom and the right Clip values to 0, you make the element invisible.

Chapter 10

Animating and Formatting Text Boxes

In This Chapter

▶ Addressing text formatting properties

▶ Assigning HTML tags to text

▶ Animating cool text effects

*I*n this Chapter, I discuss all of the different attributes and properties for using text boxes in your animation. Sometimes you may want to use text to convey a message. In Edge Animate, you can format and animate text so that it flows within your composition.

Although limited in capacity, the text box editor in Edge Animate is still rather feature-rich. While you can format each text box to show text with properties such as italics and bold, you can't make only some of the words appear italic and bold. It's an all-or-nothing proposition on that front. You can, however, tweak your animation in various ways to look the way you want. Here are some typical examples:

✔ By placing some text boxes creatively, you can arrange elements on the Stage so it appears that one word in a paragraph is italic while other words are not.

✔ While working in the text box editor, you can press Enter to start a new line of text. You can even format paragraphs to have an indent.

✔ You can change the look of your text by applying additional formatting properties such as alignment, paragraph spacing, vertical alignment, word spacing, and text shadows — and animate all these properties.

Although text shadows don't appear in Internet Explorer 9, they work fine in Chrome, Firefox, Safari, and other modern browsers.

Applying Text Properties

When you create a text box, the Properties panel expands to include Text tools (as shown in Figure 10-1). Then you can tweak the text as described in this section, using basic or advanced formatting, HTML tags, and animation of some attributes.

You can nest a text box within another element that isn't a text box (such as a rectangle). Note, however, that you can't nest one text element inside another.

Figure 10-1:
Use the Text
properties
to format
text.

Basic text formatting

The basic formatting attributes for text are shown in Figure 10-1. You can format text the following ways:

- **Choose a font:** Choose any font from the drop-down list or add a new font. For more information about adding and selecting fonts, see Chapter 12.

  See Figure 2-7 for a list of default fonts available from the Properties panel.

- **Set font size:** You can format the text to any px, percent, or em size that you want (Figure 10-2):

  - **Percentage units** represent percentages of the parent element's font size. For Edge Animate, use % in relative terms. For example, if you set one text block at 100% and another text block at 50%, then the latter font appears half as big as the former. For fonts, the parent element is the Stage itself.

- **Px** is the abbreviation for pixel units. Pixels are fixed units. One pixel is equal to one dot on the computer screen (the smallest division of your screen's resolution).

    The px unit is a fixed unit, generally used when you want to print.

- **Ems** are scalable units used in websites and can adopt to screen resolutions. An em is equal to the current font-size, for instance, if the font-size of the document is 12pt, 1em is equal to 12pt. Ems are scalable in nature, so 2em would equal 24pt, .5em equals 6pt, and so on.

If you want maximum scalability, you may want to use ems in your Adobe Edge Animate CC compositions.

Figure 10-2:
Use px, %, or em to Format Text Size.

- ✔ **Adding font weight:** You may have noticed Edge Animate doesn't have any icons to trigger bold formatting. Instead, Edge Animate uses *font weight,* which you can find directly beneath the font size. Use font weight to format your text with thin, light, normal, medium, or bold settings (as shown in Figure 10-3).

    To see the differences in the settings, first use 100 (Thin) and then use 900 (Black), you should see a dramatic change in style.

- ✔ **Adding color to the text:** You can format the color of your text just as you would the background color of an element (as shown in Figure 10-4). For more information on using the color graph, see Chapter 9.

Figure 10-3:
Use Font
Weight for
bold text.

Text color

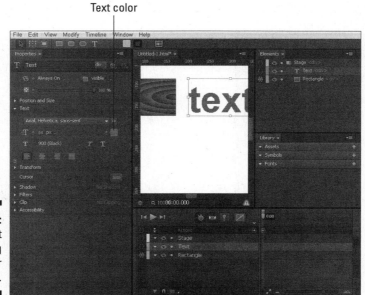

Figure 10-4:
Format Text
Color using
the color
graph.

✔ **Underlining and italicizing text:** You can underline and italicize text,
but it's an all-or-nothing deal. You can underline and/or italicize all text
in a box or none. The procedure looks like this:

> **1. From the Stage, single-click the Text Box element.**
>
> Don't double-click. Doing so opens the editor box, which you don't need just now.
>
> **2. Choose italic, or underline, or both (as indicated in Figure 10-5).**
>
> Any text in the text box now shows your chosen formatting.

✔ **Aligning text:** You can align text to the left margin, to the center, to the right margin, or justified (as shown in Figure 10-6).

Figure 10-5: Applying italics and/ or underlining to text.

Italics   Underlining

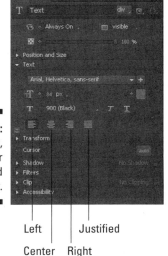

Figure 10-6: Left, center, right, or justified text.

Left   Justified

Center   Right

✔ **Adding shadows:** You can apply Shadow properties to your text for additional visual effect.

Shadows on text don't appear in Internet Explorer 9.

For more information on using Shadow properties, see Chapter 9.

One thing that you cannot format from the Properties panel is bullet points. However, if you need to use bullets in your text, you can add them from one of the .js files. The JavaScript file you need to open is *untitled*.js, where *untitled* is the name of your project. Don't confuse this file with the _edge-Action.js or the _edgePreload.js files. With the correct .js file open, search for your text. Then edit the text as shown here:

```
{
        id:'Text_1',
        display:'none',
        type:'text',
        rect:['13px','64px','99.7%','50.2%','auto','auto'],
        text:"Introduction to bullet list:<ul><li>First bullet text</
            li><li>Second bullet text</li><li>Last bullet text</li></ul>",
        align:"left",
        font:['Verdana, Geneva, sans-serif',[112.5,"%"],"rgba(0,0,0,1.00)","
            normal","none","normal"]
    },
```

You can add in HTML-style tags within the JavaScript, using <ul> to start the bullet list, and <li> for each item in the list. Don't forget to close each item with </li> and end the list with </ul>.

Using HTML tags

Using HTML tags for your text can help with search engine optimization (SEO) and browser parsing so people can find your animation online more easily.

In practice, assigning HTML tags to your font barely affects your animation's standing (beyond a slight improvement) in search engine results. Even so, it's good practice to use the correct HTML tag for certain types of text, as outlined in the following definitions. For the most part, assigning a tag to your text doesn't visibly change anything; except if you use 'address' (which makes your font italic). It's considered a best practice to use the HTML tags to adhere to coding standards — and it also helps with accessibility, as when someone uses a screen reader.

You can find the HTML tags up near the top of the Properties panel when you have a text box selected. Simply click the drop-down arrow near div to open the menu as shown in Figure 10-7.

Directly to the right of the HTML tags menu, you can find Class and Actions icons. (For more information about these properties, see Chapter 6.)

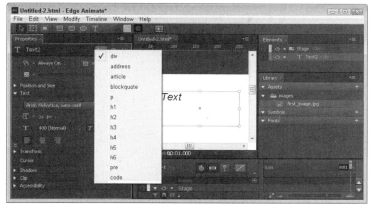

Figure 10-7:
Assigning
HTML tags
to text.

You can assign the following HTML tags to text blocks:

- ✔ `div`: This is the default setting for text boxes. In CSS3, it defines a section in a document.

- ✔ `address`: Address text is usually depicted with italics, which Edge Animate does format for you. Use this tag to define contact information.

- ✔ `article`: Use the `article` tag to define content that can stand alone and that you can distribute apart from the rest of your content.

- ✔ `blockquote`: Use this section to define a section of text that you quoted from elsewhere.

- ✔ `p`: This is the standard tag used to format paragraphs.

- ✔ `h1` through `h6`: These are standard header tags. Use `h1` for the topmost header and then `h2` for second-level headings and so on.

- ✔ `pre`: Text appears in a fixed-width font (usually Courier), and it preserves both spaces and line breaks.

- ✔ `code`: Use this tag when you want to display computer code.

You can assign one HTML tag to each text block. Therefore, you may want to use one text block for your headers (`h1`) and another text block for your paragraphs (`p`). Using HTML tags for text is considered a good practice for web development because

- ✔ It helps with screen readers, which the visually impaired use to "read" a screen. The screen reader uses text-to-speech software to express content audibly.

- ✔ Using HTML tags is considered good general coding practice.
- ✔ HTML does help, even if minimally, with SEO.

Advanced Text Formatting

Adobe Edge Animate CC offers Advanced Text Formatting properties that you can use to fine-tune the presentation of your text. Just click the icon indicated in Figure 10-8 to reveal them in the Properties panel.

Figure 10-8:
Using the Advanced Text Formatting options for spacing.

Advanced Text Formatting

The Advanced Text Formatting options include

- ✔ **Letter spacing:** Defines how far apart the letters are, and how far each one is from the others. You'd be surprised how much onscreen space you can save by a judicious use of this option.

- ✔ **Word spacing:** Defines how much space appears between words.

- ✔ **Line height:** Defines how much space appears between lines of text. You can use this option to provide just enough space (neither too cramped nor or too spaced out).

- ✔ **Text indent:** Using this option, you can indent the first line of a text block to make it look more like a paragraph in a book.

You can create animations that use all of the Advanced Text Formatting options to achieve a more professional, polished look.

Animating Text

Now, before you get carried away with the idea of animating your text, keep in mind that you can animate some text properties but not others. To give you a sense of which is which, this section lists the attributes you can animate — and those you can't.

The animation sequences you create can use any property that has a keyframe diamond next to it. If you don't see the diamond, then you can't create a keyframe with that property.

Built-in animation properties

Text properties that you can animate include

✔ Size

✔ Color

✔ All the spacing (Advanced Text Formatting) properties, including

   • Letter spacing

   • Word spacing

   • Line height

   • Text indent

The following procedure provides an example of animating text so that it changes size, color, and spacing:

1. **Use the Text tool to draw a text box on the Stage and type in some text.**

   Note that if you press Enter, you start a new line. To close the text box editor, click the X or click the Stage.

2. **Format the text by changing the color, size, and letter spacing as shown in Figure 10-9. Simply select the text box, and leave the text box editor closed, to format the text.**

   You have to double-click the text box to open the editor, so use only a single click to select the text box.

3. **Toggle the Pin and move the Playhead down the Timeline away from the Pin.**

Figure 10-9:
Editing the
text
properties.

Letter spacing   Size   Color

4. Reset the properties that you changed in Step 2 back to their defaults.

As you change each setting, the properties appear in the Timeline (as shown in Figure 10-10).

Figure 10-10:
Properties
appear-
ing in the
Timeline.

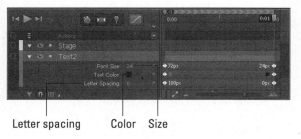

Letter spacing   Color   Size

You can preview the animation on the Stage or in the browser.

The keyboard shortcut for previewing in the browser is Ctrl+Enter.

Other animation effects

Text properties that don't show a keyframe diamond (and so can't be directly animated) include

✔ Weight

✔ Italics and underlining

✔ Alignment

Even though Edge Animate doesn't have keyframes for these properties, you can still create animation sequences that mimic that behavior.

In the following steps, I show how to create a workaround for animating properties that don't have keyframes assigned to them — in this case, animating a change in the weight of text:

1. **Create a text box on the Stage and type in some text. Then close the text box editor.**

2. **Set the font weight to 100 (Thin). (See Figure 10-3.)**

3. **Toggle the Pin and slide the Playhead down the Timeline away from the Pin.**

4. **Change the opacity from 100% to 0%. (Refer to Figure 8-13.)**

   You just created an animated sequence in which your text disappears.

5. **Copy and paste the text element.**

   By doing so, you're placing an identical text box on top of the existing text box.

6. **For the new text box, set the Opacity to 0% and the font weight to 900 (Black).**

7. **Slide both the Pin and the Playhead together (place the cursor over the orange bar with chevrons, then click and drag) down the Timeline so that the Pin is at the end of the first animation sequence and the Playhead is farther down the Timeline.**

8. **Adjust the Opacity back to 100% to create an animation sequence in which the bold text gradually appears.**

You can view this animation from the Stage or preview in a browser. You should see the thin-weighted font fade out and then see the text fade back in with a heavier weight.

If you want more of an abrupt change from Thin to Bold, here's how to do that:

1. **Create a text box, type in some text, and then close the text editor.**

2. **From the Properties panel, change the Visibility from Always On to On.**

3. **Change the font weight to Thin.**

4. **Copy and paste the text box.**

5. **In the Elements panel (top-right of the interface), rename the first text box to** Thin **and the second text box to** Bold **so you can remember which is which.**

6. **Select the Bold text box and set the Visibility to Off.**

7. **Drag the Playhead and the Pin (don't toggle the Pin) together down the Timeline to the point at which you want the font weight to change.**

8. **From the Elements panel, choose the Thin text box and set the Visibility to Off.**

9. **From the Elements panel, select the Bold text box, set Visibility to On, and set the weight to 900 (Black).**

Because you never toggled the Pin, you didn't create any keyframe animation sequences. However, you did create keyframe diamonds in the Timeline (as shown in Figure 10-11).

Figure 10-11:
Keyframe animations without an animation sequence.

When you preview this animation, you should see the thin text appear and then abruptly change to bold.

You can use these same two procedures to mimic animations for italics, underlining, and alignment. The accompanying sidebar describes an experiment of mine.

Mimicking the *Star Wars* Text Crawl

I was going through the Adobe Edge Animate CC Facebook page (this was in mid-April 2013) and I saw a post about someone creating an animation that looked just like the text crawl you see at the beginning of *Star Wars* movies. I attempted to re-create this effect, using just Edge Animate.

The only thing I couldn't truly replicate was using a 3D transform tool to make the text appear as if it were lying back on a flat surface and moving away from the viewer. Instead, I shrank the text gradually as it entered from the bottom of the screen, slowly scrolled up, and then exited the top of the screen. You can see the final result here: `http://goo.gl/znZ8N`

Chapter 11

Using the Elements Panel

In This Chapter

- Using the Elements panel to organize and work with elements
- Using the Timeline in conjunction with the Elements panel

The Elements panel is located in the top-right corner of the screen. You can do a number of things from the Elements panel, including selecting elements, opening actions for an element, setting the visibility of an element, locking an element, and nesting one element into another element. You can also name, or label, elements from the Elements panel.

The Elements panel remains empty until you create your first element, such as a text box or a rectangle, or you import an image. However, you can always see the Stage in the Elements panel.

Operating in the Elements Panel

The Elements panel provides a useful means to help organize and work with elements. From the Elements panel, you can do several things:

- Add actions
- Set visibility
- Lock elements
- Nest elements

The Elements panel updates along with the Timeline and vice versa, which is discussed in the next section. You can find the Elements panel in the top-right corner of the interface (as shown in Figure 11-1).

Figure 11-1:
The default
view of the
Elements
panel shows
the Stage.

Managing Stage actions

Chapter 5 discusses actions in detail, along with triggers that you can add to the Stage, but here I discuss how to use actions for the Stage from the Elements panel.

Adding Stage actions

To open the Actions box from the Elements panel, simply click the Open Actions icon, which is shown in Figure 11-2 along with a full list of all possible actions that you can add to the Stage.

The first nine actions listed in Figure 11-2 are unique to the Stage. The remaining actions — from click to focus — are used for elements as well. You can find a description of those actions in Chapter 5.

For some of these Stage actions, a designer with no coding experience may want to shy away from using certain actions that are code-intensive. However, even code-wary designers can use some Stage actions, such as keydown and keyup, to good effect. After a list of definitions, I provide some quick steps for using keydown and keyup.

Here is a brief description of what you can do with each of the Stage actions:

- ✔ **creationComplete:** Fires immediately after a Symbol is created and initialized but before autoPlay occurs.
- ✔ **beforeDeletion:** Fires just before a Symbol is deleted.
- ✔ **compositionReady:** Fires after the composition is ready to play but before autoPlay occurs.
- ✔ **keydown:** Fires after the user presses an assigned key (find the example code after Figure 11-2).
- ✔ **keyup:** Fires after the user stops pressing an assigned key.
- ✔ **scroll, orientationchange, and resize:** These are page-level events.
- ✔ **onError:** Fires when an event handler causes a JavaScript error.

For more information on these Stage actions, see the Adobe Edge Animate JavaScript API, which is available at

`www.adobe.com/devnet-docs/edgeanimate/api/current/index.html`

```
creationComplete
beforeDeletion

compositionReady
scroll
keydown
keyup
orientationchange
resize
onError

click
dblclick
mouseover
mousedown
mousemove
mouseup
mouseout

touchstart
touchmove
touchend

mouseenter
mouseleave
focus

swipeleft
swiperight
```

Figure 11-2:
Create
Stage
actions
from the
Elements
panel.

The following example code works with a keydown Stage action. All of the code preceded by double slashes (//) are notes to help explain what the code does. The actual code starts with `if`. After you choose keydown on the Actions menu, you must then choose how you want that action triggered. In this example, I chose Play. Before I chose Play, however, I placed the cursor directly after the bracket (and then pressed Enter on the keyboard to start a new line, then pressed Tab for the correct spacing), because that is where I want to insert the Play code (highlighted in bold). In this example, the animation plays when the user presses the spacebar.

```
// insert code to be run when the user presses a key.
// The variable "e.which" tells you the key code of the key that was pressed,
//          e.g. 32 = space
if (e.which == 32) {
    sym.play();

    // do something
}
```

The following example code uses keyup, which works in the same manner as keydown. Now, when the user releases the spacebar, the animation stops.

```
// insert code to be run when the user stops pressing a key.
// The variable "e.which" tells you the key code of the key that was pressed,
              e.g. 13 = enter
if (e.which == 32) {
    sym.stop();

    // do something
}
```

You can use a particular Stage action only once per composition.

Adding audience control

In the following procedure, I explain how to use Stage actions to allow your audience to both start and stop an animation from playing by pressing and then releasing the spacebar.

1. **Start a new composition. From the Properties panel, in the Stage section, uncheck Autoplay.**

2. **Create a simple animation on the Stage, such as a rectangle moving from left to right.**

3. **From the Elements panel, click Open Actions next to Stage and choose keydown.**

4. **In the code box, place the cursor after the bracket (press Enter to start a new line and then Tab over) and then choose Play from the menu on the right side.**

   Your code should look like the example shown earlier in the Technical Stuff note.

5. **In the code box, click the + icon (near the top left) and choose keyup.**

   This step creates a second action for the Stage.

6. **Place the cursor after the bracket, like you did in Step 4, but this time, choose Stop.**

7. **Close the code box to save your changes.**

If you preview from the Stage, the animation simply plays as though you didn't add the actions. To see your Stage actions in operation, you must preview them in a browser. To get the animation to start, press and hold the spacebar. To stop the animation from playing, release the spacebar.

Setting Visibility

The third icon in the Elements panel, after the actions and the color bar, looks like an eye. You can click this icon to set the visibility of an element. Figure 11-3 shows elements that are visible and that aren't visible. When an element isn't visible, the eye turns into a circle.

Select elements

Figure 11-3:
Setting
element
visibility.

When you turn the visibility off for an element, it no longer appears on the Stage. However, keyframes for invisible elements still appear in the Timeline.

If you preview the animation in a browser, all of the elements appear, regardless of how the element visibility is set.

Don't confuse the *Visibility* feature with the *Display* feature, which is discussed in Chapter 8. Here are the differences between the two:

- ✔ **Visibility:** Refers to showing or hiding elements on the Stage. You can hide elements on the Stage to reduce clutter. All invisible elements still appear when you preview in a browser. Visibility is used as part of the editing process for uncluttering the Stage.

- ✔ **Display:** Refers to whether the element appears or not, both on the Stage and in the Preview. Display is used in the animation creation process.

When you click the eye-icon of a parent element that contains nested elements, the child element's visibility is also affected, as shown in Figure 11-4. However, clicking the eye of a child element doesn't affect the parent element. You can set the visibility of nested elements separately. If you turn off the visibility of a parent element, the child element's Visibility icon is dimmed.

Figure 11-4:
The child
element
whose
parent is
invisible
appears
with a
dimmed eye.

Dimmed eye

Locking elements

You can *lock* elements from the Elements panel. Locking an element means that you can't edit that element.

This is useful if you have an element that overlaps another element and you don't want to accidentally select and start editing or moving that element.

When you want to lock an element in place so that you don't accidentally change it, click the circle to the right of the eyeball (Visibility icon). Locked elements have a lock icon next to them, as shown in Figure 11-5.

Locked element

Figure 11-5:
Lock
elements
so that you
don't acci-
dentally
edit them.

Nesting elements

When you nest elements, you create a hierarchy of parent and child elements. The top-level element becomes the parent and the second-level element becomes the child. Nesting is useful if you want the parent element to affect the child element in terms of position and size and other properties.

To nest one element within another, simply click and drag one element into another element. The element that you click and drag becomes the child, and the element that you dragged it into becomes the parent.

The parent element has a drop-down arrow that you can use to display or hide the child elements. Figure 11-6 shows nested elements, with the drop-down arrow showing the child elements and a parent element with the child element rolled up.

Figure 11-6:
Nest
elements
to create
parent and
child
elements.

Edge Animate has nesting rules:

✔ You *can*

- Nest rectangles into other rectangles.
- Nest images into a rectangle.
- Nest text boxes into rectangles.
- Have tiers of nest boxes.

✔ You *can't*

- Nest one text box into another text box.
- Nest images into a text box.
- Nest rectangles into text boxes.

Coordinating with the Timeline

The Timeline and the Elements panel work hand-in-hand. When you make changes in one, you see the same changes appear in the other. For example, if you name an element in the Elements panel, that name appears in the Timeline. However, if you nest elements, you can see that effect in the Elements panel, but you won't see the nesting in the Timeline. Rather, in the Timeline, you see the keyframe properties for an element, which you don't see in the Elements panel.

Features that are coordinated between the Elements panel and the Timeline include the following:

✔ Color-coordinated elements

✔ Copy and paste elements

✔ Naming elements

The Elements panel and the Timeline both have narrow colored bars for each element. These colored bars provide you with a visual clue about which element is which when you're looking back and forth between the Elements panel and the Timeline.

When you have several keyframes in the Timeline, the color coding becomes a significant aid in coordinating which elements in the Elements panel correlate with which keyframes in the Timeline (see Figure 11-7).

Figure 11-7: Color-coordinated elements in the Elements panel.

Copying and pasting

Just as you can copy and paste elements from the Timeline, you can copy and paste elements from the Elements panel: Simply right-click an element and choose Copy (or press Ctrl+C). Then right-click and choose Paste (or press Ctrl+V).

When you copy and paste elements, Edge Animate follows these rules:

✔ When you paste an element, it retains the same properties as the one that you copied.

✔ Keyframe animation sequences associated with a copied element don't copy over.

✔ If you copy a parent element, you also copy the child element; therefore, when you paste, you create copies of both the child and the parent.

> ✔ If you copy a child element, you don't also copy the parent element.
>
> ✔ When you paste an element, Edge Animate gives it the same name as the copied element but appends Copy to the end (see Figure 11-8).

Figure 11-8:
Copied
elements
have the
same name
except for
the word
Copy.

Naming elements

Giving elements names other than Text, RoundRect, or RoundRect2 is useful if you have a complicated Timeline with many elements. By naming elements, you create an easy way to find and select elements from both the Timeline and the Elements panel.

Give elements relevant names. For example, if you have a rectangle that you want to use as a menu bar, name that element, *Menu bar*. If you name it Long Rectangle Along the Top, not only does Edge Animate truncate that name (along with adding underscores between each word; because spaces in names are not allowed), but also it may become confusing later if you add a second long rectangle along the top of your animation.

The "Name" is used by Edge Animate as an ID in the HTML markup. What you type in as "Name" in the Elements panel shows in the ID attribute of the HTML element in the HTML markup. IDs have specific naming conventions, one of them is that IDs cannot contain spaces. They also can't start with a number; here's a URL that provides additional information:

www.w3.org/TR/html4/types.html#type-id

To name your element, simply double-click it from the Elements panel, and then type a name as shown in Figure 11-9.

Figure 11-9:
Double-click
an element
to name it.

Follow these rules for naming elements:

- ✔ Give it a short name so you can see the full name in the Elements box.

- ✔ Give it a relevant name and not something cute and funny. That way, you know what that element is six months later when you reopen your project.

- ✔ Don't use spaces or odd characters when naming an element. If you do, a blue icon appears, with the information shown in Figure 11-10.

Figure 11-10:
Use only
unaccented
letters and
numbers
with no
spaces.

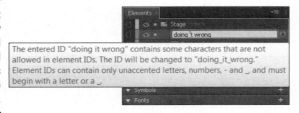

Chapter 12

Using the Library Panel

In This Chapter

▶ Importing images without adding them to the Stage

▶ Applying Symbols effectively

▶ Selecting fonts

*T*he Library panel provides an easy way to work effectively with images, Symbols, and fonts. In this chapter, I discuss how to add images to the Library panel without adding them to the Stage.

I also provide details on working with Symbols— which may appear daunting at first, but once you get the hang of it, you realize Symbols are true timesavers. That's especially true if you tend to use the same types of Symbols (such as buttons or menu items) on a regular basis.

Last, but certainly not least, I delve in to the details on working with and adding fonts to Adobe Edge Animate CC. By using the web, you can find and use thousands of fonts, and most likely you can use them all in your animation.

Positioning Images

The Library panel is a great place to view all of your assets, or images, in one spot. You can use the Library panel in association with images in the following ways:

- ✔ Import multiple images at once without having them appear on the Stage.

- ✔ Drag images onto the Stage from the Library panel.

- ✔ Image filenames remain consistent in the Library panel even if you rename them in the Elements panel.

- ✔ You don't delete or rename images in the Library panel.

You can find the Library panel on the right side of the interface (see Figure 12-1).

Figure 12-1:
Use the
Library
panel for
Assets,
Symbols,
and Fonts.

Adding images

You can add images a few different ways in Edge Animate, including the following:

- ✓ Drag and drop from your desktop to the Stage.
- ✓ Import from the main menu (refer to Chapter 3).
- ✓ Use the Library panel.

You can use the Library panel to import more than one image at a time. Simply gather all the images you want to use for your project into a single folder; then click the + icon next to Assets. When you do so, you can then navigate your hard drive to find and select images to import into your composition. After you select the images you want to import, they appear in the Library panel (as shown in Figure 12-2).

Figure 12-2:
Use the
Library
panel to
import
images
without
them
appear-
ing on the
Stage.

One of the differences between importing images from the Library panel and importing them via the main menu is that the images don't appear on the Stage and the Timeline. That way, you have your images ready for use, but they don't litter your Stage.

After you have images in the Library panel, you can click and drag them onto the Stage. You can double-click the name of the image to rename it if you so desire.

If you right-click an image from the Library panel, you can open the images folder associated with your composition, as shown in Figure 12-3.

Figure 12-3: Navigate to the folder from which you imported the image.

Deleting and renaming images

Believe it or not, you don't delete nor rename images in the Library panel. Instead, you must use either the Timeline or the Elements panel — and before doing that, you have to add the image to the Stage. You can add an image to the Stage from the Library panel with a click and a drag.

When you move an image from the Library panel to the Stage, it becomes an element and — like all elements — it appears in both the Elements panel and the Timeline. Once an image becomes an element, you can rename it and/or delete it, as with any other element.

Even if you rename or delete an image element, it remains in the Library panel, but you can rename it or delete it from the Timeline and the Elements panel. To completely remove an image, first remove all instances of the image from the Stage. Then, from the Library panel, choose Reveal in finder. Then you can delete the images from your hard drive.

Administering Symbols

You can create complex Symbols with rich functionality that you may need when you start developing complicated compositions. On the flip side, you can also create basic Symbols for everyday use.

Basically, Symbols allow you to create nested animations with independent timelines and interactive capabilities. In this section, I discuss turning elements into Symbols; editing Symbols; working with Symbols and labels; and finally how to save, export, and import Symbols.

Although Symbols do have a different workflow from that of elements, once you're comfortable working with them, you won't have any problems at all.

Creating Symbols

To create a Symbol, follow these steps:

1. **Create an element such as a text box, a rectangle, or an imported image.**

   See Chapter 3 for more information on creating elements.

2. **Convert the element to a Symbol.**

   You have three choices on how to convert that element into a Symbol:

   • Right-click the element from the Stage (as shown in Figure 12-4) to access a list of options. From that list, choose Convert to Symbol.

   • Select an element on the Stage and then click the + next to Symbols in the Library panel (as shown in Figure 12-5).

   • Use the keyboard shortcut: Ctrl+Y or ⌘+Y (Mac).

3. **Name the Symbol in the Create Symbol box (see Figure 12-6).**

   You have to play by the rules when you name a Symbol: no spaces and no accented letters or numbers. You can use an underscore, though.

   Leave Autoplay Timeline checked if you want any animations you create for this Symbol to automatically play in the Timeline. Uncheck this box if you don't want any animations to automatically play.

   If you want a particular part of your composition to play only if an action is triggered, then you do not want a Symbol to play automatically in the Timeline. For example, you can create a Symbol that plays only if your audience clicks a button.

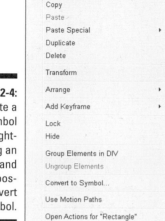

Figure 12-4:
Create a
Symbol
by right-
clicking an
element and
then choos-
ing Convert
to Symbol.

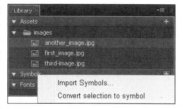

Figure 12-5:
Click the
+ next to
Symbols to
convert an
element to a
Symbol.

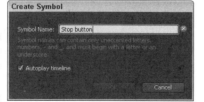

Figure 12-6:
Name your
Symbol.

After you create a Symbol, it appears in the Library panel (as shown in Figure 12-7). You can then drag it on the Stage for repeated instances, save it for use in another composition, or copy and paste it directly into another project.

Figure 12-7:
Symbols
appear in
the Library
panel.

When you create a Symbol, a new section, called Playback, appears in the Properties panel (see Figure 12-8).

Figure 12-8:
The
Playback
properties
appear
when you
select a
Symbol.

I discuss the Playback properties in the section, "Adding playback actions," later in this chapter.

Editing Symbols

After you create a Symbol, you can edit it with a right-click and then choose Edit Symbol. If you right-click from the Stage, you see the options shown in Figure 12-9.

If you right-click a Symbol from the Library panel, you see another set of options, as shown in Figure 12-10.

Figure 12-9:
Right-click
from the
Stage for
one set of
edit options.

Figure 12-10:
More
options to
choose
from in
the Library
panel.

While you're in Edit mode for a Symbol, the Stage turns gray and bread-crumb-type navigation appears in the top-left corner of the Stage, as indicated in Figure 12-11. In this example, Stop_button is the name of the Symbol. When you're editing a Symbol while the Stage is gray, edits you make affect only the Symbol's independent Timeline and not the composition's overall Timeline.

While in Edit mode for Symbols, you can get back to the Stage simply by clicking Stage from the breadcrumb navigation (as highlighted in Figure 12-11).

Click Stage

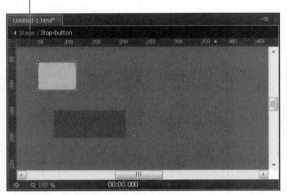

Figure 12-11:
Navigate
back to
Stage by
clicking
Stage.

Adding features

Symbols have their own Timeline, which works in conjunction with the main Timeline. As a result, Edge Animate provides specific features for use with Symbols, including the following:

- ✔ A Scrub check box
- ✔ Playback actions for Symbols
- ✔ Labels

Disabling animation

A Symbol's Timeline allows you to stop a Symbol's animation sequences from playing while you view an animation from the Stage.

In the Playback section of the Properties panel, you can find a Scrub check box (see Figure 12-12). The Scrub check box controls how animation appears on the Stage:

- ✔ If you leave the Scrub box checked, the Symbol's animation sequences unfold on the Stage.
- ✔ If you uncheck the Scrub box, the Symbol's animation sequences don't appear on the Stage.

Regardless of the Scrub box, you see all the animations when you preview in the browser.

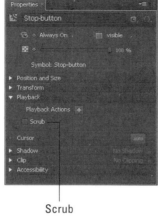

Figure 12-12: Uncheck the Scrub box to stop Symbol animations from playing on the Stage.

Scrub

Adding playback actions

Adding playback actions to Symbols is easy to do from the Properties panel. You can think of playback actions as a type of trigger for Symbols. Figure 12-13 shows the list of options that you can use, including Play and Stop.

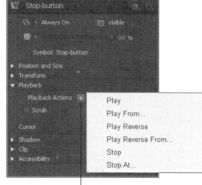

Figure 12-13: Add playback actions to insert a type of trigger for Symbols.

Playback actions

When you select a Symbol from the Stage and then choose a playback action, Edge Animate inserts an icon into the Timeline, as indicated in Figure 12-14. In addition to inserting a playback action from the Properties panel, you can also create a playback action from the Timeline, as highlighted in the figure.

Figure 12-14:
An icon
appears in
the Timeline
when you
select a
playback
action.

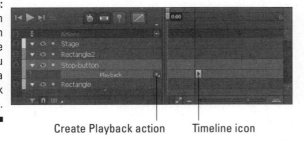

Create Playback action   Timeline icon

For best use of playback actions, create an animation sequence for the
Symbol; otherwise there's nothing to stop, play, play from, and so on.

To edit the playback action from the Timeline, simply double-click the icon,
you can then edit the time and the action (shown in Figure 12-15).

Figure 12-15:
Edit the
playback
action by
double-
clicking the
icon in the
Timeline.

You can also use labels with playback actions, as discussed next.

Labeling

You can use labels (which I cover in detail in Chapter 5) in association with
playback actions. The difference between using labels with elements as compared to Symbols is that you have to place the label in the Timeline while in
edit mode for the Symbol. Otherwise the label option (as shown in Figure 12-15)
appears dim. Follow these steps to use labels with playback actions:

1. **Create a Symbol on the Stage that has an animation sequence.**

2. **Right-click the Symbol and choose Edit Symbol.**

3. **Position the Playhead in the Timeline where you want the label to
   appear.**

4. **On the main menu, click Timeline and then Insert Label.**

5. **Name your label in the Timeline.**

6. **Exit Symbol Edit mode by going back to the Stage (click Stage from the breadcrumb navigation found above the Ruler).**

   The label you just created disappears from the Timeline, but don't worry, it's still there.

7. **Add a playback action and then open it for editing.**

   When you choose From or At playback actions, the label option becomes active, as shown in Figure 12-16 where I named the label Start Show.

   When you close this box, the name of the label appears in the Timeline next to the Playback Action icon.

Figure 12-16:
Choose a Symbol label instead of using a specific time.

You can preview playback actions on the Stage (provided you left Autoplay checked while editing the Symbol), or you can preview in the browser.

To change the location of the Symbol label in the Timeline, go back to Symbol Edit mode and drag the label up and down the Timeline.

Exporting and importing Symbols

Adobe knows that as an animator, you probably like to reuse commonly used Symbols, such as a slideshow, so Adobe made it very easy for you to:

✔ **Save Symbols:** Right-click an element and choose Convert to Symbol (shown earlier in Figure 12-4).

✔ **Export Symbols:** Right-click a Symbol from the Library panel or the Stage and then choose Export (shown earlier in Figure 12-10).

✔ **Import Symbols:** In the Library panel, click the + icon and choose Import Symbols (see Figure 12-17).

Figure 12-17:
Import
Symbols
from the
Library
panel.

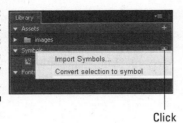

Figure 12-17:
Import
Symbols
from the
Library
panel.

Click

You can copy and paste a Symbol from one project to another. Simply select the Symbol from the Stage, copy it, and then open another project and paste it in.

Managing Fonts

Adobe Edge Animate CC provides myriad ways to use and add different fonts to your composition. In this section, I discuss the following:

✔ Selecting different default fonts from either the Properties panel or the Library panel

✔ Adding new fonts from a variety of sources

When it comes to font choices, you won't be at a loss.

Selecting fonts

Adobe Edge Animate CC allows you to choose fonts from a default fonts list, as shown in Figures 2-7 and 12-19, which is accessible from the Properties panel after you create and select a text box (refer to Chapter 10 for more on animating and formatting text). These fonts include the standards, such as Georgia, Verdana, and Times New Roman.

The Library panel also has another set of fonts from which you can choose. To open this menu, follow these steps:

1. **Click the + next to Fonts in the Library panel, as shown in Figure 12-18.**

   From here, you can choose an Edge Web Font, or click the Custom tab to add a new font. If you choose an Edge Web Font, simply select the font that you like and then click Add Font at the bottom of the box.

Figure 12-18:
Click the +
to start the
process of
adding a
web font.

Click

2. **If you clicked the Custom tab, then click the + next to the Font Fallback List.**

Doing so opens up another list of fonts you can choose.

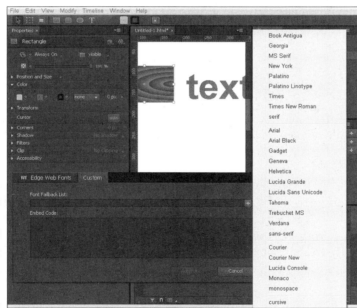

Figure 12-19:
Font
Fallback
List from
the Library
panel.

3. **Choose a font from the list; then click Add Font.**

The font you chose appears in the Library panel, as shown in Figure 12-20.

After you add a font in the Library panel, you can click and drag the name of the font onto the Stage. When you do so, Edge Animate creates a text box for you that is pre-populated with text.

Figure 12-20:
Fonts that
you add
appear in
the Fonts
section of
the Library
panel.

After you drag a font name onto the Stage, that font also becomes available in the Properties panel when you have a text box selected.

You can also add web fonts from Font Squirrel, `fonts.com`, and other types of available web fonts to your Edge Animate composition — using the same basic procedure described in the next section on using Google web fonts.

Adding Google web fonts

If you're a fan of Google web fonts, or you're simply tired of using the same old font that everyone else uses, then you can add a Google web font to your Edge Animate composition.

As of this writing, Google boasts 624 (and counting) different web fonts from which you can choose.

To add a Google web font, follow these steps:

1. **Use a web browser to visit the Google Web Font site (**`www.google.com/webfonts`**) and pick a font you like.**

2. **When you find a font you like, click Quick-Use, as shown in Figure 12-21.**

Figure 12-21:
Select a
Google web
font.

Select

Depending on the font you chose, you may have the option to customize the font with various attributes.

You also see a Page Load indicator, as shown in Figure 12-22. This tells you whether the font loads quickly or slowly onto your web page. My example font has a fast page-load time.

Figure 12-22: Page Load indicator.

Consider using fonts that have a fast page-load time for a couple reasons:

- If your page takes more than a few seconds to load, visitors will leave. They want the page to load quickly.

- Google uses page-loading times in its algorithms to determine search results. You don't want your search results hurt based on the fonts you chose.

- Also, use only styles that you really need. The more styles you add, the slower the page load.

3. **With the font customized, scroll down the page until you see a bit of code, as shown in Figure 12-23; copy this code.**

Figure 12-23: Copy the Google web font code.

4. **If Edge Animate isn't open, open it now.**

5. **In the Library panel, click the + Symbol next to Fonts.**

   The Font box opens. Click the Custom tab.

6. **In the Embed Code box, paste the code that you copied in Step 3.**

7. **Type the name of the font in the Font Fallback List, as shown in Figure 12-24.**

Figure 12-24:
Copy the
Google
web font's
code into
the Embed
Code box
and name
the font in
the Font
Fallback
List.

8. **Click Add Font.**

   You're done!

Now that you've added a custom font, when you click the font drop-down arrow from the Properties panel, you can select your custom font from the list (see Figure 12-25).

Selected font

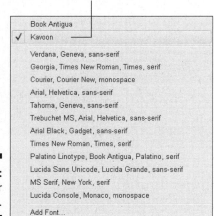

Figure 12-25:
Finding Your
custom font.

Part IV
Putting Your Animation to Use

Visit www.dummies.com/extras/adobeedgeanimatecc for great Dummies content online.

In this part . . .

✔ Structuring your project

✔ Publishing your work

✔ Putting your project on the web

✔ Visit `www.dummies.com/extras/adobeedge` `animatecc` for great Dummies content online.

Chapter 13

Creating a Project Structure

In This Chapter

▶ Automating the project structure

▶ Editing files

▶ Structuring folders and files for use with other software

*A*dobe Edge Animate provides the means for you to create animations for the web, for use with InDesign and Muse, and for tools like Apple's iBooks Author. You can save your compositions in any number of ways, depending on how you set your publishing settings.

In this chapter, I discuss the folder structure that Edge Animate creates and the files within those folders. I make these explanations worthwhile by explaining what you can do with all these files.

Understanding the Files Edge Animate Creates

When you save your Adobe Edge Animate project, the software creates several different files and folders. In addition to a special folder for your images, Edge Animate creates an edge_includes folder. I cover all these folders here in this section along with details about the different files that Edge Animate creates.

Even if you are strictly an animator and don't know a single thing about code, I still recommend that you gain a familiarity with what makes Adobe Edge Animate tick. After all, you never know when you may have to dig in to the file and folder structure to find something in particular or to tweak a line of code. Here, I walk you through the basics, so you can understand what Edge Animate creates as output.

Figure 13-1 shows a sample file and folder structure.

Figure 13-1:
Edge
Animate
creates an
entire file
and folder
structure
for you.

Saving your composition

You can work and preview compositions in Edge Animate without saving your work. However, the software doesn't create files or folders until you click Save. When you do save your work, Edge Animate creates an entire structure of folders and files for you.

To save your work, click File on the main menu and then choose Save or choose Save As to save under a different filename (see Figure 13-2).

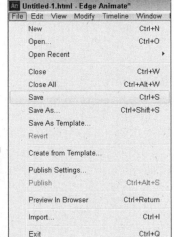

Figure 13-2:
Saving your
work from
the File
menu.

Before you save your work, create a folder on your hard drive in which you want to save your work. You don't necessarily have to create a special folder just for your images, though this is generally considered a best practice. Even if you import your images from several different locations, when you save your work, Edge Animate groups all your assets together and organizes them for you in a folder structure.

Animate files

When you save your work, one of the files that Edge Animate creates is called an *Animate file*. All Animate files are designated with the extension .an. For example, myfirstproject.an, or index.an.

Figure 13-3 shows how the Animate file appears (it has the purple square icon next to it) in your folder structure in Windows.

Figure 13-3:
You can recognize the Animate files by the purple square icon.

If you click the .an file from the folder structure, Edge Animate boots up, and your project opens.

JavaScript files

Edge Animate actually creates two sets of JavaScript files for you when you save your project:

- ✔ One set of files is found in the edge_includes folder, as I discuss later in the chapter in the section "Edge_includes folder."

- ✔ The other JavaScript files are found alongside the Animate file and the HTML file.

 Figure 13-4 shows an example of what these JavaScript files look like in the folder structure.

Figure 13-4:
JavaScript plays an important role in making animations.

If you try to open these JavaScript files by clicking them, you may get an error message. The different example JavaScript files shown in Figure 13-4 do the following:

- ✔ index_edge: In this example, the name of the project is *index*. Therefore, the name for each JavaScript file starts with the name of the project.

    Within this particular JavaScript file, you can find definitions for symbols.

- ✔ index_edgeActions: This file contains JavaScript code for the actions you created within the composition.

    For more information on adding actions to your composition see Chapters 5 (working with actions in general) and 11 (working with stage actions from the Elements panel).

- ✔ index_edgePreload: This file contains JavaScript code for the preloader.

    For more information on preload, see Chapter 14.

Don't open and play around with the JavaScript files unless you've had experience coding JavaScript. Designers and animators without coding experience really don't have to open these files at all.

If you want to open these files just to see what the code looks like, open them with Notepad or other similar plain text applications. In Windows 7, you can right-click the JavaScript file and then choose Edit from the menu. When you do so, the JavaScript file opens in Notepad.

You can edit JavaScript code directly from something like a plain text editor. The changes that you save do affect your composition.

You can find the code that you write or edit for actions, triggers, and so forth while in Edge Animate in the JavaScript_edgeActions file. For example, say that you add an action to a rectangle (such as Play From) so that the code in the Edge Animate code editor looks like this:

```
sym.play();
// play the timeline from the given position (ms or label)
sym.play(1000);
```

If you save the project and then open the JavaScript_edgeActions file in a plain text editor, you should see the above code in that file. You can now edit this code. If you want the action to start playing at the 2-second mark instead of the 1-second mark, simply edit 1000 to 2000. Then save and close the file.

You can then check the changes by clicking the HTML file to preview in a browser. The changes appear in Edge Animate the next time you open the project.

If you save edits to the JavaScript file while the composition is still open in Edge Animate, a File Changed dialog box appears, as shown in Figure 13-5.

✔ If you click Yes, Edge Animate keeps the changes that you made outside Edge Animate.

✔ If you click No, Edge Animate doesn't keep changes that you saved outside Edge Animate.

Figure 13-5:
You need to reload the composition for saves outside Edge Animate.

If you want to edit your files outside Edge Animate in a plain text editor, close and save the composition beforehand. That way, you don't run the risk of losing other changes that you might make within Edge Animate while simultaneously editing the JavaScript.

HTML files

Because the HTML language is relatively easy to learn, HTML files are probably the "friendliest" files for non-developers to work with. So, it's a good idea for you to know at least the basics of HTML. Knowing such basics makes it much easier for you to help place animations within existing web pages.

The HTML file appears alongside the Animate file and some of the JavaScript files. You can instantly recognize the HTML file from the folder structure, because its icon appears the same as your default browser's icon, as shown in Figure 13-6.

Figure 13-6:
You can
recognize
the HTML
file by the
browser
icon.

You can do a few different things with the HTML file:

✔ **Open it for viewing.** Simply click the file, and your animation opens in your default browser and begins to play.

✔ **Open it for editing.** If you right-click the HTML file, you can open the file using Notepad, or some other plain text editor, or even an HTML editor. If you open it for editing, you can do things like edit the title tag (see Chapter 6) or copy and paste portions of the code so that you can insert your animation into existing web pages (see Chapter 15).

For the most part, the HTML file is a shell to house the calls to the JavaScript file. For web browsers to display your animation correctly, they need to know where to find the files that execute your composition. That's how the HTML file comes into play. You use the .html file, or at least parts of it, to put your composition online.

You can tell that Adobe Edge Animate is using HTML5 by looking at the DOCTYPE tag in the HTML file — a piece of code put at the top of an HTML file that tells the browser what standard the page is written in. In HTML5, the DOCTYPE looks like this:

```
<!DOCTYPE html>
```

In HTML4, DOCTYPE looks like this:

```
<!DOCTYPE HTML PUBLIC "-//W3C//DTD HTML 4.01//EN"
    "http://www.w3.org/TR/html4/strict.dtd">
```

HTML5, in many ways, is about simplifying and reducing the amount of code used.

You can edit the *title* tag within the HTML file. The title tag defines what is shown in the tab of your browser. If you plan to embed your composition into one part of a web page, the title tag in your Edge Animate composition may not have an effect. The title tag looks like this:

```
<title>Untitled</title>
```

You can find this code within the head section, near the top, of the file. If you do edit the title tag within the HTML file and save the file, the changes do appear in Edge Animate.

HTML is written with tags. A *tag* is a bit of code enclosed by carrots. For example, the title tag looks like this: `<title>`. Each tag has an opening tag and a closing tag. The closing tag is similar to the opening tag, except it has a slash in it, like this `</title>`.

You most likely don't want your first animation to appear as "Untitled" on the Internet, so you probably want to update that, if you didn't already, from the Properties panel. To do so, simply overwrite Untitled to something more suitable, such as

```
<title>My First Slideshow</title>
```

After you save the HTML file and then refresh or reopen your composition in the browser, the title should now appear in the tab as shown in Figure 13-7.

Figure 13-7:
Update the title tag so that it doesn't say Untitled.

If you plan to edit your composition outside Edge Animate in a separate editor, it's a good idea to save and close Edge Animate before doing so. Otherwise, you run the risk of losing edits and changes that you may make in Edge Animate while editing the code files.

Image folders

Edge Animate creates an image folder when you save your composition, which can inadvertently result in you having two sets of the same images in your folder structure. This happens if you put your images in the same folder in which you save your composition, rather than in a separate folder named Images.

It's best practice to place your images in a folder labeled Images. That way, Edge Animate doesn't create a second set of images in your folder structure.

Having two sets of the same images can lead to confusion; especially if you want to go back and edit them later.

If you decide you don't want two sets of the same images in the same folder directory and want to delete the redundant set, make sure you don't delete the folder that Edge Animate created. If you do, you will find your images missing from your composition.

Edge_includes folder

The edge_includes folder contains additional JavaScript files. The difference here is that they are .min files.

The .min.js files found in the edge_includes folder are *minified* (compressed) JavaScript files. For example, white spaces and comments are stripped out, and they use shorter variable names. That's why when you open one of these files, it may look like a large wall of text. These compressed files allow for faster loading times, which can earn you bonus points from browsers like Google that benchmark stuff like that.

These files tend to be very long, and I don't cover them here except to mention that (a) they're important to your composition and (b) they shouldn't be tampered with or edited for danger of breaking your composition.

It's highly recommended that you don't open nor edit the .min.js files found in the edge_includes folder. Unless, of course, you're trained in such matters.

Creating Edge Animate Files for Use with Other Software Tools

Adobe Edge Animate plays well with other software tools. From the main menu, you can click File and then Publish Settings to choose which kinds of files Edge Animate creates. You choose these settings based on what you want do with the file:

✔ Put it on the web.

✔ Use with other Adobe tools, such as InDesign.

✔ Prepare files compatible with OS X.

When you choose all the Publish settings you want (see Figure 13-8), Edge Animate creates another whole set of folders and files. I go into more detail on publishing options in Chapter 14.

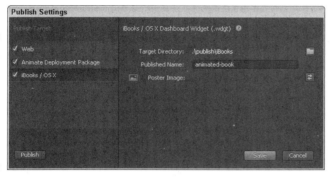

Figure 13-8: Choose the settings best suited for how you want to use the composition.

At the top level of the folder structure, you now see a Publish folder, as shown in Figure 13-9.

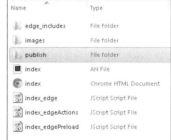

Figure 13-9: Find the Publish folder in the Folder directory.

Within the Publish folder, you find

✔ An Edge Animate package for use with other Adobe tools

✔ A .wdgt folder for use with iBooks Author

✔ A web folder that contains all the files and folders you need to publish to the web

Figure 13-10 shows the folders within the Publish folder.

Figure 13-10:
The fold-
ers within
the Publish
folder.

Edge Animate package

The Edge Animate package folder contains an .oam file (see Figure 13-11). You can use .oam files with InDesign, Muse, and other Adobe Tools. Basically, Edge Animate compresses the JavaScript and HTML files used for your animation into a format that InDesign can use (the .oam file).

Figure 13-11:
Use .oam
files with
other Adobe
tools.

iBooks folder

The iBooks folder contains a .wdgt folder. You can use this folder with Apple's iBooks Author. The .wdgt folder contains another whole series of folders and files, as shown in Figure 13-12. All you need to do is copy or import the .wdgt file for use with iBooks Author.

Figure 13-12:
The files
within the
.wdgt folder.

Name	Type
edge_includes	File folder
images	File folder
Default	PNG image
index	Chrome HTML Document
index_edge	JScript Script File
index_edgeActions	JScript Script File
index_edgePreload	JScript Script File
Info.plist	PLIST File

Adobe Edge Animate and Adobe Fireworks

Adobe Edge Animate works very well with Adobe Fireworks both in exporting and in importing one into the other. To get started, you must first download the Edge Animate extension from John Dunning's website: `http://johndunning.com/fireworks/about/EdgeAnimate`.

Once you're on Dunning's site, you can read all about the great integration features between Edge Animate and Fireworks. Dunning's Fireworks extension supports elements for use in Edge Animate, such as rectangles, text, bitmaps, symbols, circles, layers, shadows, and so on. Dunning also includes notes on which types of elements Fireworks exports as flattened images. He even explains how to export an element as a flattened image if that is what you want. This extension also enables you to export elements with percentage properties as opposed to pixels. Dunning also provides a short list of limitations that Fireworks won't export properly, such as text elements shifting vertically, depending on the size and the font.

Something that you may find really exciting is the ability to export multi-state Fireworks projects as an Edge Animate symbol. Fireworks does this by exporting the animations as either a series of PNG files or a single sprite image.

The figure shows where to click to download the Fireworks extension for use with Edge Animate.

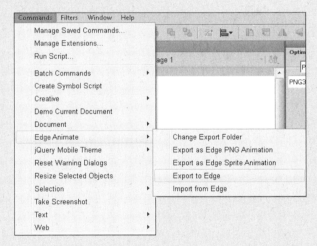

After you have the extension installed, it appears under the Commands menu in the Fireworks interface, as shown here.

You can also import Edge Animate projects into Fireworks. Basically, Fireworks asks you to select the .html or .an file that you want to import. Fireworks then creates a new document based on the same size and color as the Edge Animate document.

Web folder

This folder contains the standard set of Edge Animate files and folders. Edge Animate saves all the files and folders in one folder, which makes it easy for you to work with.

Chapter 14

Preparing Your Animation for Publication

*I*t isn't enough to simply create your animation project and then click Save. Oh, no. First you need to optimize your files for the specific task(s) for which you want to use your animation. Edge Animate provides publishing settings specifically for use on the web, for use with other Adobe tools, or for use with Apple's iBook Author. Throughout this chapter, I provide the details for each of these settings.

In addition to the Publishing Settings, you can set up a preloader. A preloader is used when your animation takes a long time to load. It's a great idea for providing some kind of visual clue to your audience that your animation is simply taking a bit of time to load and that it isn't broken.

I start this chapter suggesting different ways to handle audiences who still use Internet Explorer 8 or older. Animations don't work properly in those versions of IE, but you can create prompts for that segment of your audience to use Google Chrome Frames to avoid missing out on seeing and interacting with your composition.

Guarding Against Internet Explorer 8 and Older

Internet Explorer 8 still has a strong hold on Internet usage, particularly in the United States. Therefore, it's in your best interest to create web content that all Internet users can see. There's nothing worse for a web designer than to create content that appears broken or inaccessible to a large segment of the population.

It's imperative that you safeguard your animations from appearing broken by implementing a down-level Stage in association with the Edge Animate poster feature.

To use these features, read on!

Using the poster

You can use a *poster* with the down-level Stage. A poster, in its basic form, is a still image of your composition. You can use the poster instead of your composition when your audience is using an older web browser such as Internet Explorer 8 or earlier.

You don't have to know which browser your audience is using because Edge Animate codes that for you. All you have to do is create the poster and implement the down-level Stage to create backup content in the event your audience isn't using a modern browser (IE 9 or later, Chrome, Firefox, and Safari).

Browser, browser, who's got the browser?

Internet Explorer 9, which is the most current version of Microsoft's web browser, does play well with HTML5 and CSS3. As of this writing, Internet Explorer 10 is currently in preview and is generating interest with web enthusiasts. However, because of mostly corporate use and people who simply don't upgrade their browsers, plenty of web surfers still use versions of Internet Explorer that don't support Adobe Edge Animate CC features, especially when it comes to animations and certain types of formatting.

Desktop usage of Internet Explorer 8 and older becomes staggeringly apparent when you look at the statistics. According to many different articles, Internet Explorer is still one of the most-used web browsers in the United States, Canada, Australia, the U.K., China, and South Korea. However, it has been cited that Google's Chrome browser leads the pack in worldwide use.

As for different versions of Internet Explorer, use of IE 9 is still considered rare. When I checked the analytics of my own corporate site, which is visited mostly by corporate America, more than 33% of all visitors were using Internet Explorer between October 2011 and October 2012. Among those using IE, 56% were using version 8. Only 30% of IE users had upgraded to version 9. During that same period, 11.37% were still using IE 7, and 1.84% were using IE 6.

A responsive web design is squarely focused on mobile (tablet and phone) usage. The mobile browser war is being fought amongst Opera, Android, and Safari in regard to usage. All three of those browsers have roughly equal usage share between them, with Nokia's browser, BlackBerry, and others rounding out the bottom percentages.

Creating a poster is best done when you finish creating your animation. Follow these steps:

1. **Find a still shot that represents the point you want to make with your animation.**

   This point is most likely at the very beginning of the animation or the very end.

2. **Place your Playhead at the point you want to capture.**

   This allows you to preview your poster.

3. **Click the camera icon as shown in Figure 14-1.**

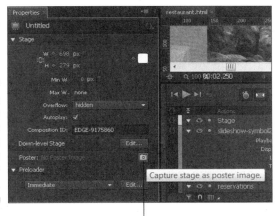

Figure 14-1:
Click the camera icon to open the Capture a Poster Image box.

Camera icon

A new box appears with a couple options, as shown in Figure 14-2.

4. **Capture your poster image:**

   • You can capture a new poster image at the current Playhead position by clicking Capture.

   • If you already have a poster image, but want to replace it with a new one, you can click Refresh.

   Doing so overwrites any previously saved poster files.

   Edge Animate saves the poster as a .png file in your images folder.

Figure 14-2:
Click
Capture
to Create
the poster
or click
Refresh to
overwrite an
old poster.

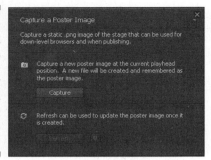

TIP

In the bottom-right corner of the Capture a Poster Image box, there is a Playhead icon. You can click that icon to move the Playhead to the position where the previous poster was taken. For example, if the Playhead was at the beginning of the Timeline for the last poster you created and you want to take the new poster image at that same location but the Playhead is now at a different point in the Timeline, simply click that Playhead icon to create a new poster at the same location as the last time you created a poster.

After you click Capture, a new box appears, as shown in Figure 14-3.

Figure 14-3:
After creat-
ing a poster,
you put it to
use through
Publish
Settings
or edit the
down-level
Stage.

From here, you can open the Publish Settings, which is described later in this chapter in the section, "Using the Publishing Settings and Publish." You can also choose to Edit Down-Level Stage, which I describe in the next section.

Using the down-level Stage

The down-level Stage is put in use when your audience uses a browser that doesn't fully comply with the advanced animation features of Adobe Edge

Animate CC. Given the current worldwide usage of Internet Explorer, especially in the United States, using a down-level Stage is in the best interest of all web content designers and animators.

Whether you click Edit from the Down-level Stage section of the Properties panel (Figure 14-4) or you reach the Down-level Stage section while creating a poster, the settings are the same.

Figure 14-4: Click Edit to open the Down-level Stage properties.

Click Edit

If you click the Edit button for the down-level Stage but don't have a poster created, Edge Animate prompts you to create a poster. To get back to the Stage, simply click Stage in the breadcrumb navigation (as indicated in Figure 14-5).

Stage

Figure 14-5: Click Stage to get back to your composition if you don't have a poster created.

Once you do have a poster created and you get to the Down-level Stage properties, you can set several properties (as shown in Figure 14-6):

- ✓ **Text:** You can use the Text tool to add text to the poster. Simply select the Text tool and then create a text box on the Stage.

- ✓ **Position and Size:** You can set where you want the poster image to appear within the Stage. You can use either X and Y coordinates, or simply use the auto W and H settings, per the default. Using Auto for width and height places your poster in its original dimensions. You can even toggle the px switch to use percentages instead of fixed coordinates.

- ✓ **Image:** From this section, you can swap out the current poster image for another image. Simply click the double-arrow icon to select another image from your library assets.

- ✓ **Link:** You can turn your poster image into a clickable link. Simply insert the URL you want members of your audience to visit when they click the image. You can also click the drop-down arrow to choose whether the new URL opens in the current browser window, a new window, _top, or _parent.

Figure 14-6:
Configure
the Down-
level Stage
properties.

Using the Preloader

Adobe Edge Animate CC has a *preloader.* The preloader defines what appears before anything else. For instances when your animation may take a long time to load, it's a good idea to use something like an hourglass timer. By using a timer, you alert your audience that the animation is loading and that they will need to wait. You can add a timer through the Preloader section on the Properties panel (shown in Figure 14-7).

In addition to choosing preloader art, you can also choose when JavaScript and images load, either as soon as they can or only when needed. I explain this further in the following sections.

Figure 14-7:
Use the
Preloader
option for
animations
that take
time to load.

Preloader option

Choosing either the Immediate or Polite option

Two different buttons appear in the Preloader properties. The first button (Figure 14-8) enables you to choose either:

✔ The *Immediate* option loads all JavaScript, graphics, fonts, and everything else all at once when the audience opens your composition.

✔ The *Polite* option loads the JavaScript (js) as page-load events fire, such as an action (say, when someone taps a button).

Figure 14-8:
The Polite
option loads
js as page-
load events
fire.

Options

Choosing the preloader art

Edge Animate provides a few different pieces of artwork that you can use as an animated timer. If your animation takes a long time to load onto the screen, your audience may start to think that it's broken or that they landed on the wrong URL. To prevent your audience from leaving, show some sort of hourglass timer that tells your audience to pull up a chair and stick around for a while. To get started, click the Edit button, as shown in Figure 14-9.

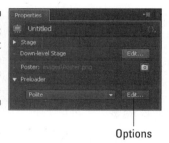

Figure 14-9: Click Edit to open the preloader's art options.

Options

When you click the Edit button, you can work on the preloader from the Stage, this is similar to when you edit a Symbol in that it is separate and independent from the main Timeline. For more information on Symbols, see Chapter 12.

The settings in the Properties panel update while you edit the preloader. You can now Insert Preloader Clip-Art, as shown in Figure 14-10.

Figure 14-10: Open the menu with preloader art.

Choosing the preloader art

From the preloader art menu, you can choose from several different animation hourglass-type icons, as shown in Figure 14-11. After you select an animated piece of art, click Insert near the bottom of the window.

Each type of preloader art has different dimensions and file sizes. It's a good idea to choose art that fits within the Stage of your composition.

If you don't like any of these ideas, Edge Animate provides you with the option of swapping out the art, which I describe next.

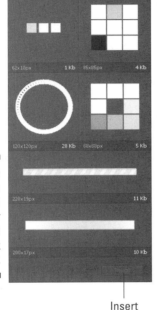

Figure 14-11:
Choose an
animated
preloader
clip and
then click
Insert.

Insert

Adding preloader art, just like anything else, increases file size. You probably don't want to add a large preloader to a composition that is already large. You can see how large the preloader is (size affects page-loading speeds) when you open the drop-down menu to select and insert the preloader gif (Figure 14-12).

Figure 14-12:
Edge
Animate
provides a
visual graph
depicting
preloader
art size.

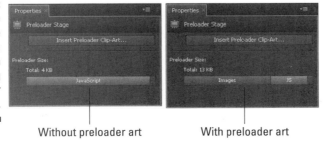

Without preloader art   With preloader art

Editing the preloader clip art

After you insert one of the clip art options, the Properties panel displays new settings, as shown in Figure 14-13. You can edit the following properties:

- ✔ **Position the art by X and Y axis points.** You can choose between pixel or percent.

- ✔ **Edit the width and height.** You can choose between pixel or percent.

- ✔ **Swap out the current image.** This is also how you can use custom preloader art, which I cover in more detail in the next section.

- ✔ **Add a link.** You do so by adding a URL in the box and set the target window from the drop-down arrow.

Figure 14-13:
Properties
for pre-
loader art.

You can also edit the preloader art directly from the Stage, as shown in Figure 14-14.

Select Timeline

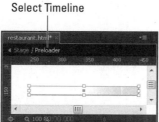

Figure 14-14:
Edit the
preloader
art from the
Stage.

Using custom preloader art

If you don't like any of the preloader clip art that Edge Animate provides, you can use your own art instead. After you select one of the preloader clip art options and then close that menu, you can swap out the preloader image from the Properties panel. When you click the Swap Image icon (as indicated in Figure 14-15), you can choose from images in your Library Assets. This enables you to choose your own custom art.

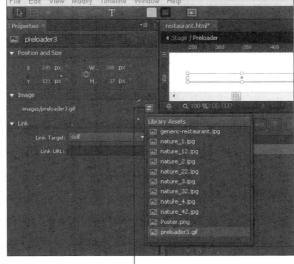

Figure 14-15: Swap out the pre- loader clip art with your own art from Library Assets.

Select art

Using the Publishing Settings and Publish

The rest of this chapter covers the publishing settings. This includes the web options and publishing your composition for use with other Adobe tools and iBooks. To open the publishing settings, from the main menu, click File⇨Publish Settings, as shown in Figure 14-16.

Click File

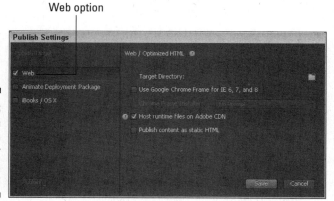

Figure 14-16:
Open the
Publish
Settings
from the File
menu.

Using the web options

After you click Publish Settings on the File menu, the Publish Settings box appears. From within that box, you see three options on the left side. When you select the Web option, more web settings appear on the right (see Figure 14-17).

Web option

Figure 14-17:
Use the
Web Publish
Settings for
online
animations.

The advantage to using the Web Publish Settings is that it allows Edge Animate to perform different types of optimization and minification to the files. When you click the Publish button, Edge Animate generates a lighter file output, which means the file is significantly reduced as compared to simply saving the composition.

The Web Publish Settings include

- ✔ **Target Directory:** Click the folder icon to choose where you want the web files saved.

- ✔ **Use Google Chrome Frames:** Check this box to create a Google Chrome Frame for when your audience is using Internet Explorer 8 or earlier. If your audience doesn't have Google Chrome Frame installed, you can prompt them to install it.

  There are three options on how to display the prompt, as shown in Figure 14-18. A Google Chrome Frame provides the means for members of your audience to view your animation when they use IE 8 or earlier, versions that don't properly support Edge Animate.

- ✔ **Host runtime files on Adobe CDN:** If you choose this option, you benefit from faster downloads and easier-to-manage output with runtime hosting provided by Adobe via Akamai servers. Uncheck this option if your content needs to run offline.

- ✔ **Publish Content as Static HTML:** Creates an HTML file with additional div tags. This provides more options for working with the HTML file, such as adding it to an existing web page and helps with SEO.

Edge Animate generates the following code when you publish your project as a static HTML page. In addition to a div tag for the Stage, tags for the other elements appear:

```
<body style="margin:0;padding:0;">
                <div id="Stage" class="EDGE-10260726">

        <div id="Stage_Rectangle" class="edgeLoad-EDGE-10260726" title="Use as
            Alt Tag"></div>
        <div id="Stage_Text" class="edgeLoad-EDGE-10260726 Text Box">Text</div>
        <img id="Stage_swirl" class="edgeLoad-EDGE-10260726 swirl image"
            alt="Alt Tag" title="Accessibility"
                src="images/green%20swirl.jpg"></img>
    </div>
</body>
```

You can copy and paste the code within the body tags to insert your animation into an existing web page. Just remember to upload the associated JavaScript files and the images as well. See Chapter 15 for additional information on how to embed your animation into another HTML file.

Type of prompt

Figure 14-18:
Choose
the type of
prompt, or
No Prompt,
for your
audience
to install
Google
Chrome
Frame.

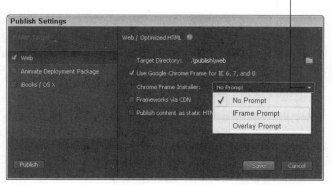

Using the Edge Animate Deployment Package

Use the Edge Animate Deployment Package if you're publishing your composition for use with other Adobe software tools such as InDesign, Muse, and others. When you select the Edge Animate Deployment Package from the Publish Settings, you can choose different settings from the right, as shown in Figure 14-19. When you select these options and then click Publish, Edge Animate creates an .oam file for use with other Adobe software.

Select package settings

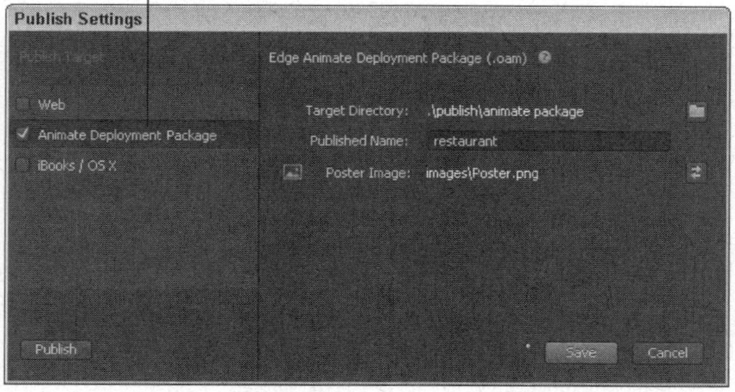

Figure 14-19:
Choose
where to
save the
file, what to
name it, and
the poster
image for
.oam files.

The settings for the Edge Animate Deployment Package include

✔ **Target Directory:** Click the folder icon to choose where to save the .oam file.

✔ **Published Name:** Name the .oam file in this box.

✔ **Poster Image:** You can swap out the poster image by clicking the double arrow icon.

When you finish with the settings, click Save to exit the window, or click Publish to generate the files.

Publishing as iBooks / OSX

Use the iBooks / OS X setting if you're publishing your composition for use with Apple's iBooks Author. When you select the iBooks / OS X from the Publish Settings, you can choose different settings from the right, as shown in Figure 14-20. When you select these options and then click Publish, Edge Animate creates an .wdgt file for use with Apple's software.

Select compatible device

Figure 14-20: Choose where to save the file, what to name it, and the poster image for .wdgt files.

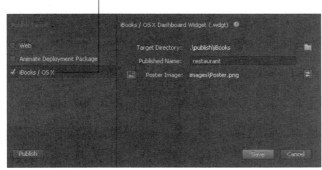

The settings for the iBooks / OS X include

✔ **Target Directory:** Click the folder icon to choose where to save the .wdgt file.

✔ **Published Name:** Name the .wdgt file in this box.

✔ **Poster Image:** You can swap out the poster image by clicking the double arrow icon.

When you finish with the settings, click Save to exit the window, or click Publish to generate the files.

For Edge Animate to generate these special files, you must either click Publish on the File menu (Figure 14-15) or click Publish from the Publish Setting box. Clicking Save or Save As doesn't generate the special files.

Chapter 15

Putting Your Project on the Web

*P*lacing your composition online can mean many things to many different people. The process is different depending on the type of site to which you want to add your composition. You can use your Edge Animate project as its own stand-alone site or page. You can embed your composition into an existing web page. If you use the Joomla! content management system (CMS), you can add your animation using a wrapper module. If using WordPress is more your style, you can use an Edge Suite extension.

No matter how you plan to use your animation online, using a good FTP (File Transfer Protocol) solution is the recommended means to uploading your files, which is necessary for most of the sections in this chapter. If you don't already use FTP, I can suggest using FileZilla (http://filezilla-project.org), which many other companies and individuals have suggested to me over the years. FileZilla is free and intuitive to use. If you have trouble figuring something out, documentation is easily available (http://wiki.filezilla-project.org/Documentation). FileZilla is continuously updated and supported as open-source software.

This book doesn't cover buying domains or getting a web host. I assume that you, or your client, already have a web host and domain. If you don't have a web host or a domain, I suggest looking into that before moving forward. Personally, I've used Bluehost (www.bluehost.com) for more than five years and have never had a problem. Its customer service is fast and responsive, and the service representatives can generally help you with any situation. You don't have to take my word for it, though; you can use WebHostingChoice (http://webhostingchoice.com) as a starting point to research the top web hosts.

Posting Your Composition as a Standalone Page

A good example of a stand-alone page or website is an informative and interactive set of graphics and text. Informative graphics can have rollovers for more information or an intuitive navigation menu that is presented using cues mixed among the text and images (as opposed to a menu bar running along the borders of the site).

Refer to Chapter 14 for how to get your animation ready for publication. Now is a good time to review how to use the publishing settings, in particular the section on using the web options.

Uploading your animation through your own hosted site

If you host your own site, simply copy and paste your files into your site's directory. The only file that you don't have to copy over is the `.an` file (the Animate file). If Edge Animate generates a `debug.log` file, you don't have to copy over that file either. For more information on the files and folders that Edge Animate creates, see Chapter 13; Chapter 14 provides information on the publishing settings for deploying to the web.

I highly recommend using the publishing settings (see Chapter 14) and transferring the files and folders that Edge Animate generates within the `publish\web` folder structure to your web host. This folder structure doesn't contain the `.an` file. It contains only optimized files for web use.

When you copy over the files, be sure to include the images and the `edge_includes` folder and all of the files in those folders.

After you copy over the files and folders, your Edge Animate composition should appear online. You can find it at the URL according to how your directory is set up and based on the name of the HTML file. For example, if the name of your HTML file is `slide-show-animation.html`, you can find your composition at `www.yourwebsiteurl.com/slide-show-animation.html`.

Uploading to your hosted site through FTP

If you want to put your animation online through a web host, I recommend using good FTP software such as FileZilla. To the uninitiated, using FTP may sound a little scary, but it's no more complicated than using folders and files just like the ones on your desktop computer.

Creating a new directory for your composition

To keep your files organized, create a new folder, or directory, in your overall site's directory to store your animation compositions. To do so in FileZilla, simply right-click where you want the new folder to be and then choose Create Directory, as shown in Figure 15-1.

Create the new folder in the root folder that contains your site. For example, you probably have a folder called `public_html`, which is where you store your site's files and additional folders. Or your root folder may be simply called *yoursite*.com; it all depends on how your site was originally set up.

Figure 15-1:
Create a
new direc-
tory for your
animation.

Name your new directory something generic, like *animations,* that way you can use this folder again for future animation compositions.

Uploading your files

With the new folder set up, it's time to import, or upload, your animation. If you're using FileZilla or similar FTP software, uploading the files is a matter of a simple drag-and-drop or copy-and-paste action. You can also click File⇨Import on FileZilla's menu bar.

After you create the new directory and upload the files, your directory should look similar to Figure 15-2.

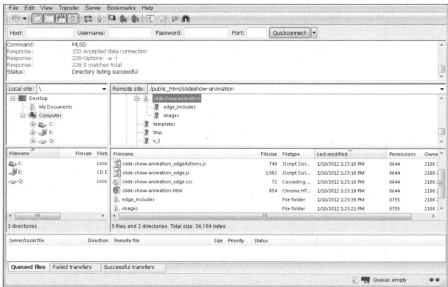

Figure 15-2:
Your
animation
directory.

Finding your animation online

Now, to find your animation online, simply follow the specific URL path that you set up. In this example, the URL is similar to

```
http://www.yoursite.com/slideshow-animation/slide-show-animation.html.
```

Adding Your Project into an Existing Web Page

Often your end goal for your animation is to embed it in an existing web page, such as an animation slideshow on a restaurant site. Here is a step-by-step guide on how to embed your animation in an existing web page:

1. **Find the HTML file you want your composition to appear in.**

2. **Open the Edge Animate HTML file. Copy everything between** `<!--Adobe Edge Runtime-->` **and** `<!--Adobe Edge Runtime End-->`, **which is found in the** `<head>` **tags.**

3. **Paste the code in the** `<head>` **tags of the web page in which you want your animation to appear.**

4. **Copy this code, which appears between the** `<body>` **tags:**

```
<div id="stage" class="EDGE-7347542">
</div>
```

5. **Paste the code into the HTML file of the web page where you want the animation to appear.**

6. **Save the updated HTML file.**

7. **Upload the Animate files and folders into the same folder as the HTML file that now contains your animation.**

   See the previous section on uploading your files for more information.

8. **Preview, test, and fine-tune how the animation appears in the page.**

When you copy over code, don't copy the `<title>` tag from your Animate HTML file. Doing so may conflict with the `<title>` tag on the HTML file that you're copying into. Also, don't copy the `<body style="margin:0; padding:0;">` code from your Animate HTML file. Doing so might conflict with the `<body>` tag on the HTML page that you're copying into.

Don't break the path that connects the HTML file, the JavaScript files, and the image folder. If the paths don't remain consistent, your animation will not work properly.

There's a very good chance that you'll need to fine-tune the CSS or other design parameters of the web page to ensure that the animation appears as you want it to look in the page. Each web page is unique. However, whoever originally designed the web page most likely knows what to do to make sure your composition looks good on the page.

Putting Your Composition into a Joomla! Site

If you use Joomla! as a content management system (CMS), how do you get your composition to show up on your site? The answer is pretty simple: You make a *wrapper module*. A wrapper module in Joomla! enables you to create an *iFrame*. An iFrame allows you to add content from another URL into your Joomla! article. The following section explains how to do this.

The first thing you need to do is upload your Edge Animate files, as described earlier in this chapter. That effectively puts your animation online. But that doesn't help with placing your animation in your Joomla! site; it simply appears online as though you posted it as its own page.

The easiest and quickest way to put your animation in Joomla! — for example, in an article or on the front page — is by using a wrapper module.

The following procedure creates a wrapper module for your animation and uses that module in an article to get your animation to appear on your Joomla! site.

1. **To create a wrapper module, go to the Joomla! main menu and click Extensions⇨Module Manager (Figure 15-3).**

Open the Module Manger

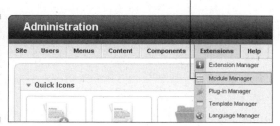

Figure 15-3:
Open the
Module
Manager
from the
main menu.

2. **Click New, as shown in Figure 15-4.**

Click to create new module

Figure 15-4:
Creating a
new module
in Joomla!.

3. **Choose Wrapper from the list of available modules.**

4. **Configure the module as shown in Figure 15-5:**

   a. Fill in the Title field.

   b. Name the Position.

   c. Set the Status to Published.

   d. Insert the URL in the appropriate field.

   e. Set the Height (you can leave the Width at 100%).

   f. Assign the module to all pages down at the bottom in the Menu Assignment box (not shown in Figure 15-5).

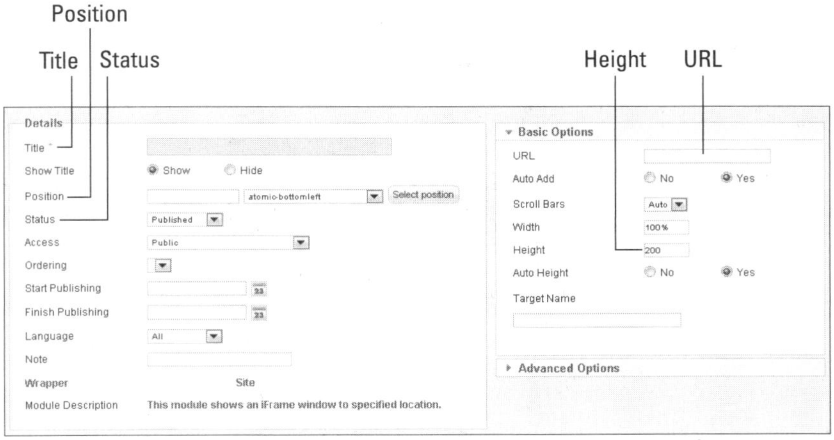

Position

Title | Status   Height   URL

Figure 15-5:
Configure
the Wrapper
module.

5. **Click Save & Close from the top-right corner.**

6. **Insert this wrapper module into the article in which you want your animation to appear.**

   Within Joomla!, navigate to the appropriate article and then insert the wrapper module by typing **{loadposition *customposition*}** where you want the animation to appear, where *customposition* is the position name you used in Step 4b.

You can find an Edge Suite plug-in for WordPress. This plug-in enables you to add your Edge Animate composition into a WordPress site. You can find the Edge Suite plug-in for WordPress at `http://wordpress.org/extend/plugins/edge-suite`

From that page, you can find links to helpful tutorials on how to use the plug-in.

Part V
Creating Sample Projects

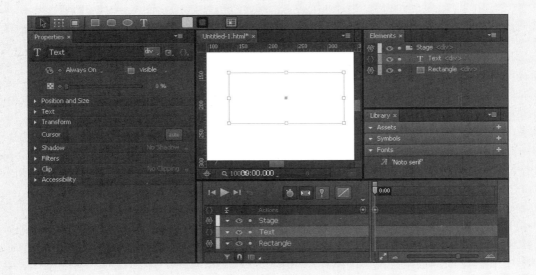

In this part . . .

- ✔ Constructing animations
- ✔ Designing projects
- ✔ Visit www.dummies.com/extras/adobeedge animatecc for great Dummies content online.

Chapter 16

Creating an Interactive Slideshow Animation

Creating an interactive and animated slideshow is a great way to acquire some of the Adobe Edge Animate CC basics. In this chapter, I cover how to work with several images in a composition. I also discuss how to time the images fading in and fading out. In addition, I show you how to add a loop to a slideshow so that it keeps playing. To include some basic interactivity to the slideshow, I conclude with a discussion on how to add Play and Stop buttons.

Overall Steps for Creating a Slideshow

This chapter provides detailed steps for creating a slideshow with a loop and buttons for starting and stopping. Here's a quick rundown of the general steps:

1. Determine the size of the Stage. This is especially important if you want to embed the slideshow into an existing web page.

2. Gather your images and size them the same size as the Stage.

3. Import all of the images through the Library panel in Edge Animate.

4. Drag the first image onto the Stage.

5. Set the Opacity properties for the image to fade in and then fade out.

6. Place the second image on the Stage.

7. Copy the first two keyframes you made for the first image.

8. Select the second image, and then paste the first keyframes so that they apply to the selected image.

9. Repeat Steps 6 through 8 for the remaining images.

10. Add in a Stage trigger to play from the beginning when the animation reaches the end.

11. Add the Play and Stop buttons and set their actions.

12. Add Cursor attributes to the buttons.

That's the overall procedure in a nutshell. You can find the details on each of these steps throughout the remainder of this chapter.

Setting Up Images and the Stage

Before you even open up Adobe Edge Animate CC, I highly encourage you to organize the images that you want to use in your slideshow. You also want to figure out how big you want to set the Stage. After you have done that, then you can open up Edge Animate and start importing the images.

1. **Determine how big to make the Stage. If you want to place the slideshow into an existing web page, determine the available space in the page.**

2. **When you know how big you want to make the Stage, size the images accordingly.**

   Slideshows look best when you size all the images the same.

3. **Create a folder on your desktop for your overall slideshow project. Within that main folder, create another folder called Images. Place all your images within that folder.**

4. **Open Edge Animate and size the Stage per Step 1.**

   See Chapter 3 for more on how to size the Stage.

5. **Import all your images at once through the Library panel (see Chapter 12).**

After completing these first steps, you can proceed to animating the first slide.

If your image is bigger than the Stage, parts of the image appear dimmer than other parts. The parts that appear dimmer are the parts that are off the Stage (see Figure 16-1). You can resize the Stage or the images to make a good fit. You can also change the Overflow property for the Stage to Visible, but that won't help if you want to place the slideshow within an existing web page and you have tight space considerations.

Figure 16-1:
Make sure the Stage and the images are the same size.

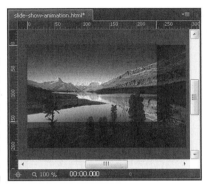

Animating the First Slide

Edge Animate is feature-rich, and you can create a composition multiple ways. For example, when creating your slideshow, you can use the Visibility property to make images appear or disappear from the Stage. However, for now, I want to use opacity. I have a couple reasons for doing so. First, I go into detail on using visibility in a later example in Chapter 19; second, I want to show how to use opacity effectively. When you use opacity to fade elements in and out, also using visibility is redundant and unnecessary. The following procedure picks up where I left off in the previous section.

1. **Drag your first image from the Library panel onto the Stage.**

2. **From the Properties panel, set the Opacity to 0.**

   This starts your image off as appearing invisible, as shown in Figure 16-2.

3. **Toggle the Pin and drag the Playhead down the Timeline to the 1-second mark.**

Opacity

Figure 16-2:
Using the
Opacity
setting to
conceal the
image.

4. **Set the Opacity to 100%.**

   If you preview the slideshow at this point, you see the image fade in over the course of 1 second. You now have your first animation.

5. **Select this animation and copy it.**

6. **Configure the image to fade out:**

   a. Place your cursor over the yellow bar with the chevrons, as shown in Figure 16-3.

   b. Click and drag that keyframe so that the Playhead is at the 2-second mark and the Pin is at the 1-second mark.

   c. From the Properties panel, adjust Opacity back to 0.

   This makes your image fade out.

Another way to do Step 6 is to copy the transition from the Timeline. Then, use Paste Inverted (from the main menu, click, Edit➪Paste Special➪Paste Inverted).

Figure 16-3:
Click and
drag the
Playhead
and Pin
down the
Timeline.

You should now have two animations. The first one fades the image in, and the second one fades the image out. If you preview the animation, you'll see the image slowly appear and then disappear.

The next section shows how to animate the second slide.

Animating the Second Slide

If you've been following along since the beginning of this chapter, you currently have a Stage and a set of images in your Library that have the same size dimensions. You've also created two transitions during which your first image fades onto the screen in 1 second and then fades out.

Now it's time to create the second set of transitions for use with the second slide:

1. **Drag the second image for your slideshow from the Library panel onto the Stage.**

2. **Place the Playhead at the 2-second mark in the Timeline.**

3. **Copy the first two transitions from the previous procedure.**

   You can select them both at the same time by clicking on the rollup bar, as shown in Figure 16-4.

Figure 16-4:
Place the
cursor over
the top bar to
select both
keyframes.

4. **Make sure you have the second image selected and then paste in the transitions.**

   This applies the same keyframe attributes to the second image as you set for the first image. At this point, if you preview the slideshow, you see the first image fade in and then out, and then the second image fades in and fades out.

5. **Experiment with meshing the two images so that as the first image fades out, the second one starts to fade in.**

   To do so, select the second set of transitions and drag them down the Timeline so that it starts at the 1-second mark, as shown in Figure 16-5.

   If you preview the slideshow now, you see the second image start to appear as the first image disappears.

Figure 16-5:
Blend the fading out of the first image with the fading in of the second.

6. **Repeat Steps 1 through 5 for your remaining images.**

Scrub the Playhead to about the 1.5 mark in the Timeline. Doing so allows you to see both images at approximately 50% opacity. You can see a combination of both images on the Stage at once, as shown in Figure 16-6.

Figure 16-6:
Viewing both images at once.

Adding the Finishing Touches

Up to now, you have a decent slideshow animation. However, it's missing interactivity. Also, it stops when it reaches the end. In this section, I show you how to add a loop to your animation so that it keeps repeating. I also show you how to add Play and Stop buttons so that your audience can interact with the slideshow.

Adding a loop

Here's how to add a loop to your slideshow:

1. **Place the Playhead at the end of the Timeline.**
2. **Click the Insert Trigger icon from the Timeline, as shown in Figure 16-7.**

Figure 16-7:
Insert a trigger into the Timeline.

When you click the Insert Trigger icon, the Trigger dialog box opens.

3. **Click Play From on the right side of the box.**

   This populates the code, as shown in Figure 16-8.

   By default, Edge Animate uses 1000 as the timestamp from which to play. If you want your slideshow to repeat from the very beginning, edit this to 0.

4. **Close the box to save.**

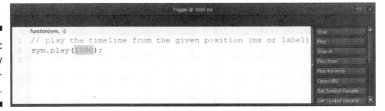

Figure 16-8:
Click Play From to create a loop.

To preview the loop, you must watch the animation from a browser (File➪Preview in browser). The Stage doesn't support the trigger.

Adding Play and Stop buttons

Now you have a slideshow that continuously repeats, but what if your audience wants to stop the slideshow? In that case, it's good to provide some buttons that your audience can interact with. The following procedure shows you how to add a Play button and a Stop button. For this procedure, I'm assuming that you already have images that represent the buttons.

Here's how to add actions to your buttons. You can repeat this process for the Stop button and the Play button:

1. **Place your button on the Stage where you want it to appear (this doesn't have to be an image. It can be a text box or an image).**

2. **Right-click the button image and choose Open Actions.**

3. **From the menu, choose Click.**

    This opens a second menu.

4. **From this menu, choose the action for the button.**

    You can choose Play or Stop here.

    This populates the dialog box with code, as shown in Figure 16-9.

Figure 16-9:
Click Play
to have the
animation
start playing
where it
left off.

To test that your buttons work, you must preview the animation in a browser.

Adding the Cursor attributes

If you previewed a button in the preceding section to see whether it works, you may have noticed that your cursor didn't change from the standard arrow to a hand when you hovered over the button, indicating that it is indeed a button.

In the next procedure, I show you how to add Cursor attributes to the buttons to provide a visual clue to your audience that they can click the buttons. This procedure assumes you already have an image on the Stage with actions set.

1. **Select the element (image of the Play or Stop button) on the Stage.**

2. **From the Properties panel, click the Cursor attribute icon.**

    This opens the Cursor attribute menu (Figure 16-10).

Cursor attribute

Figure 16-10:
Add a
Cursor
attribute to
your
buttons.

3. **Choose the pointing hand icon.**

    This icon appears when you hover the mouse over the button in a web browser.

To see your Cursor attributes in action, you must preview the animation in a browser. The Stage doesn't support Cursor attributes.

Chapter 17

Synchronizing Elements in an Animation

*I*n this chapter, I explain how I created an animation of a car driving into a brick wall. I affectionately named this composition "Car Go Boom." To get the animation to work, I drew the road and some lane markers. I then imported an image of a car, sans the wheels. I had to remove the wheels from the car so that I could create an animation of the wheels turning. I also imported an image of a brick wall so that the car had something to hit. Finally, I added an effect of the car bouncing off the wall and then some text saying "Boom" — hence I made "Car Go Boom."

My intention in this chapter is to give you a resource for synchronizing elements, using the rotating tool, and effectively using easing.

Drawing Elements onto the Stage

To get started, use the Rectangle tool to draw the road (refer to Chapter 3 for more on drawing elements). Simply draw a black rectangle along the bottom portion of the Stage.

While drawing your objects, make sure the pin isn't toggled and that Edge Animate doesn't automatically create keyframes; otherwise each element you draw and each change you make are recorded as animated keyframes. That could be fun to watch later — to see the iterative process of creating, coloring, placing, and sizing the rectangles — but it probably wouldn't look too good in the final animation.

If you want to get fancy, you can draw lane markers:

1. **Draw a small rectangle.**
2. **Use the color picker (refer to Chapter 9) to change the color to yellow.**
3. **Angle the lane marker to a –10 skew (refer to Chapter 7).**

4. **Place the lane marker in the middle of the road.**

   You can use the guide lines that magically appear to align the element in the center.

5. **Copy and paste the lane marker as many times as you need to.**

   Repeat until the road has a sufficient number of lane markers, as shown in Figure 17-1.

Figure 17-1:
Stage is set
with a road
and lane
markers.

If, after placing all the lane markers in the road, you decide you want smaller markers, you can adjust their sizes all at once:

1. **Select one of the markers.**
2. **While pressing Shift on the keyboard, select the other markers.**
3. **In the Properties panel, adjust the size by changing the Width.**

   The Height should stay proportional if the Link Scale is on.

You can also import the brick wall at this time so that it's at the far end of the road.

Now it's time to import and synchronize a car wheel.

Rotating an Element

Adobe Edge Animate CC isn't the equivalent to stop-motion animation. That is, you don't have to create a keyframe for each rotation of a wheel. If you have to do that, you may as well create a claymation composition.

Here's how to make your wheel roll:

1. **Import an image of a car wheel and position it right above one of the lane markers.**

2. **Activate the pin and adjust the Playhead in the Timeline so that you can create a transition.**

3. **Use the mouse to move the wheel off the Stage.**

4. **Change the Rotate attribute (refer to Chapter 7) to 360 degrees (see Figure 17-2).**

   Your composition should now look like Figure 17-3.

You can preview this animation on the Stage.

Rotate properly

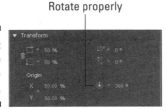

Figure 17-2: Set the Rotate property to 360.

You can also use the Properties panel (instead of the mouse) to roll the wheel off the Stage instead of the mouse. To do so, in the Position and Size section, set the L property so that the wheel is just off the Stage (refer to Chapter 8 for more on positioning and sizing). If you have Global selected, then you would simply set the X property.

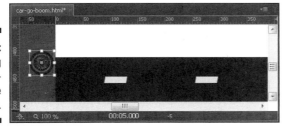

Figure 17-3: Positioning the element off the Stage.

Synchronizing More than One Element

Now that you've practiced making one wheel roll down the road, it's time to import the car image and copy and paste the first wheel to create a second wheel.

If you've been following the chapter, now is a good time to delete the first animation you made of the wheel rolling down the road by itself. To do so, select that keyframe in the Timeline and delete it. When you delete the keyframe, the object isn't deleted. To delete the object, you need to select it from the Stage, and then delete it.

Before you start importing new images and copying and pasting the wheel, be sure to toggle off the pin and make sure the stop watch isn't red so that you don't start creating automatic keyframes. You don't want each import, change, and move animated.

Aligning the wheels:

1. **Align the car image so that the wheel well is aligned with the wheel.**

2. **Copy and paste the first wheel to create a second wheel. Place the second wheel in the empty wheel well.**

Now it's time to synchronize the car and the wheels so that they all travel together down the road.

While you import your images, you may need to use the Send Backward feature (to find this feature, open the Modify menu from the main menu, then choose Send Backward) to send the image of the wheel behind the image of the car. Figure 17-4 shows the different options available for arranging your elements.

Figure 17-4:
The Modify menu for arranging the order of objects.

Modify	Timeline	Window	Help			
Arrange			▶	Bring to Front	Ctrl+Shift+]
Align			▶	Bring Forward	Ctrl+]
Distribute			▶	Send Backward	Ctrl+[
				Send to Back	Ctrl+Shift+[
Group Elements in DIV		Ctrl+G			
Ungroup Elements		Ctrl+Shift+G			
Convert to Symbol...		Ctrl+Y			
Edit Symbol					

Adobe Edge Animate CC does support images with transparent backgrounds. To keep the transparent background of your image, save it as a .png file; otherwise, you may have square white edges along the perimeter of your wheels, which could look funky as the car is cruising down the road.

At this point, your composition should look like Figure 17-5 (the wall isn't shown), with the road drawn and the three images (car and two wheels) in place and selected.

Figure 17-5:
Preparing
for synchro-
nization.

1. **Enable Auto Keyframe mode (the stopwatch appears red), toggle the Pin and move the Playhead in the Timeline to where you want the animation to end.**

   For example, if you want the car to take 5 seconds to cross the Stage, move the Playhead out to the 0:05 mark and keep the pin at 0.

2. **Select the two wheels and the car by clicking on them with the mouse while holding down Shift so that you have all three elements selected.**

3. **Use the mouse to click and drag the three objects until the front end of the car hits the wall.**

   Don't worry if your hand is a little shaky while dragging the objects. That actually improves the appearance of a car driving down the road and smacking into a wall.

4. **From the Timeline, make sure the Playhead is at the point in time when the car hits the wall, leaving the Pin at the beginning of the animation.**

5. **Select only one of the wheels and change the Rotate attribute to 360.**

6. **Select the other wheel and set the Rotate attribute to 360.**

If you play the animation now, the car should appear to be traveling down the road and stopping when it meets the wall.

Using Easing

In this section, I describe how to create the appearance of a car bouncing off a brick wall by using easing. For more information on easing, refer to Chapter 4.

Keep an eye on where the Playhead and Pin are in the Timeline. Also keep an eye on the Pin to see whether it's toggled and whether the stopwatch icon is activated to create automatic keyframes.

Here's how to add easing to an element. The following steps continue from the example in the preceding section:

1. **Place the Playhead at the end of the animation where the car meets the wall.**

2. **Select the elements to which you want to add an easing attribute.**

   In this case, you select the car and two wheels.

   Now you can edit the easing attributes by using the Easing tool in the Timeline as highlighted in Figure 17-6.

Figure 17-6: Using the Easing tool.

3. **Click the Easing tool icon (Figure 4-11).**

   This opens several options for using easing.

4. **Choose one of the options and then choose a more detailed option.**

   If you click different options, the graph on the right updates showing a representation of the easing effect.

   For this example, choose Ease Out and then Bounce.

Notice that three of the five easing attributes are named with either *In* or *Out* or *In Out*. Here's a brief description of those terms:

✔ **In:** The easing effect takes place at the beginning of the animation.

✔ **Out:** The easing effect takes place at the end of the animation.

✔ **In Out:** The effect happens at both the beginning and the end of the animation.

If you play the animation now, you should see the wheels rotating, the car moving down the road, and when the car meets the wall, you should see it bounce back and forth. Okay, so it's more like the car ran into a trampoline rather than a brick wall, but you discovered how to use easing. Now is a good time to experiment with all the different easing attributes.

It can be difficult to see the full easing effect watching the animation play in real time. You can watch the animation in slow motion by scrubbing the Playhead back and forth in the Timeline. Doing so allows you to see the car bounce in slow motion.

Timing Some Text

Just for practice, try adding text to appear at the point when the car hits the wall.

1. **Place the Playhead and Pin in the Timeline at the point where you want the text to appear.**

   If you want to time the text to appear just after the first crash, scrub the Timeline so that you see the car hit the wall and then start to bounce back — that's where you want to place the Playhead and Pin. That way, the text appears as the car bounces back and forth off the wall.

2. **Insert a text box (refer to Chapter 10) and type some text, such as Boom.**

3. **Reduce the Opacity setting (refer to Chapter 8) to 0 (see Figure 17-7).**

   This gives the appearance that the text isn't there, as shown in Figure 17-8.

4. **Make sure the Pin is toggled and move the Playhead a smidgen down the Timeline.**

Opacity

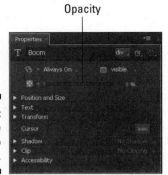

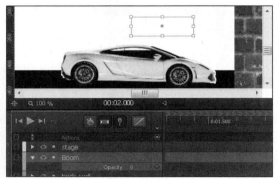

5. Change the Opacity to 100%.

This gives the appearance that the text pops into view as the car hits the wall. Figure 17-9 shows the Stage with the text.

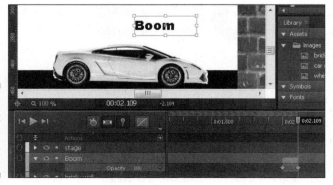

You can change the name of the elements to better suit what they actually represent. For example, if you have several text boxes in your animation, numbering them isn't the best way to keep track of them. Instead, you can rename them for better representation. In this case, renaming the text box as **Boom** helps you remember what that element is.

Chapter 18

Building an Interactive Tutorial

*A*dobe Edge Animate CC is a great tool for e-learning specialists and teachers. You can build interactive and animated tutorials from which students can learn. In this chapter, I show you how to create a tutorial with several steps. Students can use forward and back arrows to move forward in the lesson or to move back a step. I also show how to add a Symbol to the composition, which is used for a quick tip that students can tap to show or hide additional information.

During the course of this chapter, I discuss a few pitfalls that I encountered when first creating this tutorial. My intention is that you can learn from my mistakes, and avoid creating the same mistakes. Also, as you advance in working with Edge Animate, you may discover that some of my ideas aren't completely necessary. For example, when it comes time to create a Symbol, I suggest that you create your first Symbol in a separate project, save it as a Symbol, and then import it into your main composition. Doing so for your first few projects may save you some headaches. However, as you become more familiar with Edge Animate, you may find that this extra step is no longer necessary.

I originally created this tutorial with dimensions appropriate for use on an iPad; however, the tutorial works great on mobile devices such as Amazon's Kindle Fire and Android phones. It also works great on desktop browsers such as Internet Explorer 9, Firefox, and Chrome.

This chapter starts with the assumption that you've already:

✔ Created a wireframe

✔ Gathered your assets and fonts

✔ Sized the Stage (iPad screen dimensions: 768 x 1024)

You're ready!

Steps for Building an Interactive Tutorial

To get a sense of what this chapter shows you how to build, here's the first step of the tutorial. The function of the tutorial is to teach how to complete a task through a series of steps. The student taps on elements to proceed through the tutorial.

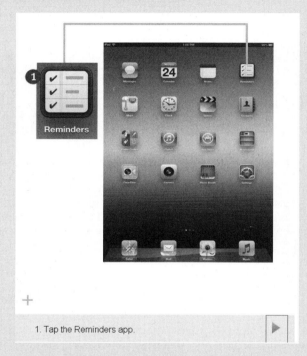

1. Tap the Reminders app.

Here are the overall steps presented in this chapter:

1. Gather your assets.

2. Size your Stage.

3. Format the navigation bar.

4. Add a text box for the instructions.

5. Add placeholders for the navigation arrows.

6. Create and animate the callout lines using clipping.

7. Use labels in the Timeline to show where new steps begin.

8. Add actions to the navigation arrows so students can move back and forth through steps.

9. Create a Symbol for the quick tip text.

Placing the Navigation Bar

First, you place the navigation bar, which enables the student to advance the lesson or to backtrack to a previous step, along the bottom of the screen.

1. **Use the Rectangle drawing tool to create the navigation bar along the bottom of the Stage. Use the color picker to set the background color (see Chapter 9).**

2. **Create a text box for the instructions (Chapter 10).**

3. **Draw a rectangle to house the forward arrow in the lower-right corner (Chapter 3).**

4. **Place the image of a forward arrow inside the rectangle.**

5. **Use the guides to help evenly align the elements (text box, arrow box, and arrow) within in the navigation bar.**

   Figure 18-1 shows how helpful the guides are when you need to align several elements. You can place as many guides as you need.

Figure 18-1:
Use the
guides to
help align
elements.

Place the guides and then leave them. Don't delete them or move them. You want these guides in place throughout the process of creating the tutorial. Each step uses different arrow elements (forward_arrow_step_1, forward_arrow_step_2, forward_arrow_step_3) and leaving the guides in place helps you remember where to place them. Placing your arrows in slightly different positions for each step may create the appearance of the arrows jumping around, even if the arrows change placement in tiny increments. Right now, you're placing only the forward arrow, but in the next step, you add the back arrow.

Animating the First Step of the Tutorial

Now that you've created the navigation bar, you can turn your attention to animating the first step.

1. **Place the first main graphic on the Stage.**

   Each step has a different main graphic. You want to size the main graphics roughly the same size for consistency. In this example, the main image switches between the iPad's home screen and reminder screen.

2. **Use the guides to determine the placement of the main image (see Figure 18-2).**

   That way, all main graphics appear in the same location.

Figure 18-2: Use the guides to help place the main graphic images.

Resist the temptation to simply move the guides you placed for the navigation bar for use with main graphics.

Using clipping for the callout lines

Now it's time to draw the *callout lines*. The callout lines are used to provide a reference as to where the student should tap the screen. In this example, I use rectangles to draw the callout lines, and I use clipping to animate them.

This procedure shows how to animate the callout the lines:

1. **Use the Rectangle tool to draw a long, skinny bar and then set the background color, as shown in Figure 18-3.**

Figure 18-3:
Draw the first callout line.

2. **Copy the first callout line and paste it to create the second line.**

   Each segment of the line is its own element. By copying and pasting, you keep the same width and color and save yourself the trouble of redrawing and reformatting the line.

3. **Name each line segment accordingly so that each one isn't Rect1Copy or whatever.**

   Use **northlinestep1**, **horizontallinestep1**, and so on. You want to keep these names straight so that you can find them easily later to make tweaks.

4. **Use clipping (refer to Chapter 9) to animate the callout line appearing on the Stage.**

   Select the element and then the Clipping tool, toggle the Pin, and move the Playhead down the Timeline. Start the keyframe with the element completely clipped, and end the keyframe with the element completely unclipped.

   Figure 18-4 shows a partially clipped callout line.

Figure 18-4:
Use clipping to create the animation of the callout line that's appearing.

You can preview the clipping animation from the Stage.

Create segments in the Timeline for each step

Now that you have Step 1 complete, it's a good idea to start adding labels to your Timeline (see Chapter 5). The labels should represent where Step 1 begins, another for Step 2, and so on. This is like creating segments in your Timeline, which is helpful for a couple of reasons:

✔ These labels come in handy when you set the actions for the forward and back arrows.

   The labels help you visualize where Step 1 is taking place, where Step 2 happens, and so forth.

Using labels is considered best practice because using time code may prove trickier when working with actions. For instance, you can move the label to affect timing without having to edit the action, whereas when using time codes, you can't. Labels also provide visual clues in the Timeline on what is taking place at that time.

Using Stage triggers to stop the tutorial from advancing

Your tutorial keeps playing unless you add a Stage action to trigger the animation to stop playing. You want the animation to stop playing so that the student controls when to advance the lesson. Otherwise, the animation keeps playing through each step.

This procedure shows you how to stop the animation after each step:

1. **Place the Playhead where Step 1 finishes.**

2. **Click the Insert Trigger icon, as indicated in Figure 18-5.**

   Doing so opens the Trigger code box.

Figure 18-5:
Create Stage
triggers to
stop the
animation
from playing
at the end of
each step.

3. **From the Trigger code box, choose Stop from the right side, as shown in Figure 18-6.**

Figure 18-6:
Choose Stop
to stop the
animation
from
playing.

4. **Close the box to save the trigger.**

Now when you preview the animation, it stops after Step 1 is finished. To test this, repeat the steps and procedures in this section for Steps 2, 3, and so on.

Adding the Interactivity

After you complete animating each step in your tutorial, you need to add the forward and back buttons, which allows students to advance at their own pace. After the procedure on adding actions for the arrows, I show you how to add a quick tip button as a SymbolSymbol.

Creating the forward and back arrows

If you are like me, you may want to create a SymbolSymbol for the back and forward arrows. I'm here to tell you that is overkill. The navigation arrows are too simple to warrant use of a SymbolSymbol. Besides, SymbolSymbols are best used when you want to create animations that are *independent* of the main Timeline. The navigation arrows aren't independent of the main Timeline; in fact, they work directly with the main Timeline in regard to the labels that represent where each step begins. A better reason for creating a SymbolSymbol is for the quick tip, which I discuss in the next section.

Here is a list of points to keep in mind when working with the navigation arrows:

✔ Each step needs its own arrow element.

✔ Don't use more than one click (or tap) action per element.

✔ Avoid using the touch commands. Click works best even for touch screens. The touch commands can lead to double-clicking. This is more true for tablets like the Kindle Fire. On the iPad, double-clicking does not happen as often.

Add labels to your Timeline for use with the navigation arrows. If you use a label in an action that doesn't exist, your animation plays from the beginning of the Timeline.

Here's the procedure for adding actions to your navigation arrows:

1. **Set the visibility of each arrow element.**

   You don't want the arrows to always be visible. As you add an arrow for each step, turn the visibility to On at the beginning of the step and Off right before the end of the step. See Chapter 8 for more information on the Visibility property.

2. **Name each arrow element accordingly (**forward_arrow_1, forward_ arrow_2, **and so on).**

   This way, you can find them easily later on.

   Now you're ready to edit the action.

3. **Right-click the arrow and choose Open Actions.**

4. **Choose Click from the menu.**

5. **Choose Play From in the right column.**

6. **Edit the code so that a click starts playing the animation from the appropriate location.**

   For example, for the forward arrow in Step 1, you want the student to advance to Step 2 (see Figure 18-7).

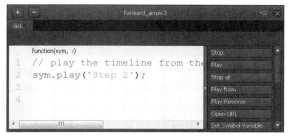

Figure 18-7: Use labels in the actions for ease of use.

7. **Set the cursor attribute for the element (see Chapter 5).**

   This is only necessary if your audience might use a desktop or laptop computer along with a mouse. If you plan for the tutorial to only appear on tablets, then this isn't necessary.

Now that you have the first arrow created, you can copy the element for re-use on each step. When you are ready to place the arrow to advance to Step 3 of the tutorial (the first arrow advances the student to Step 2), move the Pin and Playhead to where Step 2 starts in the Timeline and then paste in the element in the same spot (using the guides) as where the first arrow was placed.

Then edit the click action (so that it advances to Step 3 instead of Step 2, etc.) and remember to set the visibility for each arrow. For example, at the beginning of Step 2, the first arrow's visibility should be Off, and the second arrow's visibility should be On.

You can follow this same procedure for the back arrows. The first back arrow should appear at the beginning of Step 2 so that the student can backtrack to Step 1.

Creating the quick tip

The quick tip in this tutorial is an excellent example of how and when to use Symbols in Adobe Edge Animate CC. The quick tip works independently of the main Timeline and thus has actions and labels that don't affect the main

Timeline. You can even create this Symbol in an entirely different project than you've been working on so far, which is exactly what I propose you do until you gain enough experience working in Edge Animate to create Symbols within the main composition.

The quick tip in this example is a plus Symbol. When students tap that Symbol, additional text flies out, and they can close that extra text by tapping on an X. Here's how you do that:

1. **Start a new project.**

2. **Add an element to the Stage that you want to serve as the icon for the quick tip.**

3. **Create a keyframe animation in which text flies out from the Symbol.**

   For example, create a text box directly over the quick tip Symbol and shrink it down to almost nothing.

4. **Create a keyframe animation so that it moves up and to the left of the quick tip and slowly enlarges to 100%. Set the visibility to On for the duration of the transition.**

5. **Add a Stop Stage trigger right after that keyframe.**

6. **Create a second keyframe animation (after the Stage trigger) so that the enlarged text shrinks back down to nearly 1% and moves back to over the Quick Tip Symbol. Set the visibility to On at the beginning and then to Off at the end.**

7. **Add a second Stop Stage trigger at the end of the second keyframe.**

8. **Insert labels into the Timeline to show where the text enlarges and where the text shrinks.**

   At this point, your Timeline should look similar to Figure 18-8.

   Now you need to add an action to the Quick Tip element.

Figure 18-8:
Timeline
showing
keyframes
for the
Quick Tip
animations.

9. **Right-click the Quick Tip element, choose Open Actions, choose Click, and then edit the code (see Figure 18-9).**

10. **Create a means for the student to close the text:**

   a. Import an X icon image and place it in the top-right corner of the text box.

   b. Set the visibility to On at the point in the Timeline when the text completely enlarges.

   c. Set the visibility to Off when the text starts to shrink, as shown in Figure 18-10.

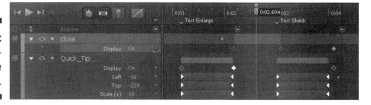

11. **To enable the student to close the text box, add an action to the X icon element, as shown in Figure 18-11.**

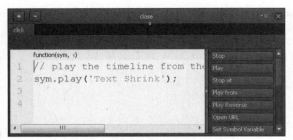

Figure 18-11:
Code for
closing the
text box.

You're ready to convert this project into a Symbol.

12. Right-click and choose Convert to Symbol.

13. In the dialog box, name the Symbol and uncheck Autoplay Timeline, as shown in Figure 18-12; then click OK.

This stops the Symbol from automatically playing when the main animation starts to play.

Figure 18-12:
Name the
Symbol and
uncheck
Autoplay
Timeline.

14. Copy this Symbol and paste it into the main composition (or you can export the Symbol if you want to import it into several different compositions).

And that's how you create an animated Symbol that plays independently of the main Timeline.

Chapter 19

Animating an Interactive Children's Book

- -

In This Chapter

▶ Getting organized to animate an interactive children's book

▶ Formatting text and effectively using shadow

▶ Creating navigation links

- -

*T*his chapter presents a basic outline on how to create an animated children's book. What I don't do is provide step-by-step directions on animating the actual story. Writing and animating the story are up to you. The writing part, well, that's completely up to you; but by reading this book, you find out how to animate the story. This chapter provides tips on how to add subtle refinements to your animation project and how to organize and plan a children's book.

Overview Planning

To animate an interactive children's book, the first thing you gotta do is write the story. (I realize that's probably common sense, but I've been guilty of wanting to jump ahead a few steps in times past, so I thought I'd add that as a gentle reminder.) So, step one is to write the story and create a storyboard that outlines how the book progresses.

Before you start animating, the second item to check off is gathering your assets. Whether that means hiring an illustrator to create the artwork, doing it yourself, buying stock art from various websites, or using copyright-free images off the Internet is up to you. Regardless of your methods, be sure to get at least one image that you can use for the background, or multiple background images if your story takes place in more than one location. Having a consistent background image helps in placing your characters and text boxes, and it facilitates an interactive table of contents.

My thinking process on how to create the table of contents

Probably one of the most important techniques to learn while creating an animated book is proper development of the table of contents (TOC). I stumbled onto this one when I first tried to create an animated children's book. My initial plan was to make the TOC a Symbol. I wanted the TOC to behave independently of the main Timeline so that it appeared and disappeared based on the audience's interaction.

The tricky part was creating links in the TOC so that the audience could jump from chapter to chapter (or page to page). The easiest way to do so is to use Play From actions utilizing labels from the main Timeline. The problem is that Symbols behave independently of the main Timeline and, therefore, don't recognize labels from the main Timeline.

My second thought was to use URLs in the action, but for that to work, I would have to create each chapter as its own Edge Animate project, which would create tons of files and tons of uploading (because I would have to upload each project separately and each project would have its own URL). I suppose for very lengthy books that approach is a viable option,

but most children's books aren't lengthy — think of *Goodnight Moon* as compared to *Game of Thrones*.

Finally, I ditched the idea of using a Symbol for the TOC. Instead, I created a segment in the main Timeline in which I placed my TOC animations and links. You can read the details on how I did this later in the chapter.

I do realize that most children's books do not contain chapters. If your book does not contain chapters per say, every time you read the word "chapter," simply replace it with the word "page." If your book is extremely short, you may want to skip creating a TOC. For longer books that need more than one sitting to read, I recommend a TOC.

If your book becomes very long, loading times may be affected. If it takes too long for your book to load, consider dividing the book into multiple Edge Animate files (different projects) to reduce the file size. If you do make multiple files for your book, you need to use URL links in your TOC instead of linking to labels from the Timeline.

In addition to the artwork, think about what kind of font(s) you want to use in your book. Now is a good time to review the section in Chapter 12 on working with fonts.

Once you have your storyboard created and your artwork is ready to go, it's time to start thinking about how to organize your Timeline in Adobe Edge Animate CC. Decide how to create segments in the Timeline, how to use labels to help you visualize where Chapter One starts, where Chapter Two starts, and so on. Think of the keyframe animations for each chapter as segments. You also want to segment some time for the table of contents (TOC). At first blush, you may think about creating a Symbol for the TOC, but for this example, I show you how to use labels from the main Timeline to create links for the TOC, which is why the TOC is part of the main Timeline and not a Symbol.

Symbols are used to create animations that are independent of the main Timeline. Symbols have their own set of labels for their own Timeline. Symbols don't recognize labels from the main Timeline.

Finally, before you start animating, here are few things to consider doing:

- ✔ Set the Visibility of elements to turn on when you want them to appear and turn off when you want them to disappear.
- ✔ Add labels in the Timeline to signify when different chapters (or pages) start and for use with Play From actions.
- ✔ Create different text boxes for headers, body paragraphs, and each different link or navigation button.

Formatting the Text Boxes

Although Adobe Edge Animate CC has many features, settings, and properties for text, it isn't intended for text-heavy projects, which is fine for children's books that may contain only a few lines of text on each page. Edge Animate is also good for creating children's books because you can enable interactivity by creating links with the text boxes and other elements.

Creating a different text box for each element

For Edge Animate CC, you must create a separate text box whenever you want to use different formatting for the text. For example, if you use different font sizes or colors for the chapter headings than you use for the main text, you need to create different text boxes for the different types of text.

You also have to create separate text boxes for each link in the TOC. Although it may seem easier to create a single text box with a long list of chapter titles, doing so won't work in this example. Each text box can contain only one Play From action, which you use to create the links. So, each chapter title in the TOC must have its own text box.

Using shadow on text appropriately

Say that your background image consists of blue skies and white puffy clouds. If you use a light-colored text, your text may become lost or hard to read over the white clouds. Or say that you want to use the color blue for the TOC link and place it in the top-left corner of the Stage on top of a blue sky — using blue on blue may make it hard for your audience to read or even see the text.

To help with this, I recommend placing a subtle shadow on the text to make it easier to read (see Figure 19-1).

Figure 19-1: Add a shadow to your text for easier reading.

To create the shadow, follow these steps:

1. **Check the Pin to make sure it's not toggled and be sure that Edge Animate doesn't automatically create keyframes as you perform these steps.**

2. **Select the text box.**

3. **From the Properties panel, toggle No Shadow to enable adding shadows, as shown in Figure 19-2.**

Figure 19-2: Enable the Shadow properties.

Enable properties

4. **Change the shadow color to black and set each of the properties to 1, as shown in Figure 19-3.**

Figure 19-3:
Configure
the shadow
for subtlety.

Shadow properties

You now have a shadow on your text, which makes the text easy to read when it's placed over images, as shown in Figure 19-4.

Figure 19-4:
Text with
a slight
shadow is
easier to
read.

Creating a Segmented Timeline

Although I don't go into the specifics of animating an interactive children's book (after all, the story you tell and how you tell it are up to you), I do want to provide a list of items to keep in mind while animating your story:

✔ Label the start of each chapter (or page) to create a segmented Timeline. This makes it easy to see where each part of the book starts. You can use the labels for your Play From actions as well. Also, insert a label for where you want your TOC animation to start.

✔ Set the Visibility property for each of your elements to On (instead of using the default Always On) at the appropriate times.

✔ Animate each segment to tell your story.

✔ Place a Stage trigger to stop the animation at the end of each segment. Otherwise the story keeps playing, and the audience loses control over when they want to move forward.

✔ Turn the Visibility of elements to Off just after the Stage Stop trigger for each segment. (Unless, of course, you want those same elements visible in the next segment.)

✔ If you plan to use a consistent background image throughout the story, you can leave that element's Visibility setting at Always On so that the image is visible when the TOC opens — and so your audience doesn't experience a blank Stage when they open the TOC.

Navigating the Story

In this section, I discuss a couple ways for your audience to navigate through your story. I present how to build an interactive table of contents (TOC) and discuss how to place navigation links for your audience to advance the story or return to a previous page.

Place the forward and back navigation links as you animate each chapter or page. That way, when you preview the story in a browser, you can test the navigation as you edit each chapter or page. You may wait until you finish animating the story before you add the TOC, simply because you may not have all your labels in place until the end.

Placing the next and back navigation

Consistency is always the key to good navigation. Don't make your audience guess where or how to move the story forward. If you want to use more creative text than "Next" or "Back" to indicate the navigation, be sure you make clear what your audience needs to do to advance the story. For example, add something like "Find out what happens to the bear by clicking the beehive."

If that approach is still too dry, you can do something along the lines of, "The bear swatted at the beehive with his paw. Can you help him get the honey by knocking down the bee hive?" Then make the beehive glow for a moment. Such visual clues will clearly signal the audience to click the beehive to advance the story.

Using standard and consistent buttons for navigation is a tried-and-true approach, and this is how you do it:

1. **Use the Stage guides to align your navigation buttons or text.**

   The Stage guide helps you consistently place the elements in the same location for each page (see Figure 19-5).

Figure 19-5:
Use the guides to help place elements.

2. **Make sure the Pin is not toggled, and place the text or image on the Stage.**

3. **Advance the Playhead to the point in the Timeline where you want the navigation element to appear — for example, at the end of Chapter One.**

4. **From the Properties panel, turn the visibility On for the navigation element (see Figure 19-6).**

Visibility

Figure 19-6:
Turn the visibility from Always On to On.

5. **Right-click the element and add an action to the element (click Play From) and use the label for Chapter 2, for example (see Figure 19-7).**

Action   Label   Action

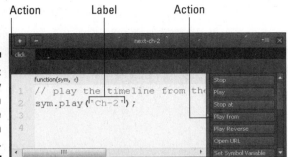

Figure 19-7:
Add a Play
From action
for the
Navigation
link.

6. **Slide the Playhead down the Timeline to the end of the first chapter and just after the Stop Stage trigger. Change the visibility to Off, as shown in Figure 19-8.**

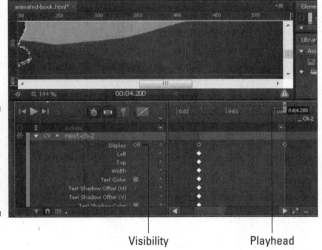

Figure 19-8:
Turn the
visibility to
Off after the
Stage Stop
trigger.

Visibility   Playhead

Repeat this procedure, using a unique element, for each navigation element. You can create the back navigation in the same manner.

Building the table of contents

Using a TOC is a nice touch that adds another level of professionalism to your interactive book.

Create a TOC only if it truly benefits your audience. For example, if you create a book in which your audience may want to skip around to different parts, a TOC can be useful. A TOC may also be useful if the story takes more than one sitting to read; however, if your audience can read through the book in 5 to 15 minutes, a TOC isn't necessarily beneficial. Figure 19-9 shows the TOC that I talk about in the following sections.

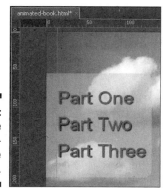

Figure 19-9:
An example
of format-
ting a table
of contents.

Formatting the table of contents

Before you start formatting the TOC, advance the Playhead to a point in the animation where the visibility for all other elements is turned off. This gives you a clear working space for formatting the TOC. For example, move the Playhead to the far end of the Timeline.

Make sure that the Pin isn't toggled and that Edge Animate is not set to start automatically creating keyframes. Otherwise Edge Animate creates keyframes as you format the TOC.

How to create a table of contents:

1. **Draw a rounded rectangle to create a container for the TOC. Place it along the left side of the Stage.**

2. **From the Properties panel, in the Corners section, choose the 4-corner formatting option.**

3. **Format the corners so that those at top-right and bottom-right are slightly rounded (see Figure 19-10).**

4. **Format the top-left and bottom-left corners to appear square (simply click the box for that corner) to create a tabbed look (see Figure 19-10).**

Formatting option

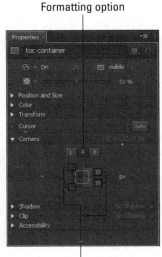

Figure 19-10:
Creating a
tabbed look
for the TOC
container.

Square corners

5. **Use a 50% Opacity setting for the background of the rounded rectangle so that the background image is visible through the element (see Figure 19-11).**

Opacity

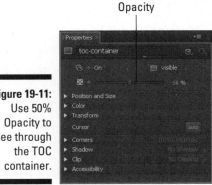

Figure 19-11:
Use 50%
Opacity to
see through
the TOC
container.

6. **Create a separate text box for each chapter or page of the book and place them vertically within the rounded rectangle.**

Use the guides to help you align the text boxes, as shown in Figure 19-9.

7. Format the text in a traditional blue color to signify it's a link, as shown in Figure 19-12.

Figure 19-12: Format the color of the text in a traditional blue link color.

8. Select the rounded rectangle and the text boxes and move them off the Stage to the left (see Figure 19-13). Remember not to animate this step.

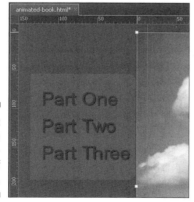

Figure 19-13: Slide the TOC elements off the Stage.

After you complete formatting the TOC, you can start to animate it so that the audience can interact with it.

Animating the TOC

The animation for the TOC consists of the TOC sliding out from the left when the TOC link is clicked. (Placing the TOC link is the last procedure in this chapter, right after this one.) When the audience clicks one of the TOC links, the TOC disappears from the Stage. Here are the steps for this process:

1. **Insert a label in the Timeline to designate where you want to start the TOC animation.**

    You use this label later for the TOC link.

2. **Move the Playhead down the Timeline to where you inserted the TOC label.**

3. **Toggle the Pin to start automatically creating animated keyframes.**

4. **Move the Playhead down the Timeline to indicate the length of time that you want the TOC to take to slide onto the Stage, as shown in Figure 19-14.**

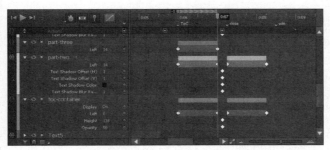

Figure 19-14: Toggle the Pin and move the Playhead down the Timeline to animate the TOC sliding in from the left.

5. **Select all the TOC elements and move them onto the Stage. This creates a keyframe animation.**

6. **For each TOC element**

    a. Select the element and right-click it (for example, choose Open Actions and then Click) to add an action (for example, Play From).

    b. Type the label as shown in Figure 19-15.

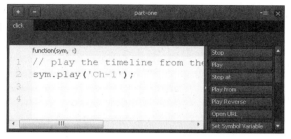

Figure 19-15:
Add a Play
From click
action to
create a
link.

7. **Add a Cursor attribute for each of your TOC elements (Figure 19-16).**

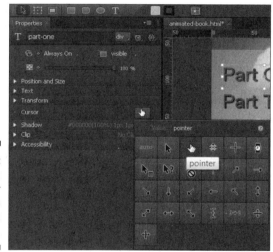

Figure 19-16:
Add a
Cursor
attribute to
your TOC
items.

8. **Place a Stage Stop trigger at the end of the TOC segment in the Timeline.**

9. **Move the Playhead slightly past the Stage Stop trigger and then turn off the visibility for each of the TOC elements.**

You have now created the animation for the TOC. The next step is to create a way for the audience to open the TOC.

Placing the TOC text box link

In this section, I present a procedure on how to create a means for your audience to access the TOC. At the beginning of the animation, the TOC is not visible. You want to create an element that enables the reader to open the TOC. If you don't want to use a text box to create the link to open the TOC, you can just as easily use an image or a drawn element. Whatever you choose to use, make sure it signifies that, by clicking (or tapping) it, the audience knows it's opening the TOC.

Here's how to create an element that opens the TOC:

1. **Place the Playhead in the point in the Timeline where you want the TOC link to appear.**

   For example, you may want the TOC link to appear directly after an opening title screen or at the end of the first page or chapter.

2. **Find a place on the Stage where you want the TOC link to consistently appear — for example, in the top-left corner of the screen.**

3. **Draw a text box and type** Table of Contents, **or whatever you think is appropriate.**

4. **From the Properties panel, change the visibility from Always On to On.**

5. **Add an action to the TOC element (right-click the element, then choose Open Actions⇨Click⇨Play From, and then type in the TOC label), as shown in Figure 19-17.**

Action   Label   Action

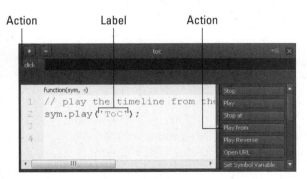

Figure 19-17: Adding a Play From action that specifies Click for the TOC element.

6. **Move the Playhead down the Timeline to the point in the animation where you want the TOC element to turn off and change the visibility setting to Off from the Properties panel.**

Here's a trick for getting the TOC element (the link) to disappear when the TOC is open:

1. **Make sure the TOC animation (when it slides in from the left) is at the very end of the animation, after all the chapters.**

2. **Set Visibility for the TOC element link to On at the beginning of the book.**

3. **Set Visibility to Off at the end of the project's last chapter, but before the start of the TOC animation.**

4. **Place a Stage Stop trigger at the end of the last chapter.**

   Otherwise the TOC animation plays at the end of the last chapter.

Place Stage Stop triggers at the end of each chapter to stop the animation; otherwise the story continues to play. For more information on Stage Stop triggers, refer to Chapter 5.

Chapter 20

Animating Navigation Menus

· ·

In This Chapter

▶ Creating an animated drop-down menu

▶ Importing your slideshow project as a Symbol for use in a one-page site

▶ Using mouseovers as actions

▶ Using Open URL actions

▶ Creating a navigational header for a larger site

▶ Creating a one-page site

· ·

*E*dge Animate is good for creating one-page sites and headers within larger sites. Within these headers, you can add navigation to other parts of the parent site. The example in this chapter shows how to create an animated header for a company with three main business units. The animation includes the feature of rollover text for each business unit and links for the visitor to dive deeper into the site.

A great example of a one-page site is a restaurant site. Restaurant sites tend to have a limited amount of text and an abundance of imagery depicting the dining room, the staff, and of course the food. Don't let the term one-page site trick you though; even though the site won't have multiple pages, you can still present the appearance of many different pages just by swapping out the text and adding a slideshow. In this chapter, I show you how to create such a site, using an animated drop-down menu.

Creating a One-Page Website

You can create an entire website with Adobe Edge Animate CC, provided you keep it relatively simple. I'm not suggesting that you can create a complex site with tons of text and hundreds of pages; you are better off using another tool for that task. However, it's completely plausible to create simple websites with limited text with Adobe Edge Animate CC.

As I mentioned, an excellent example of a one-page website is a restaurant site because it tends to have limited text, perhaps a paragraph or two per page, and it tends to rely on imagery to convey its message. The heavy use of imagery lends itself to slideshow animation (refer to Chapter 16 for more on creating slideshow animation), which you can import into your one-page site as a Symbol.

The following sections provide details on creating animated drop-down menus with top-level and sub-level menu items (as shown in Figure 20-1). I also show how to set up the actual content, through the example of importing a slideshow Symbol.

Figure 20-1:
Create
animated
drop-down
menus
with Edge
Animate.

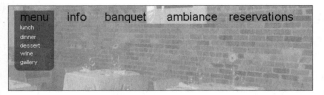

Creating the top-level menu items

The following procedure describes how you can set up the top-level menu items:

1. **Place the guides on the Stage to evenly align the menu items.**

   You can use Modify⇨Distribute (from the main menu) to help align elements as well.

2. **Create a separate text box element for each top-level menu item.**

3. **Add a cursor attribute to each element.**

4. **Change the visibility to On for each element, even though the top-level menu items are always visible.**

5. **Insert a label in the Timeline to indicate where the sub-level menu animation occurs.**

6. **Place a Stop Stage trigger (see Chapter 5) before the first sub-level animations begin, as shown in Figure 20-2.**

Figure 20-2:
Use a Stop
Stage
trigger to
prevent the
animation
from playing
before the
visitor clicks
a link.

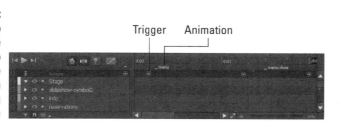

7. **Right-click the first top-level menu item and add an action (Open Actions⟳Click, Play From) to start playing from the first sub-level animation segment of the Timeline, using the label that you inserted in Step 5 (see Figure 20-3).**

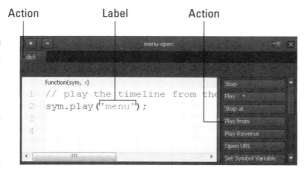

Figure 20-3:
Add a Click,
Play From
action to
create a link
to the sub-
level menu.

Now you need to create the sub-level menu.

Creating the sub-level menu items

The sub-level menu opens when the visitor clicks a top-level menu item. You can animate how the sub-level menu opens. In the following procedure, I show how to create an effect in which the drop-down menu appears to literally drop-down, with each sub-level menu item appearing one at a time as the menu opens. You achieve the drop-down menu animation effect with the Clipping tool, as shown in Figure 20-4. I then turn the visibility to On for each sub-level menu item as the clipping animation reveals each item. I describe this procedure in detail in the following section.

Figure 20-4: Use Clipping to reveal the sub-level menu items container.

Opening animation for the sub-level menu

To create the sub-level menu, follow these steps:

1. **Move the Playhead to the point in the Timeline where you inserted the label for the first sub-level menu item.**

2. **Create a separate text box for each sub-level menu item.**

   In this example, I changed the font color to white to make it easier to read against a multi-colored background (see Chapter 10).

3. **Add a Cursor attribute to each text box element.**

4. **Draw a rectangle box over the menu list to act as a container.**

   In this example, I used a 50% Opacity setting with a black background. I also rounded the bottom corners but left the top corners square. These settings are shown in Figure 20-5.

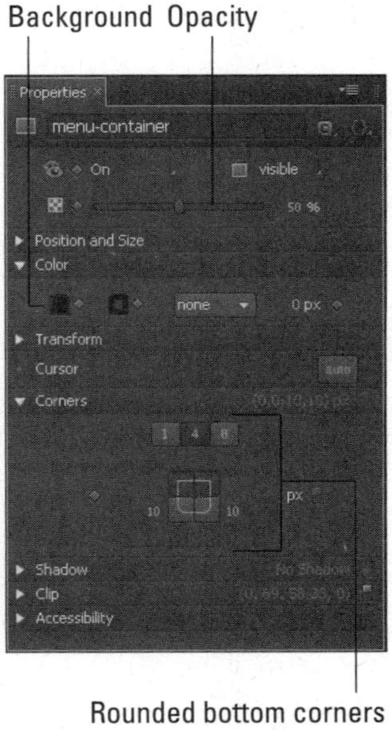

Background Opacity

Figure 20-5: Format the menu container from the Properties panel.

Rounded bottom corners

5. **Toggle the Pin and select the menu container.**

6. **Use the Clipping tool to create an animated effect of unveiling the rectangle, as though it were sprouting from the top-level menu item.**

   See Chapter 9 for more on clipping.

7. **Time the visibility for each sub-level menu item as the rectangle box reveals itself.**

   The best way to do this is to scrub the Playhead along the Timeline manually to view when the clipping effect passes over each sub-level menu item. As the rectangle element unclips while you move the Playhead down the Timeline and passes over the sub-level menu item, change the Visibility setting for each of those elements to On. Figure 20-6 shows how that appears in the Timeline.

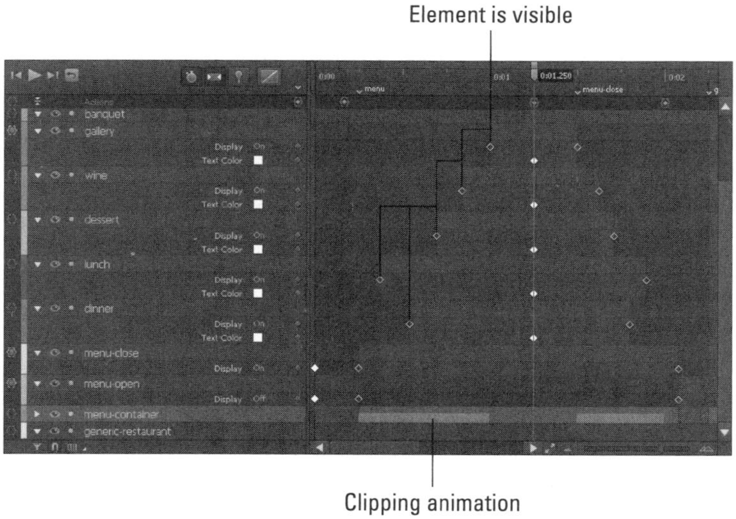

Element is visible

Figure 20-6: The keyframes appear staggered along the course of the clipping animation.

Clipping animation

8. **Add a Stop Stage trigger at the end of this animation.**

At this point, you have an animation for opening the sub-level menu. To finish, you need to create the closing animation for the menu. I describe how to do so next.

Closing animation for the sub-level menu

In addition to creating an animation for when the menu opens, you can create an animation for when the menu closes. This animation occurs while the menu is open and the visitor clicks the top-level menu item.

The following procedure describes how you can create the closing animation:

1. **Insert a label in the Timeline to indicate where you want the close menu animation to begin, such as at the end of the open menu animation.**

2. **Swap out the top-level open menu element with a close menu element.**

    a. Copy the top-level menu item.

    b. Turn the visibility to Off.

    c. Paste the menu item.

    d. Turn the visibility to On.

    e. Update the action to close the sub-level menu items (see Figure 20-7).

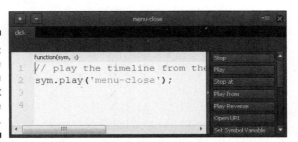

Figure 20-7:
Update
the action
to reflect
closing the
menu.

3. **Reverse the animation sequences you made to open the menu to reflect closing the menu.**

    a. Use the Clipping tool to create an animation in which the menu container (the rectangle) appears to roll up.

    b. Time the visibility of the sub-level elements so that they appear Off (that is, disappear) as the clipping occurs (Figure 20-8).

4. **At the end of the menu-close menu animation, add a Stage trigger in the Timeline to play from the beginning of the Timeline (see Figure 20-9).**

    This brings your visitor back to the beginning of the Timeline, where the click action for the top-level menu opens the sub-level menu.

5. **Just after the Stage trigger that you inserted, turn off the visibility for the menu-close element (top-level menu item text box) and the menu-container element (the rectangle).**

Element is not visible

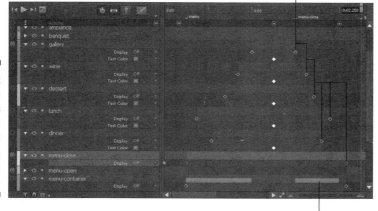

Figure 20-8:
Time the
elements
so that the
visibility is
Off during
the clipping
animation.

Closing animation

Figure 20-9:
At the end
of the close
menu ani-
mations, add
a Stage trig-
ger to play
from the
beginning.

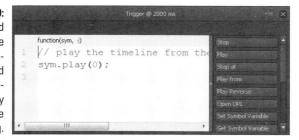

At this point, you have animations for when the menu opens and closes. In the next section, I show you how to create an animation for when visitors click a menu item.

Navigating to new content

In this project, you create a one-page site with a menu. Although the site is considered a one-page site, that doesn't mean all of the content is static. You can still make new content appear, as though visitors were clicking through to a new page, even though they remain on the same page. You can use the following procedure to create this navigation by inserting a slideshow as a Symbol.

1. **Create a slideshow as described in Chapter 16.**

   You can skip adding the buttons if you want; I don't use them in this example. Instead, I use an infinite loop so that the slideshow keeps repeating (at the end of the slideshow animation, insert a Stage trigger to play from the beginning).

2. **Convert the slideshow into a Symbol (refer to Chapter 12) and export it.**

   Be sure to leave Autoplay selected. That way, when the visitor clicks the Gallery link from the menu, the slideshow automatically starts to play.

3. **Import the Symbol into this current project through the Library panel by clicking the + icon (see Figure 20-10).**

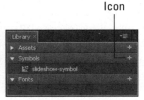

Figure 20-10: Click the + icon next to Symbols to import a Symbol.

4. **Insert a label in the Timeline to indicate where the sub-level menu item's content is animated.**

   In this case, name the label **Gallery**.

5. **Add an action (Click, Play From) for the sub-level menu item, using the label** Gallery **as shown in Figure 20-11.**

Figure 20-11: Select the sub-level menu item and add a Click, Play From action.

6. **Place the Playhead over the Gallery label in the Timeline.**

7. **Drag the Symbol from the Library panel onto the Stage.**

8. **Change the visibility for the Symbol from Always On to On.**

Now when your visitor clicks Menu➪Gallery, the slideshow automatically starts to play. When your visitor clicks another menu item, the slideshow goes away.

Navigating with Mouseovers and Open URL Actions

So far in this book, I've discussed navigating in terms of being within an animation's Timeline, using actions with clicks and Play From. In this section, I branch out and move toward navigating with the Open URL action. This works great when your animation is embedded within a larger — parent — site. By using an action with Open URL, you can place links within your animation to other pages of the parent site. That way, your visitor can navigate within your animation to access other parts of the site.

Another type of action I haven't discussed much so far is mouseovers. *Mouseovers* (aka *rollovers)* are great for when a click isn't necessary. For example, you can allow your visitor to scroll through a list of items, and as she scrolls, new information appears on the screen. That way, the visitor doesn't have to click through each item to see more information. In the following procedures, I show you how to use an effective mix and Open URL actions and mouseover actions to create a functional and effective navigation menu, or a *header,* that you can embed into a larger site.

This example focuses on a business with three main departments. The three departments are listed vertically on the left, with room on the right for text that describes the different departments. When the visitor rolls over the different departments, different text appears on the right. When the visitor clicks the logo or one of the text links, she is taken to a page within the larger, parent site.

Placing the artwork and the text

You can use the following procedure to set up the project and get started:

1. **Gather your assets, including the URLs you want to link to and the text you want to appear.**

2. **Size your Stage according to the space you want it to consume on the parent site.**

3. **Use the guides on the Stage to create partitions, using the rule of thirds — that is, with one-third of the space on the left and two-thirds on the right.**

   In Figure 20-12, you see that I even added guides to create margins for the text. Vertically, use the Stage to create three rows for the left column.

4. **Place the Always On elements on the Stage, such as the logos and the names of the business units on the left.**

   You may also want a consistent header at the top on the right.

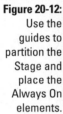

Figure 20-12:
Use the guides to partition the Stage and place the Always On elements.

Lorem ipsum dolor sit amet, consectetur

Business Unit A

Business Unit B

Business Unit C

Duis condimentum justo tristique urna pulvinar adipiscing. Vivamus non sodales magna. In hac habitasse platea dictumst. Sed volutpat tincidunt tortor, id vehicula tortor venenatis id. Etiam commodo auctor risus, sit amet eleifend diam gravida vel. Maecenas consectetur mi at leo imperdiet dictum. Sed condimentum porttitor sem eget viverra. Vivamus ultricies quam euismod nisi vehicula interdum ac et nisi. Vivamus hendrerit consectetur lacinia. Suspendisse at massa erat. Praesent odio

Read more about ABC, DEF or GHI.

5. **Add some kind of animation to the logos to draw attention to them.**

   I discuss how to make elements spin in Chapter 7. Later in this chapter, you find out how to add an Open URL action to the logos.

6. **Add a Stage Stop trigger after the initial animations.**

   If you don't add the Stage Stop trigger, all the mouseover text appears in order. And you don't want that to happen.

With the Stage set, it's time to add the text that you want to appear when a visitor rolls a mouse pointer over one of the business units.

Adding the mouseover text

In this example, I use text that appears before the visitor clicks anything. This text is then replaced when a mouseover or click action occurs.

Follow these steps to add the rollover text:

1. **Draw a text box on the right within your guides and type the initial text.**

2. **Change the visibility from Always On to On.**

3. **Segment your Timeline with labels for use with the mouseovers. Each label represents where in the Timeline the mouseover text appears. Insert the first label.**

4. **Place the Playhead in the Timeline where you inserted the first label.**

5. **Draw a text box on the Stage within your guides and type or paste the text.**

6. **Set the visibility to On for the text.**

7. **Insert a second label into the Timeline for the second business unit's text.**

8. **Just before the second label, add a Stage Stop trigger, as shown in Figure 20-13.**

Figure 20-13:
Insert Stage
Stop trig-
gers in the
Timeline
after each
business
unit text.

Triggers

9. **Place the Playhead in the same spot as the second label.**

10. **Turn off the visibility for the first business unit text.**

11. **Place a text box for the second business unit's text on the Stage. Turn the visibility to On.**

12. **Repeat Steps 1 through 11 for the third business unit's text.**

A nice aspect to using mouseovers is that the rollover text doesn't go away if the visitor moves the mouse off the element — that is, of course, if she doesn't mouse over another element that has a mouseover action.

Adding the mouseover and open URL actions

Use the following steps to add the mouseover and open URL actions.

1. **Right-click the top-left element for the first business unit to open the Actions panel.**

2. **Add a mouseover.**

3. **Add a Play From action and use the label for the first business unit text. Test it in a browser to confirm that when you roll over the element, the text changes on the right.**

   You can add animations to the text on the right to ensure that your audience notices that the text changes. Chances are that the text updating is fairly obvious.

   Overusing animation can be just as bad as no animation at all. Be careful not to overdo it.

4. **Select the logos and add a cursor attribute.**

   It's a good idea to start adding a cursor attribute first (before adding the link) for all links. I usually discover that I forgot to add it when I test the link. When the cursor doesn't change, I think I didn't add the link, but then when I click it and the link works, I realize I simply forgot to add the cursor attribute.

5. **Add the Click, Open URL action for the logo. Update the URL in the code to where you want your visitor to go, as shown in Figure 20-14.**

Action

Figure 20-14:
Use the
Open URL
Action to
navigate
within the
parent site.

URL   Action

At this point, you may realize that the spinning logo link may not be enough to prompt visitors to click, especially if they're looking for a traditional-colored text link to click. In this case, you can add a text link within the rollover text, as I describe next.

Adding text links

It's a good idea to add a colored text link in your rollover text so that, for example, your audience can clearly navigate to the About Us page for a particular business unit to find more information. This is how you add the link:

1. **Move the Playhead over the first label.**

2. **Add a new text box under the business unit text and set the visibility to On. Don't forget to set the visibility to Off right after the Stage Stop trigger.**

3. **Right-click the text box element to add a Click, Open URL action, as you did for the logo.**

4. **You can color the link any way you like, but the traditional hyperlink blue is R: 0; G: 0; B: 255.**

   See Chapter 10 for more information on formatting text.

5. **Repeat Steps 1 through 4 for each business unit.**

You may even want to add text links within the initial text box just in case visitors don't hover over the mouseover elements or don't click the logos. If you decide to do so, remember to use a separate text box for each link, as shown in Figure 20-15. Also, remember to use the guides to evenly align each text box.

Figure 20-15:
Each link needs its own text box element.

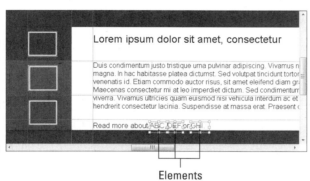

Elements

After completing the procedures in this chapter, you have an animated navigation system that you can incorporate into a larger parent site.

To post these projects online, refer to Chapter 14, where you find out how to get your animation ready for the web using the Publishing settings. Also refer to Chapter 15 for information on putting your composition on the web, including how to embed the animation in an existing web page.

Chapter 21

Building a Responsive Web Design

*T*his chapter discusses the details of formatting settings for a responsive web design. By using percentages (%) instead of pixels (px), you can create animations that automatically adjust to the size of a person's browser. Using percent also helps with formatting for different mobile screen sizes for devices such as phones and tablets.

Currently, popular mobile screen sizes range from 4 inches to 7 inches to 10 inches. Creating a separate animation for each type of device is not necessary. Instead, you can create a responsive web design as discussed in this chapter.

Starting at the Stage

To get started with creating a responsive web design, you need to set the width and height properties of the Stage to %.

You can also set the properties for maximum width and minimum width:

- ✔ For the minimum width, you can use either % or px.
- ✔ You can set the Max W property to none, px, or %. The default is None.

  To change the Max W property, click the drop-down arrow and then uncheck the None box, shown in Figure 21-1.

Figure 21-1:
Change
the Max W
property by
clicking the
drop-down
arrow.

When you change the W and H properties from px to %, little white icons (*ticks*) appear on the Ruler, as shown in Figure 21-2. You can slide those ticks up and down the Ruler to simulate the effect of a person adjusting the browser's window size.

Properties   Tick

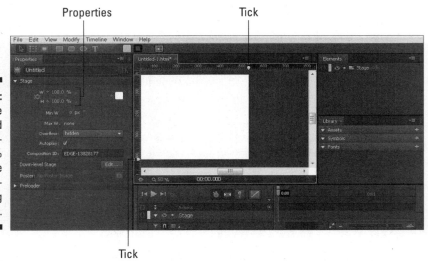

Figure 21-2:
Change the
Width and
Height prop-
erties to %
to enable
browser-
resizing
simulation.

Tick

If you have elements on the Stage that are also set to %, you see those elements adjust in size as the browser window is resized.

To test the width percentage settings for your design, experiment by using px instead of % for the minimum width:

1. **Start a new project and set the Stage width and height to 100%.**
2. **Set the Min W to 600 px and leave Max W at None.**
3. **Import an image and place it on the Stage.**
4. **Set the image width and height to %.**
5. **Slide the tick down the ruler and watch as the image resizes.**

When you slide the tick past the minimum width, the image and Stage stop scaling down in size. If you preview this in a browser, you'll see that the image becomes cropped when you size the browser smaller than the minimum.

The little caret (shown in Figure 21-3) that appears in the Ruler indicates the px width of the Stage when you use the percent setting.

Stage width

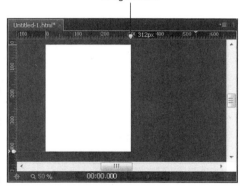

Figure 21-3:
The caret
indicates
the Stage
size in px.

Setting the Layouts

You can apply the same percentage settings to elements for a responsive web design as you can for the Stage. You can set these properties a few ways. One way is to change the properties from pixel to percentage for each element individually from the Properties panel. However, that option can be time-consuming, and it isn't necessary. Adobe Edge Animate CC provides two different means for setting global parameters: *layout defaults* and *layout preferences*. The layout preferences are geared toward scaling and sizing for each individual element in relation to the parent element. The layout defaults set the value for each element as either percent or pixel.

Set the layout defaults first and then override them as necessary with the layout presets.

Although the terms layout defaults and layout preferences may sound similar, they have different meanings, as I explain in the following sections. I cover the layout preferences in more detail in Chapter 8.

Using the layout defaults for responsive design

If you know that you want to use the same settings for all the elements and images that you use on the Stage, you can set the layout default values, as shown in Figure 21-4. You can open the Layout Defaults menu from the toolbar.

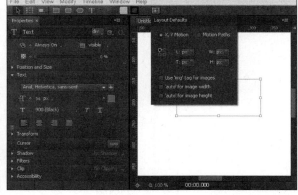

Figure 21-4:
Go to the toolbar to open the Layout Defaults menu.

For a responsive web design, you can use a combination of px and % settings, depending on what you want to dynamically resize and what you want to be static.

To start off designing for responsiveness, I recommend the following settings:

✔ Set all of your elements to % (L, T, W, and H).

✔ Select the Use 'img' Tag for Images box.

✔ Select 'auto' for Image Height.

Changing the layout defaults to percentages sets the properties for all elements — text boxes, rectangles, ellipses, and images — to respond when the browser window is resized.

To keep your image size proportional (so that it doesn't stretch oddly wide or long) when the browser is resized, set either the image width or the image height to Auto (use the check boxes shown in Figure 21-4 to configure your settings), but not both — nor neither one. You have to set either the width or the height to Auto to keep the image proportional as the window is resized (refer to Figure 21-4). The exception to this is when you work with SVG files (for example, an image of a pattern). In this case, you can set both width and height to %, and the image will still look good.

If you set your elements for percent, when you resize the Stage, the elements on the Stage also resize:

➤ To stop elements from resizing when you change the size of the Stage, change all the elements back to px.

Using the layout preferences for a responsive web design

Chapter 8 covers the details on the layout preferences, which you can find in the Properties panel, as shown in Figure 21-5.

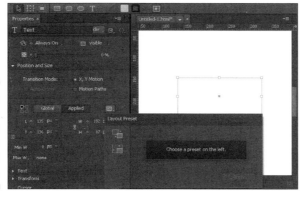

Figure 21-5:
Use the layout presets from the Properties panel.

You can override the layout defaults that you configured from the toolbar with the layout presets from the Properties panel. This is useful if you want one of your elements to behave differently than the layout defaults.

A big difference between the layout defaults and the layout presets is that the presets are intended to work with parent elements:

- ✔ Layout presets apply responsiveness to existing and/or multiple elements while layout defaults are for new compositions with no or few existing elements. In addition, the layout presets make it easier to apply certain responsive behavior such as scaling only the position, centering an image, and so on.

- ✔ If the element is not nested inside another element, Edge Animate treats the Stage as the parent element.

Here's a fun way to experiment with how the layout presets work:

1. **Draw two elements on the Stage, such as a rectangle and an ellipse.**

2. **Nest one of the elements into the other (drag and drop one element into the other from the Elements panel).**

3. **Select both of the elements and set the Layout Preset to Scale Size (see Figure 21-6) and then click Apply.**

Figure 21-6:
Select the Scale Size Layout Preset to resize the child element when the parent element is resized.

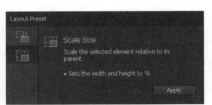

4. **Select only the nested element and resize it.**

   The parent element should remain unaffected.

5. **Select only the parent element and resize it.**

   The child element should resize along with the parent.

6. **Select the Stage and resize that to watch the two different elements resize.**

   For the next step, make sure the Stage width and height are set to %.

7. **Test the responsive web design aspect by dragging the tick mark along the ruler.**

8. **Change the layout preset for one of the elements from Scale Size to Scale Position (see Figure 21-7).**

Figure 21-7:
Select
the Scale
Position lay-
out preset
to affect the
position of
the element.

9. **Drag the tick mark in the ruler and note the difference in behavior for the element.**

Elements do not have an auto feature like images do to keep proportions. If you want an element to maintain its width or height, you have to switch back to px rather than use %.

Testing Your Animation's Responsiveness

The best way to find out how a responsive web design works is to test it before you start working on a real project. You can glean much from these experiments. For example, images can keep proportions, but drawn elements and text boxes do not if you use percentages instead of pixels. Also, drawn elements and text boxes won't wrap around images if you resize the browser causing the window to shrink. Instead, drawn elements and text boxes resize to fit the new window dimensions — and either appear over the image or disappear under the image.

You can affect whether the elements appear over or under the image by using the Arrange setting (right-click an element and choose Arrange and then select whether you want to bring an element forward or backward). This is the same as changing the order in the Elements panel.

Adobe Edge Inspect

Adobe Edge Inspect, as the name implies, is part of the Edge suite of tools. This is a very handy Chrome extension that you install into both your Chrome browser and your mobile device. To download the Chrome extension, go to `http://html.adobe.com/edge/inspect`. You do need a membership to the Adobe Creative Cloud to install this extension, which is available for free (as of this writing).

You also need to install the Inspect app on your mobile device:

✔ iOS devices: `www.adobe.com/go/edgeinspect_ios`

✔ Android devices: `www.adobe.com/go/edgeinspect_android`

✔ Kindle Fire devices: `www.adobe.com/go/edgeinspect_amazon`

For more information on installing, you can visit `http://forums.adobe.com/docs/DOC-2535`.

After you have both the extension and the app(s) installed on your devices, you can pair your computer with your mobile device, enabling you to see your computer's browser. To enable the synching, you must have all of your devices on the same wireless network.

The synch is limited to only the browser. If you switch to your desktop, your mobile device continues to display whatever was last on your web browser.

If for some reason your computer and devices don't automatically synch to each other, you have to manually input your computer's IP address (when you click the Edge Inspect button in the browser, it shows you the IP address) into your mobile device. That's what I had to do to pair my Windows laptop to my Android phone. I also had to do it for my Kindle Fire. And that's when I learned that in order to pair up multiple devices, you need to pay a $9.99 per month membership.

The benefit to using Edge Inspect is that you can view your Edge Animate projects on your mobile device when you preview your animation in the browser. This means that you don't have to upload your files to the web for testing. You also don't have to type in the URL for your project over and over. In addition, if you click any links in the browser running on your desktop machine, then all synched devices will also follow that link as well. The savings in time alone may be worth that ten bucks per month.

To test how different types of elements react to the browser window resizing, try the following:

1. **Set up the Stage for a responsive web design by setting the width and height to %.**

2. **Set the layout default to %.**

3. **Add different types of elements to the Stage, such as text boxes, images, and rectangles.**

4. **Set different layout presets for the different elements.**

5. **Nest some elements into each other.**

6. **Drag the tick on the Ruler around (both the vertical and the horizontal) and see how the different elements react.**

   You can also preview in a browser to see how the elements react when you resize the browser window.

You can also use Adobe Edge Inspect to view how your design looks on different types of devices. I discuss this in the Adobe Edge Inspect sidebar.

Part VI
The Part of Tens

Enjoy an additional Adobe Edge Animate Part of Tens chapter online at www.
dummies.com.

In this part . . .

✔ Discover ten great ways to use Adobe Edge Animate successfully.

✔ Explore the tools that can make any Adobe Edge Animate experience heavenly.

✔ Enjoy an additional Adobe Edge Animate Part of Tens chapter online at www.dummies.com.

Chapter 22

Ten Users of Edge Animate

*A*dobe Edge Animate CC has many more uses than just ten, but here I list the top ten that immediately rise to the top of my mind. You may find some of them elementary, whereas others may evoke fresh ideas for things you can do with Edge Animate, from creating basic slideshows, to creating advertisements, to creating an e-learning tool. You may even come up with a way to animate a game with Adobe Edge Animate CC.

Animating with Edge Animate

Yes, you can animate with Edge Animate. Shocking, I know. But if I didn't list animating as a use for Edge Animate, I'd be missing a big one. The animations that you create can be as simple as a sun rising over a hill or as complex as all the stars and planets moving through the universe. The only limitation is your own imagination as to what you want to create and put into motion.

Designing with Edge Animate

You can also design with Edge Animate. Although Edge Animate is not necessarily a design tool, designers can work with Edge Animate rather easily, so designing with Edge Animate is a legitimate use. You may not draw overly complex illustrations with Edge Animate, at least not with 1.0, but you can place and move elements about the Stage in a simple way to create works of art. And that, to me, is designing.

Developing with Edge Animate

Good developers who know their code wouldn't let this missing feature stop them from adding sound to their Animate project. Instead, developers who know their stuff can dive in to the JavaScript and add the code necessary to incorporate sound into their animation.

The persistent code window, as I discuss in Chapter 2, is there for developers to take full advantage of when they want to edit or add to the code. Edge Animate's code window allows you to view all the available code or just the relevant parts for a particular element. Either way, Adobe made it easy for developers to dive in and work their magic.

Learning from Edge Animate Projects

E-learning specialists and teachers may delight in knowing that it's possible to create animated tutorials with Edge Animate. In Chapter 18, I explain how to build an example of what an interactive and animated tutorial can look like. Everyone, from kids to adults, can benefit from an easy-to-use and intuitive touch-screen interface on their tablets and phones.

You can create animated tutorials that teach everything from how to use a remote control for your television to how to use a tablet. If someone needs to become skilled at something, there's a good chance you can make an animated and interactive tutorial to instruct them.

Working with Edge Animate as a Professional

As a web professional, you'll find Edge Animate useful for an endless list of items. If you have a site that needs a little energy injected, Edge Animate is a great tool for you to:

✔ Build animated logos.

✔ Build slideshows (refer to Chapter 16).

> ✔ Build one-page sites such as for a restaurant or an interactive brochure (refer to Chapter 20).
>
> ✔ Animate a children's book (refer to Chapter 19).

If you decide to animate your company's logo, try to keep it simple. Overdoing an animation and making it more complex than necessary can do more damage than good. You don't want to confuse your visitor by a logo dancing and bouncing across the screen, if there's no apparent purpose. On the other hand, giving your logo a nice little spin can gain the attention that it deserves.

Animating as a Hobby

Animating as a hobby is my favorite use for Edge Animate. While I was learning to use the tool, I made several animations for my other favorite hobby, playing video games. I created a site called GoozerNation, where a team of contributors and I discuss all things video games. After Edge Animate came out, this site started boasting Edge Animate projects in addition to just articles. Figure 22-1 shows a still shot of an animation I created using Commander Shepard from the popular video game franchise *Mass Effect.* When "Mass Effect 3" released, an Internet meme characterized a phrase that the Commander repeats during the course of the game (that is, he endorses a particular store and repeats ad nauseum that store is his favorite). My twist on the meme was that Commander Shepard's favorite site on the Internet was my own. The animation was cheesy and badly done. It mostly consisted of the Commander's mouth opening and closing, which was supposed to represent him speaking the words that appeared to his right. I even added a *Play Again* link so that people could watch it over and over.

You can view the animation here: `http://goo.gl/vuNsV` (I used Google's URL shortener to save you a bunch of typing)

Figure 22-1: Don't hold back from making cheesy animations as well as good ones.

Selling with Edge Animate

Creating advertisements with Edge Animate is another excellent use for the tool. Unlike Flash, Edge Animate uses HTML5 and JavaScript, so your audience can view your ad on Apple devices. That way, you know your ad can appear on iPads and iPhones.

Popular advertisement sizes include

- **Leaderboard:** 728 x 90
- **Medium rectangle:** 300 x 250
- **Wide skyscraper:** 160 x 600
- **Full banner:** 468 x 60
- **Large rectangle:** 336 x 280
- **Rectangle:** 180 x 150
- **Button:** 120 x 60
- **Square button:** 125 x 125

When making your advertisement in Edge Animate, try designing it with a responsive web design. That way, no matter the screen size, your ad looks good.

Specializing Your Content

I read an article the other day about how using a tablet is a great way to create an economical kiosk for customer use. For example, say that you work in a car dealership; what if you provided a tablet for customers to preview cars, features, and options while they peruse the showroom floor. You can create an Edge Animate project that allows customers to do exactly that.

Here's another example. Restaurant employees can use an Edge Animate composition on a tablet to show customers images of the day's specials. Instead of using a paper menu, the tablet can display vibrant images of the dishes, which the customer can then sort though.

Gaming with Edge Animate

You might consider making games with Edge Animate a stretch. After all, a key component to most games is sound, which Edge Animate lacks in the initial version. However, I don't think making games with Edge Animate is entirely impossible. It just takes a ton of extra coding. So, making games with Edge Animate is most likely geared toward hardcore developers and not necessarily designers or hobbyists.

With that said, I made a sort-of game using Adobe Edge Animate. The game, if you want to call it that, involves the audience clicking a basketball to make a basket (see Figure 22-2). When the audience clicks the ball, the ball launches up toward the basket with flames shooting out from it. The ball then swishes through the hoop and lands with a bounce. The audience is then invited to shoot another basket. Again, as with the Commander Shepard animation, it's completely cheesy, but in a fun kind of way. To play the game yourself, you can find it online at `http://goo.gl/9B8xg`.

Figure 22-2:
You can make games with Edge Animate, if you want to.

Using the Responsive Web Design Tools

A great use of Edge Animate is making responsive web designs. I go into detail on how to create a responsive web design in Chapter 21. This feature allows you to create animations that respond to different browser and screen sizes. I can envision a future in which many web-design jobs will make responsive web design a mandatory requirement; just think of all the different screen sizes on the market today. You have your 4-inch to 6-inch phones, 7-inch and 10-inch tablets, and any number of dimensions for laptops and desktop monitors.

Learning how to create a responsive web design may very well become essential for all web enthusiasts. If this is something that interests you, check out Adobe Edge Reflow, which is in development as of this writing but should be available sometime in 2013.

Chapter 23

Ten Online Resources

In This Chapter

▶ Finding tools

▶ Expanding skills

▶ Staying in touch

*A*s you've no doubt noticed, you can find URLs to useful websites throughout this book; all can lead you to very handy information that you can use with your Adobe Edge Animate CC project. Some of the URLs point to websites, such as Adobe, where you can access the different software in the Creative Cloud. Other URLs point you in the direction of fonts that you can use in your Edge Animate project. Then there are the educational URLs that send you to API references, the W3C, and other informative sites.

I've grouped all of these URLs into one comprehensive chapter and grouped them into ten sections for easy reference. This includes finding a web host, a content management system, and FTP software, all of which is invaluable in getting your project online.

Last, I provide two links that I hope you consider visiting. These are links to my *Adobe Edge Animate CC For Dummies* Facebook page and Twitter account. I plan to keep these accounts running for as long as there's an active audience. I'd love to hear from you and see what kinds of projects you conjure up after reading this book.

Adobe Links to the Creative Cloud

In case it's escaped your attention (not likely, but hey, it can happen), Adobe has a ton of software residing in the virtual cloud. A great place to start is at a page called "Adobe & HTML," located at `http://html.adobe.com` (see Figure 23-1).

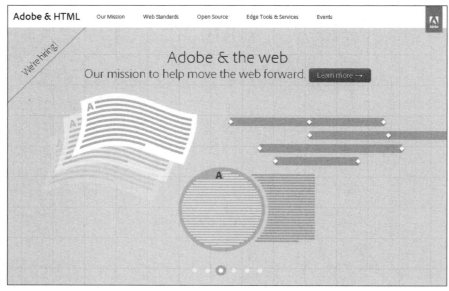

Figure 23-1:
Adobe
wants to
help you
create
the web.

At the Adobe & HTML page, you can learn about Adobe's mission for the web, how it adheres to HTML standards, how it's committed to Open Source projects, and there's a section on Edge Tools & Services. It's really an interesting corner of the Internet to check out what Adobe is doing in terms of helping you create web content. There's even a link to events, which take place around the world.

Here are more great Adobe URLs to check out:

✔ **Adobe Edge Code:** `http://html.adobe.com/edge/code`

✔ **Adobe PhoneGap Build:** `http://html.adobe.com/edge/phonegap-build`

✔ **Adobe Edge Reflow:** `http://html.adobe.com/edge/reflow`

✔ **Adobe Edge Inspect:** `http://html.adobe.com/edge/inspect`

Online Font Resources

Even though Adobe Edge Animate CC doesn't work great with tons of text, it does work well with small amounts of text, and it enables you to import tons of fonts. In Chapter 12, I show you how to import fonts from places such as Google. Figure 23-2 shows the Adobe Edge Web Fonts page.

Figure 23-2:
Adobe
offers its
own Edge
web fonts.

Here is a short list of good places to find excellent fonts:

- **Google's web fonts:** www.google.com/webfonts
- **Adobe also has Typekit:** http://html.adobe.com/edge/typekit

Referencing the APIs

For the developers out there, APIs serve as an excellent resource to find new coding information. For non-developers, APIs can at least provide background information that can help you make sense of the code you're staring at in the code window.

Here are three useful API sites:

- **Adobe's Edge Animate JavaScript API:** www.adobe.com/devnet-docs/edgeanimate/api/current/index.html
- **The jQuery site:** http://jquery.com
- **Google's Hosted Libraries Developer's Guide:** https://developers.google.com/speed/libraries/devguide

Google's Hosted Libraries page has a ton of links that you can explore to learn even more.

The W3C

At times, I've felt that the W3C is antiquated and rather slow moving in terms of keeping HTML standards fresh and relevant, but the W3C site still serves the important purpose of being an excellent resource for learning how to use HTML tags. You may find this site beneficial while learning how to use HTML and CSS with your Edge Animate projects.

A separate source from W3C is the W3C online school (`www.w3schools.com/tags`). You can click around the W3C school to learn a thing or two about HTML, CSS, JavaScript, jQuery, and more.

Adobe Fireworks

Adobe Fireworks has been around for awhile, and I've heard varying opinions on the design tool. Certain sites, like *Smashing Magazine,* still run many articles praising the software. If you do check it out and like it, you may be happy to know that it's available through Adobe's Creative Cloud. Here's the URL: `www.adobe.com/products/fireworks.html`. Plus, Fireworks works great with Edge Animate, as I discuss in Chapter 13.

You can find a great resource to find out more about Fireworks at John Dunning's site: `http://johndunning.com/fireworks`.

Browser Usage

Chapter 1 has an entire section on browser compatibility — a very important concern for most web designers and developers. Adobe Edge Animate CC does work great on all modern browsers, but that doesn't include previous versions of Internet Explorer (older than version 9). To keep up to date on the current usage of Microsoft's browser, check here: `http://en.wikipedia.org/wiki/Usage_share_of_web_browsers`.

Hopefully, this page stays fresh with new updates, and even more hopefully, that old versions of IE will disappear from users' computers so that we won't have to worry anymore about whether our animations work in everyone's browsers.

FTP Recommendation

Unless you host your own servers, or if you're simply going the way of the downloadable app, you're going to need a way to upload your animation files to the web. Luckily, FileZilla provides excellent software for you to do just that, which you can find at `http://filezilla-project.org`.

Even though FileZilla's FTP software is intuitive and easy to use, you still may have some questions. In that case, check its online documentation at `http://wiki.filezilla-project.org/Documentation`.

Web Hosts

If you're looking around for a web host so that you can show off all your animations, look no further than this site to compare all of the different offerings: `http://webhostingchoice.com`.

I can personally vouch for Bluehost, as I've been using the company for many years for several sites and I've never had a problem. And no, the company did not pay me to say that. I don't mind recommending it based on several years of great service. You can find it here: `www.bluehost.com`.

Content Management Systems

If you want to start a blog, or some kind of news site with tons of content, you may want to add some animations to it. Several different types of Content Management Systems (CMS) are out there perfectly suited to serve this task. My personal choice has always been Joomla! You can check it out at `www.joomla.org`.

Another option for a CMS is WordPress. It even has a plug-in for Adobe Edge Animate CC: Go to `http://wordpress.org/extend/plugins/edge-suite`.

Adobe Edge Animate CC For Dummies Online

In this day and age of social media, I would be remiss if I did not host a Facebook and Twitter account for my *Adobe Edge Animate CC For Dummies* book. You can find the Facebook page here: www.facebook.com/ AdobeEdgeAnimateForDummies.

And the Twitter account is here: https://twitter.com/ AnimateDummies.

I would be very happy to interact with you on both Facebook and Twitter. We can share projects, tips, and lessons learned. If you have a question about something, feel free to pose your question on either of these sites — hopefully, I'll have an answer, or maybe someone else from the community can chime in.

Chapter 24

Ten Web Design Trends

*N*ew web design trends emerge every year — rounded corners, shadows, inset text. This year is no exception; new trends continue to appear, and I expect to update this chapter when it's time to write version 2.0 of this book.

One consistent factor is that new trends in web design appear to go hand-in-hand with new coding capabilities. For example, at the beginning of web design, it was difficult to create rounded corners without using tables and several different images. These days, creating rounded corners is as easy as writing a few lines of CSS code — not to mention that you can ditch the tables and the extra images.

The web design trends presented in this chapter, for the most part, represent not only new coding techniques but also new ways for your audience to interact with your site in engaging ways. When you grab your audience's attention and get them intrigued in your web design, you're well on your way to retaining that audience. By using Adobe Edge Animate, you can create all of the design trends listed here.

More Imagery and Illustration

Are you tired and bored of looking at a wall of text? Are all those small images and icons starting to look a bit dated? Does a solid background color make you yawn? If you feel that way, there's a good chance your audience feels the same way. Adding more imagery and illustrations to your site can greatly improve your web design. To make your site look more current, add a subtle background image instead of using a white, grey, or black background.

In Chapter 3, I discuss importing images for use with your Animate composition and how to work with them. In Chapter 6, you can discover how to use images in the background and the difference between using a div tag and an img tag for the images. Chapter 8 has great information on setting Layout presets for your images. Chapter 12 goes into detail on using images from the Library panel. As you can see, this book can give you a strong start working with images in Edge Animate.

Horizontal Scrolling

Creating web designs with horizontal scrolling could take some courage— it's rarely been done — but that doesn't mean it hasn't been done before and to great effect. A simple web search for "great horizontal websites" won't leave you disappointed. You will find many great examples of art sites, galleries, and creative sites that use horizontal scrolling to great effect.

While this type of navigation is still relatively new, by creating a site in this fashion you could place yourself at the head of the pack in terms of fashionable web design.

Vertical Scrolling

Just the opposite of horizontal scrolling is vertical scrolling. While scrolling vertically has been a popular web design trend for many years, in the past year or two it has been greatly exaggerated.

Many sites, such as `boingboing.net` and `twitter.com` use a never-ending vertical-scroll technique that keeps the audience on the page. This never-ending presentation style is designed to keep audience attention on a continuous search for more content.

Fixed Headers

If you decide to design an animated web page using the never-ending vertical-scroll method, then you might want to think about adding a *fixed header* to your site. A fixed header is a navigation menu that rests at the top of the page and it remains visible as your audience scrolls down the page. This feature enables your audience to navigate quickly from where they are to a different section of your site — and always know where they are.

A fixed header is a convenience your audience can appreciate because they don't have to scroll all the way back up to the top of the page to find the menu. Features that keep user convenience in mind will also keep your audience on your site for longer periods of time.

Creative Navigation

Getting creative with your navigation is neatly complementary to using more illustrations and images in your web designs. Instead of a basic text menu, use images to denote a link. After your users learn that they can click images to advance through your site, they'll become more comfortable with looking for links in unusual places on your site. This kind of interaction opens up the opportunity to create *easter eggs* within your site. An easter egg, in this context, represents seemingly hidden content that can surprise and excite your audience when they stumble across it.

A great way to show your audience that an image or an icon is a link, is to use the Cursor attribute feature in Animate. When your audience passes the mouse pointer over a linked image, the cursor can change from a pointer to a hand, indicating a link (as discussed in detail in Chapter 5).

Storytelling

Everyone loves an engaging story. So, why not design a site or animation that tells your audience an engaging story? Instead of creating a basic restaurant website that presents only images of the food and descriptions of ingredients, why not create a fanciful background story? In addition to listing your best dishes as being locally organic, farm-raised, sustainable goodness, why not add a story about the couple who got engaged between the main course and the dessert? You could add an animation of a ring dropping into a flute of champagne, complete with rising bubbles. Site visitors might have arrived at your restaurant site looking for a good meal, but they'll stay to learn more about what goes on at the other tables. Storytelling website animations not only enhance presentation, they can connect with visitors' life experiences.

Navigating within One Page

One-page websites — once known as *brochure sites* — are making a comeback. By keeping your audience on a single page that can take on the appearance of various different pages, you can take advantage of the scrolling trend. Instead of clicking around to different pages in an attempt to find something, your audience can instead scroll through your site as they advance through your content. Links that serve as images can also help your audience jump directly to specific spots on the site when they know what they want — while still engaging someone who is casually searching.

By creating a site as described in this section, you are really taking advantage of a few current web design trends: scrolling for information, using more imagery, and implementing creative navigation. Chapters 19 and 20 provide examples of how to create a one-page site complete with navigation.

Moving Away from Flash

Adobe Flash was once the wave of the future, but that wave has crashed on the beach and a new wave is rolling in. Where Flash used to be the predominant tool for creating animations and websites, that tool's heyday has come and gone. But I'll stop short of calling it dead in the water.

Adobe Edge Animate might not quite be ready to completely replace Flash, but it's on its way to accomplishing just that. After all, you can't view Flash on i-devices such as iPhones and iPads, and who wants to create content that appears broken on some of the most popular mobile devices around?

HTML5, CSS3, and JavaScript

The world of web design and coding techniques is constantly evolving. The big trend in code is HTML5 and CSS3, which are only going to become increasingly ingrained into the web-o-sphere. Google Chrome is leading the charge, implementing the latest standards — with Firefox and Safari right alongside. Then there's Internet Explorer — currently a bit late showing up at the party — but Microsoft is making great strides in updating their browser to keep pace. In the first chapter of this book, I go into detail on HTML5 and browser compatibility.

In Chapter 14, I discuss how to safeguard your animation from appearing broken on older versions of Internet Explorer by using the Down-level Stage and the different web publishing options that Edge Animate offers. In these regards, simply using Adobe Edge Animate could be considered a web design trend itself!

Responsive Web Design

Responsive web design (RWD) is the latest rage these days. The concept behind RWD is to design one site for use on any number of devices, from desktop monitors to tablets to phones. While web designers might be split on whether to create a mobile site separately from a desktop site, or to create a single site that can respond to browser size, I see the trend tilting to the responsive camp.

The reason for this is rather simple, by creating one responsive site, you don't have to keep updating two different sites. Creating an RWD points in the direction of the future; the more advanced coding techniques and tools become, the better they'll work with RWD. Consider it one more way Adobe Edge Animate puts you in the vanguard of web design trends. (Chapter 21 goes into full detail on how to create an RWD using Animate.)

Index

Notes

Notes

Notes

Apple & Mac

iPad For Dummies,
5th Edition
978-1-118-49823-1

iPhone 5 For Dummies,
6th Edition
978-1-118-35201-4

MacBook For Dummies,
4th Edition
978-1-118-20920-2

OS X Mountain Lion
For Dummies
978-1-118-39418-2

Blogging & Social Media

Facebook For Dummies,
4th Edition
978-1-118-09562-1

Mom Blogging
For Dummies
978-1-118-03843-7

Pinterest For Dummies
978-1-118-32800-2

WordPress For Dummies,
5th Edition
978-1-118-38318-6

Business

Commodities For Dummies,
2nd Edition
978-1-118-01687-9

Investing For Dummies,
6th Edition
978-0-470-90545-6

Personal Finance
For Dummies,
7th Edition
978-1-118-11785-9

QuickBooks 2013
For Dummies
978-1-118-35641-8

Small Business Marketing Kit
For Dummies,
3rd Edition
978-1-118-31183-7

Careers

Job Interviews
For Dummies,
4th Edition
978-1-118-11290-8

Job Searching with
Social Media
For Dummies
978-0-470-93072-4

Personal Branding
For Dummies
978-1-118-11792-7

Resumes For Dummies,
6th Edition
978-0-470-87361-8

Success as a Mediator
For Dummies
978-1-118-07862-4

Diet & Nutrition

Belly Fat Diet For Dummies
978-1-118-34585-6

Eating Clean For Dummies
978-1-118-00013-7

Nutrition For Dummies,
5th Edition
978-0-470-93231-5

Digital Photography

Digital Photography
For Dummies,
7th Edition
978-1-118-09203-3

Digital SLR Cameras &
Photography For Dummies,
4th Edition
978-1-118-14489-3

Photoshop Elements 11
For Dummies
978-1-118-40821-6

Gardening

Herb Gardening
For Dummies,
2nd Edition
978-0-470-61778-6

Vegetable Gardening
For Dummies,
2nd Edition
978-0-470-49870-5

Health

Anti-Inflammation Diet
For Dummies
978-1-118-02381-5

Diabetes For Dummies,
3rd Edition
978-0-470-27086-8

Living Paleo For Dummies
978-1-118-29405-5

Hobbies

Beekeeping
For Dummies
978-0-470-43065-1

eBay For Dummies,
7th Edition
978-1-118-09806-6

Raising Chickens
For Dummies
978-0-470-46544-8

Wine For Dummies,
5th Edition
978-1-118-28872-6

Writing Young Adult Fiction
For Dummies
978-0-470-94954-2

Language &
Foreign Language

500 Spanish Verbs
For Dummies
978-1-118-02382-2

English Grammar
For Dummies,
2nd Edition
978-0-470-54664-2

French All-in One
For Dummies
978-1-118-22815-9

German Essentials
For Dummies
978-1-118-18422-6

Italian For Dummies
2nd Edition
978-1-118-00465-4

 Available in print and e-book formats.

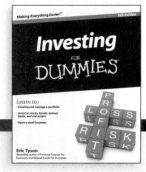

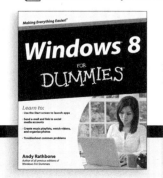

Math & Science

Algebra I For Dummies,
2nd Edition
978-0-470-55964-2

Anatomy and Physiology
For Dummies,
2nd Edition
978-0-470-92326-9

Astronomy For Dummies,
3rd Edition
978-1-118-37697-3

Biology For Dummies,
2nd Edition
978-0-470-59875-7

Chemistry For Dummies,
2nd Edition
978-1-1180-0730-3

Pre-Algebra Essentials
For Dummies
978-0-470-61838-7

Microsoft Office

Excel 2013 For Dummies
978-1-118-51012-4

Office 2013 All-in-One
For Dummies
978-1-118-51636-2

PowerPoint 2013
For Dummies
978-1-118-50253-2

Word 2013 For Dummies
978-1-118-49123-2

Music

Blues Harmonica
For Dummies
978-1-118-25269-7

Guitar For Dummies,
3rd Edition
978-1-118-11554-1

iPod & iTunes
For Dummies,
10th Edition
978-1-118-50864-0

Programming

Android Application
Development For
Dummies, 2nd Edition
978-1-118-38710-8

iOS 6 Application
Development For Dummies
978-1-118-50880-0

Java For Dummies,
5th Edition
978-0-470-37173-2

Religion & Inspiration

The Bible For Dummies
978-0-7645-5296-0

Buddhism For Dummies,
2nd Edition
978-1-118-02379-2

Catholicism For Dummies,
2nd Edition
978-1-118-07778-8

Self-Help & Relationships

Bipolar Disorder
For Dummies,
2nd Edition
978-1-118-33882-7

Meditation For Dummies,
3rd Edition
978-1-118-29144-3

Seniors

Computers For Seniors
For Dummies,
3rd Edition
978-1-118-11553-4

iPad For Seniors
For Dummies,
5th Edition
978-1-118-49708-1

Social Security
For Dummies
978-1-118-20573-0

Smartphones & Tablets

Android Phones
For Dummies
978-1-118-16952-0

Kindle Fire HD
For Dummies
978-1-118-42223-6

NOOK HD For Dummies,
Portable Edition
978-1-118-39498-4

Surface For Dummies
978-1-118-49634-3

Test Prep

ACT For Dummies,
5th Edition
978-1-118-01259-8

ASVAB For Dummies,
3rd Edition
978-0-470-63760-9

GRE For Dummies,
7th Edition
978-0-470-88921-3

Officer Candidate Tests,
For Dummies
978-0-470-59876-4

Physician's Assistant Exam
For Dummies
978-1-118-11556-5

Series 7 Exam
For Dummies
978-0-470-09932-2

Windows 8

Windows 8 For Dummies
978-1-118-13461-0

Windows 8 For Dummies,
Book + DVD Bundle
978-1-118-27167-4

Windows 8 All-in-One
For Dummies
978-1-118-11920-4

ℯ Available in print and e-book formats.

Take Dummies with you everywhere you go!

Whether you're excited about e-books, want more from the web, must have your mobile apps, or swept up in social media, Dummies makes everything easier .

Dummies products make life easier!

3 1491 01177 7921

- DIY
- Consumer Electronics
- Crafts
- Software
- Cookware
- Hobbies
- Videos
- Music
- Games
- and More!

For more information, go to **Dummies.com®** and search the store by category.

For Dummies is a registered trademark of John Wiley & Sons, Inc.

A Wiley Brand